THE NEW CAMBRIDGE COMPANION TO
WILLIAM FAULKNER

The New Cambridge Companion to William Faulkner offers contemporary
readers a sample of innovative approaches to interpreting and appreciating
William Faulkner, who continues to inspire passionate readership worldwide.
The essays here address a variety of topics in Faulkner's fiction, such as its
reflection of the concurrent emergence of cinema, social inequality and rights
movements, modern ways of imagining sexual identity and behavior, the South's
history as a plantation economy and society, and the persistent effects of
traumatic cultural and personal experience. This new *Companion* provides an
introduction to the fresh ways Faulkner is being read in the twenty-first century
and bears witness to his continued importance as an American and world writer.

John T. Matthews is Professor of English at Boston University. His previous
books include *The Play of Faulkner's Language*; *"The Sound and the Fury":
Faulkner and the Lost Cause*; and *William Faulkner: Seeing Through the South*.
Matthews's articles on Faulkner and Southern literature have appeared in such
journals as *Texas Studies in Language and Literature, American Literature,
American Literary History*, and *Philological Quarterly*.

A complete list of books in the series is at the back of this book

D1600216

THE NEW CAMBRIDGE
COMPANION TO
WILLIAM FAULKNER

THE NEW CAMBRIDGE
COMPANION TO
WILLIAM FAULKNER

EDITED BY
JOHN T. MATTHEWS
Boston University

CAMBRIDGE
UNIVERSITY PRESS

CAMBRIDGE
UNIVERSITY PRESS

University Printing House, Cambridge CB2 8BS, United Kingdom

One Liberty Plaza, 20th Floor, New York, NY 10006, USA

477 Williamstown Road, Port Melbourne, VIC 3207, Australia

314-321, 3rd Floor, Plot 3, Splendor Forum, Jasola District Centre, New Delhi - 110025, India

79 Anson Road, #06-04/06, Singapore 079906

Cambridge University Press is part of the University of Cambridge.

It furthers the University's mission by disseminating knowledge in the pursuit of
education, learning and research at the highest international levels of excellence.

www.cambridge.org
Information on this title: www.cambridge.org/9781107689565

© Cambridge University Press 2015

First published 2015

A catalogue record for this publication is available from the British Library

Library of Congress Cataloging in Publication data
The New Cambridge Companion to William Faulkner / edited by John T. Matthews.
pages cm. – (Cambridge Companions to Literature)
Includes bibliographical references and index.
ISBN 978-1-107-05038-9 (hardback) – ISBN 978-1-107-68956-5 (paperback)
1. Faulkner, William, 1897–1962 – Criticism and interpretation.
2. Southern States – In literature. I. Matthews, John T., editor.
PS3511.A86Z9226 2015
813'.52–dc23 2014043435

ISBN 978-1-107-05038-9 Hardback
ISBN 978-1-107-68956-5 Paperback

CONTENTS

CONTRIBUTORS

ALIYYAH I. ABDUR-RAHMAN is Associate Professor of English and African and Afro-American Studies at Brandeis University, where she specializes in American and African American literature and culture, critical race theory, gender and sexuality studies, and multiethnic feminisms. She is the author of *Against the Closet: Black Political Longing and the Erotics of Race* (Duke University Press, 2012) and has published widely on topics ranging from the relation of sexuality and social order in slave narratives to the impact of Civil Rights retrenchment on the formations of black families and on the current putatively "post-racial" moment. She is at work on a new book, provisionally titled "Millennial Style: The Politics of Experiment in Contemporary African Diasporic Culture."

HUGUES AZÉRAD specializes in comparative literature, aesthetics, modernism, and French poetry at the University of Cambridge, Magdalene College, where he is Fellow and College Lecturer in French. He is the editor of the contemporary poetry section of *The Literary Encyclopedia* and coeditor of *Twentieth-Century French Poetry: A Critical Anthology* (Cambridge University Press, 2010). Azérad is the author of *L'Univers constellé de Proust, Joyce et Faulkner: le concept d'épiphanie dans l'esthétique du modernisme* (Peter Lang, 2002). He has published extensively on nineteenth- and twentieth-century French and English literature, with particular attention to comparative modernism and Caribbean culture.

MARTYN BONE is Associate Professor of American Literature at the University of Copenhagen. He is the author of *The Postsouthern Sense of Place in Contemporary Fiction* (Louisiana State University Press, 2005); the editor of *Perspectives on Barry Hannah* (University Press of Mississippi, 2007); and the coeditor of a three-volume mini-series: *The American South in the Atlantic World* (University Press of Florida, 2013), *Creating Citizenship in the Nineteenth Century South* (University Press of Florida, 2013), and *Creating and Consuming the American South* (University Press of Florida, 2015). Bone has published on Faulkner and other writers of the modern South, and he is at work on a book about literary representations of the U.S. South in transnational contexts.

RANDY BOYAGODA is Associate Professor of English and University Director of Zone Learning at Ryerson University in Toronto. He is the author of a scholarly monograph on immigration and American identity in the fiction of Salman Rushdie, Ralph Ellison, and William Faulkner (Routledge, 2009) and has written two novels: *Governor of the Northern Province* (2006) and *Beggar's Feast* (2012). He also contributes reviews and commentary to a variety of publications, including the *New York Times, Wall Street Journal, National Post, Globe and Mail,* and *Financial Times* (UK). Boyagoda's latest book is a biography of Fr. Richard John Neuhaus (Random House, 2015), and he is currently at work on a new novel.

PATRICIA E. CHU is Assistant Professor of English at the State University of New York at Albany, where she works on nineteenth- and twentieth-century American literature, Anglo-American modernism, race and gender theory, Asian American literature, and African American literature. She is the author of *Race, Nationalism and the State in British and American Modernism* (Cambridge University Press, 2006) and numerous articles on American literature, including a recent study of biopolitical history and the contemporary "ethnic" novel in *American Literary History.*

GREG FORTER is Professor of English at the University of South Carolina, where he specializes in postcolonial literature and theory, twentieth-century U.S. literature, gender studies and feminist theory, critical race theory, and psychoanalytic literary theory. He is the author of *Gender, Race, and Mourning in American Modernism* (Cambridge University Press, 2011) and *Murdering Masculinities: Fantasies of Gender and Violence in the American Crime Novel* (New York University Press, 2000). He is currently writing a book titled *Atlantic and Other Worlds: Critique and Utopia in Postcolonial Historical Fiction,* a study of historical fictions about colonialism that will discuss works by Amitav Ghosh, Patrick Chamoiseau, Arundhati Roy, Toni Morrison, Barry Unsworth, and others.

SYLVAN GOLDBERG is a doctoral candidate in English at Stanford University. He holds a B.A. in English from Vassar College and an M.A. in literature and environment from the University of Nevada, Reno. His research focuses on nineteenth-century American literature and sentimentalism, addressing questions of ecocriticism, gender and sexuality, affect, and aesthetics.

JAIME HARKER is Associate Professor of English at the University of Mississippi, where she teaches American literature, gay and lesbian literature, and gender studies. Harker is the author of *America the Middlebrow: Women's Novels, Progressivism, and Middlebrow Authorship between the Wars* (University of Massachusetts Press, 2007) and *Middlebrow Queer: Christopher Isherwood in America* (University of Minnesota Press, 2013). She has coedited *The Oprah Affect: Critical Essays on Oprah's Book Club* (State University of New York Press, 2008) and *1960s Gay Pulp Fiction: The Misplaced Heritage* (University of

Massachusetts Press, 2013). She is currently working on a book on Southern lesbian feminism and feminist print culture.

PETER LURIE is Associate Professor of English at the University of Richmond. His teaching and research interests include Faulkner, film studies, nineteenth- and twentieth-century American literature, and modernism. He is the author of *Vision's Immanence: Faulkner, Film, and the Popular Imagination* (Johns Hopkins University Press, 2004) and coeditor of *Faulkner and Film: Faulkner and Yoknapatawpha 2010* (University Press of Mississippi, 2014). His book *American Obscurantism: History and the Visual in American Literature and Film* is forthcoming from Oxford University Press.

JULIAN MURPHET is Professor in the School of the Arts and Media and Director of the Centre for Modernism Studies in Australia at the University of New South Wales. His fields of expertise include film and television, cultural theory, British and Irish literature, and North American literature. He is the author of *Multimedia Modernism: Literature and the Anglo-American Avant-Garde* (Cambridge University Press, 2009); *Narrative and Media*, co-edited with Helen Fulton, Rosemary Huisman, and Anne Dunn (Cambridge University Press, 2005); *Bret Easton Ellis' American Psycho* (Continuum, 2002); and *Literature and Race in Los Angeles* (Cambridge University Press, 2001). He has edited numerous volumes and special issues of journals on media and literature, modernism, and visual technologies and has published widely in periodicals on Faulkner, Beckett, Eliot, and other modernists.

SUSAN SCOTT PARRISH is Associate Professor of English at the University of Michigan. Her work addresses the interrelated issues of race, the environment, and epistemology in the Atlantic world from 1492 through the twentieth century, with a particular emphasis on plantation zones. She is the author of *American Curiosity: Cultures of Natural History in the Colonial British Atlantic World* (University of North Carolina Press, 2006) and editor of Robert Beverley's 1705 *The History and Present State of Virginia* (University of North Carolina Press, 2013). She has just completed another book, provisionally titled *Noah's Kin: 1927 and the Culture of Modern Catastrophe*, which provides a cultural history of the most publicly engrossing U.S. eco-catastrophe of the twentieth century, namely the Mississippi flood of 1927.

RAMÓN SALDÍVAR is Professor of English and Comparative Literature and the Hoagland Family Professor of Humanities and Sciences at Stanford University, and he is currently the Burke Family Director of the Bing Overseas Studies Program there. His teaching and research focus on the areas of literary criticism and literary theory, the history of the novel, nineteenth- and early twentieth-century literary studies, cultural studies, globalization and issues concerning transnationalism, and Chicano and Chicana studies. Saldívar is the author of *Figural Language in the Novel: The Flowers of Speech from Cervantes to Joyce* (Princeton University Press, 1984; paperback 2014), *Chicano Narrative: The Dialectics of Difference* (University of Wisconsin Press, 1990), and *The Borderlands of Culture: Américo Paredes and the Transnational Imaginary* (Duke University Press, 2006). He is coeditor of *The Imaginary and Its Worlds: American Studies after the Transnational Turn* (Dartmouth College Press, 2013). He is currently at work on two book projects: *Race, Narrative Theory and Contemporary American Fiction* and *Américo Paredes and the Post-War Writings from Asia*.

MELANIE BENSON TAYLOR is Associate Professor of Native American Studies at Dartmouth College, specializing in U.S. Southern studies. She is the author of *Disturbing Calculations: The Economics of Identity in Postcolonial Southern Literature, 1912–2002* (University of Georgia Press, 2008) and *Reconstructing the Native South: American Indian Literature and the Lost Cause* (University of Georgia Press, 2012). Taylor is at work on two book projects: *Faulkner's Doom* (which interrogates the use of Indian tropes in William Faulkner's modern South) and *Indian Killers* (which studies the phenomenon of violence and murder in texts by and about contemporary Native Americans).

BENJAMIN WIDISS is Assistant Professor of English at Hamilton College. He is the author of *Obscure Invitations: The Persistence of the Author in Twentieth-Century American Literature* (Stanford University Press, 2011). He is working on a second book, *Flirting with Embodiment: Textual Metaphors and Textual Presences in Contemporary Narrative*, which explores the relationships between mass production and individual bodily presence in the aesthetic postures of an emergent post-postmodernism.

ACKNOWLEDGMENTS

A collaborative volume such as this depends on the expertise and generosity of many scholars: those whose work appears here, others whose scholarship informs it, as well as many experts who have contributed much to new knowledge about Faulkner and ways of studying his writing today that, had space allowed, would have been represented here. Our list of works cited provides a partial list of the extensive scholarship on Faulkner, but readers are encouraged to consult more comprehensive bibliographies.

Ray Ryan at Cambridge University Press had faith in my vision for this new version of the *Companion*, and Caitlin Gallagher at the Press was an exemplary guide through its production; my thanks to both. I've drawn on the counsel and counted on the liberality of many in the field of Faulkner studies, including the anonymous readers of my proposal, who improved the plan of the book. I do wish to mention the invaluable contributions over many years of two colleagues with a shared interest in Faulkner: Richard Godden, whose attention to the substance of Faulkner's texts brilliantly and unfailingly instructs and whose standard inspires; and Philip Weinstein, whose writing exceptionally illuminates Faulkner's literary imagination and who, as the editor of the original *Companion*, generously advised about this successor. I am grateful to Boston University, particularly Dean Virginia Sapiro of the College of Arts and Sciences, and my chairs in English, William Carroll, Gene Jarrett, and Maurice Lee, for continued research support during the preparation of this book. I wish to thank Mayor George Patterson of Oxford, Mississippi, not only for granting permission on behalf of the City of Oxford for the use of John McCrady's painting *Oxford on the Hill* as the cover illustration but also for personally seeing to its transit to the University of Mississippi studio. I thank as well the University's Director of Communications Photography

Robert Jordan for his exceptional efforts in creating a digital reproduction of the painting. Joyce Kim, a doctoral candidate in English at Boston University, provided expert editorial assistance in preparing the manuscript and index; I am deeply grateful for her labors. I encounter the memories of two longtime friends and colleagues in Faulkner studies on every page here: Noel Polk and Stephen Ross.

CHRONOLOGY OF WILLIAM FAULKNER'S LIFE AND WORKS

1897   William Cuthbert Falkner, first of four sons of Murry C. Falkner and Maud Butler Falkner, is born on September 25 in New Albany, Mississippi. Murry Falkner is an administrator for the railroad built by his legendary grandfather, William C. Falkner – a man known as the "Old Colonel" and widely remembered for his achievements as a soldier, landowner, lawyer, businessman, politician, and writer. (The family name was spelled "Falkner" until WF added the "u" in 1918.)

1902   The Falkner family moves to Oxford, Mississippi.

1914   After an indifferent secondary education (which ceased after the tenth grade), WF accepts a mentor relationship with Phil Stone (four years older), reading widely in classics and contemporary literature. Stone will serve for many years as a sometimes unwanted adviser, helping WF get his early works published.

1916–17 WF begins to write verse and to submit graphic and literary work for the University of Mississippi yearbook.

1918   WF and Estelle Oldham, childhood sweethearts, consider eloping, but WF seeks her father's permission, unsuccessfully. She marries Cornell Franklin. WF attempts to enlist in the U.S. Air Corps to fight in World War I, is rejected because he is too short, goes to Toronto, and (masquerading as an Englishman) joins the Royal Air Force training program. He returns to Oxford after the war, feigning war wounds and military exploits (his flight training was actually completed in December, a month after the armistice).

1919–20 WF enrolls as a special student at the University of Mississippi; studies French, Spanish, and Shakespeare; writes a play entitled *Marionettes*; completes his first volume of verse – *The Marble Faun* – which (with Phil Stone's help) will eventually be accepted for publication.

1921–23 WF works in a New York bookstore managed by Elizabeth Prall, Sherwood Anderson's future wife. He returns to Oxford to serve as university postmaster, a job he notoriously mishandles; in 1923 he is fired from it.

1924 *The Marble Faun* is published in December.

1925 WF travels to New Orleans and is introduced through Elizabeth Prall to Sherwood Anderson and his literary circle, a group associated with the avant-garde literary magazine *The Double Dealer*. WF spends six months with this group, developing a serious interest in writing fiction and completing his first novel, *Soldiers' Pay*, a "lost generation" story centering on the betrayals of a war-wounded aviator. Anderson's publisher, Horace Liveright, accepts it for publication. WF spends the second half of 1925 traveling in Europe, living in Paris, reading contemporary literature, and writing reviews; he returns to Oxford by Christmas.

1926 *Soldiers' Pay* is published in February. WF starts two new novels: *Father Abraham*, about the Snopeses, a clan of aspiring poor farmers; and *Flags in the Dust*, about the prestigious Sartoris planter family.

1927 WF's second novel, *Mosquitoes*, set in New Orleans and reflective of its avant-garde arts scene, is published in April by Liveright.

1928 Liveright rejects WF's third (and most ambitious to date) novel, *Flags in the Dust*. This novel inaugurates WF's fictional history of his own region and is accepted eventually by Harcourt, Brace, on condition that it be shortened. Throughout the 1920s, WF continues to see Estelle Oldham Franklin and her two sons during her visits to Oxford. He begins writing *The Sound and the Fury* in the spring and finishes it by early fall.

1929 Shortened and retitled, *Flags in the Dust* is published as *Sartoris* in January. WF begins writing *Sanctuary*. *The Sound and the Fury*, WF's first indisputable modernist masterpiece, is rejected by Harcourt, Brace but accepted by Cape and Smith. Estelle Oldham Franklin's divorce is finalized in April; WF marries her in June. *The Sound and the Fury* is published in October. During the fall, WF works nights at a power plant, completing a first draft of *As I Lay Dying* in less than seven weeks.

1930   WF buys Rowan Oak, an elegant but rundown antebellum mansion in Oxford. In need of funds (a need that will continue for the next twenty years), WF begins aggressively to market his short stories along with his novels, the former often paying better. "A Rose for Emily" is published in April. *As I Lay Dying* is published in October by Cape and Smith, giving WF's fictional county its name of Yoknapatawpha.

1931   Daughter Alabama born in January; she dies after nine days. *Sanctuary*, begun before publication of the two previously completed masterpieces and first conceived according to WF as a "potboiler," is heavily revised before being published in February. Its sexual violence attracts the attention of Hollywood, and WF will soon begin an off-and-on twenty-year career as a scriptwriter for Metro-Goldwyn-Mayer and Warner Brothers studios. (The two best-known films for which Faulkner earned writing credit were adaptations directed by Howard Hawks of Hemingway's *To Have and Have Not* [1944] and Raymond Chandler's *The Big Sleep* [1946].) *These Thirteen*, a collection of WF's stories, is published in September.

1932   *Light in August*, WF's first major treatment of the problem of race, is published in February by Smith and Haas. WF's father dies, causing family financial difficulties. WF accepts his first contract, from MGM, to work in Hollywood as a film scriptwriter.

1933   WF's second volume of poems, *A Green Bough*, is published in April. Daughter Jill is born in June. *The Story of Temple Drake*, a film version of *Sanctuary*, is released. The film *Today We Live*, based on WF's short story "Turn About," premieres in Oxford.

1934–35   *Doctor Martino and Other Stories*, a collection of detective stories, is published in April. WF works on *Absalom,*

Absalom!, his most ambitious novel about the South so far, as well as his most deliberately modernist work, both in Hollywood and in Oxford. He interrupts *Absalom* for a few months to complete *Pylon*, a brief novel about daredevil stunt pilots, and then returns to *Absalom* after the death of his youngest brother, Dean, in an air crash. (WF, himself an amateur aviator, had encouraged Dean to learn to fly.) *Pylon* is published in March 1935.

1936   *Absalom, Absalom!* is published in October by Random House, thereafter WF's permanent publisher.

1938   *The Unvanquished*, a collection of Civil War stories, is published in February. WF writes *The Wild Palms* (renamed by the publisher against WF's preferred title, *If I Forget Thee, Jerusalem*), a hybrid novel composed of two intertwined stories. He buys a farm outside of Oxford.

1939   *The Wild Palms* is published in January. WF is elected to the National Institute of Arts and Letters. Despite previous attention from French critics, such as Malraux and Sartre, WF only now begins to receive searching commentary from American critics. WF's short story "Barn Burning" wins the O. Henry Award.

1940   *The Hamlet*, the first novel of the Snopes trilogy, is published in April.

1942   *Go Down, Moses and Other Stories*, WF's broadest and most sustained scrutiny of black-white relations, is published in May.

1946   Dire financial pressures lead WF to a final Hollywood contract with Warner Brothers. Malcolm Cowley's edition of *The Portable Faulkner* is published in May by the Viking Press. Except for *Sanctuary*, WF's novels in their publishers' regular hardcover editions are all out of print; Cowley's volume makes a representative selection of WF's work available to a large reading public.

1948   *Intruder in the Dust*, a sequel to the Lucas Beauchamp materials of *Go Down, Moses*, is published in September. The novel's direct representation of Southern racial conflict secures large sales and signals WF's willingness to speak out on social issues. WF is elected to the American Academy of Arts and Letters.

1949   Film version of *Intruder in the Dust* is released in October. *Knight's Gambit*, a collection of detective stories, is published in November.

1950   *Collected Stories* is published in August. WF wins the Nobel Prize for Literature, travels with his daughter to Stockholm, and delivers his famous Nobel Prize acceptance speech.

1951   *Collected Stories* wins the National Book Award. *Requiem for a Nun*, a reprise of the Temple Drake materials in *Sanctuary*, written in a hybrid form that alternates between prose sections and stage drama, is published in September. France awards WF the Legion of Honor. From this point on, WF's work receives critical (indeed "canonical") attention and brings him financial security. Increasingly, he writes and speaks out on political (especially racial) issues, his position costing him support from many fellow Southerners because of his attack on racism, while disappointing liberals because of his gradualist approach to desegregation. WF travels extensively during the 1950s and early 1960s as a cultural ambassador for the State Department, making trips to Japan, Venezuela, and Greece.

1954   *A Fable*, a story of World War I cast as a version of the Passion Week of Christ's crucifixion and resurrection, is published in August, after more than a decade of intermittent work on it by WF. He describes it as "an indictment of war perhaps." It wins the Pulitzer Prize.

1955   *Big Woods*, a collection of stories, is published.

1957   *The Town*, the second novel of the Snopes trilogy, is published in May. WF teaches as writer-in-residence at the University of Virginia. He will alternate residence between Charlottesville and Oxford until his death.

1959   *The Mansion*, the final volume of the Snopes trilogy, is published in November.

1962   *The Reivers*, Faulkner's last novel, is published in June. A month later, on July 6, WF dies unexpectedly (probably of a heart attack) in a clinic at Byhalia, Mississippi, where he had been recurrently hospitalized for alcoholism and more recently for treatment following the last of many horseback-riding accidents. His funeral takes place the next day in Oxford.

1963   *The Reivers* wins the Pulitzer Prize

ABBREVIATIONS FOR TEXTS CITED

AA   *Absalom, Absalom! The Corrected Text.* 1936. New York: Vintage International, 1990.

AILD   *As I Lay Dying: The Corrected Text.* 1930. New York: Vintage International, 1990.

CS   *Collected Stories of William Faulkner.* New York: Vintage, 1977.

FAB   *A Fable.* 1954. *William Faulkner: Novels 1942–1954.* New York: Library of America, 1994.

FU   *Faulkner in the University,* ed. Frederick L. Gwynn and Joseph L. Blotner. Charlottesville: University of Virginia Press, 1959.

GDM   *Go Down, Moses.* 1942. New York: Vintage International, 1990.

JER   *If I Forget Thee, Jerusalem [The Wild Palms].* 1939. New York: Vintage International, 1995.

LA   *Light in August: The Corrected Text.* 1932. New York: Vintage International, 1990.

LG   *Lion in the Garden: Interviews with William Faulkner 1926–1962,* ed. James B. Meriwether and Michael Millgate. New York: Random, 1968.

P   *Pylon.* 1935. *William Faulkner: Novels 1930–1935.* New York: Library of America, 1985.

R   *The Reivers.* 1962. *William Faulkner: Novels 1957–1962.* New York: Library of America, 1999.

RN   *Requiem for a Nun.* 1951. *William Faulkner: Novels 1942–1954.* New York: Library of America, 1994.

S   *Sanctuary: The Corrected Text.* 1931. New York: Vintage International, 1993.

SAR   *Sartoris.* New York: Random, 1961.

SF   *The Sound and the Fury: The Corrected Text.* 1929. New York: Vintage International, 1990.

SL   *Selected Letters of William Faulkner*, ed. Joseph Blotner. New York: Random, 1977.

US   *Uncollected Stories of William Faulkner*, ed. Joseph Blotner. New York: Vintage, 1981.

JOHN T. MATTHEWS

Introduction

William Faulkner today remains among the most widely read, vigorously studied, and creatively contested writers in English worldwide. An informal tabulation of professional scholarship on U.S. writers reported in the annual bibliography of the Modern Language Association shows Faulkner second to Herman Melville, by a small margin, in the number of items published on his work in English internationally since 2008 (Nathaniel Hawthorne, Toni Morrison, and Ernest Hemingway all registered somewhat fewer). But Faulkner's stature as a subject of academic interest tells only part of the story of his importance as an international writer. As we make our way into the century after his, readers from all over the world continue to recognize Faulkner's monumental achievement in describing the extreme transformations of economic, social, and intellectual life that constituted a decisive moment in the history of global modernization. Faulkner's genius was to imagine, with staggering minuteness of detail, over a long arc of historical change, how a set of people sharing a small corner of the earth experienced profound upheavals in their world. Faulkner's enduring relevance has something to do with the way those shocks of modernization continue to be felt in the disruptions of traditional agrarian ways of life; in the century-long emergence of the global city; in reinventions of the local or regional; in the revolutionary effects of new technologies; in the ascendance of market commerce and speculative finance over the making of things; in the challenges to tyrannical political states and varieties of elite rule over minorities, including reactionary ones based on fictions of racial, ethnic, gender, regional, or religious inferiority; in the long-lasting disablements caused by European colonialism and imperialism both to victims and to perpetrators; in the blind assault on the natural world for human gain.

As scrupulously as Faulkner's descriptive powers attempt to comprehend his world, however, his writing still matters because it so extends itself artistically. By that I mean the way Faulkner stretches the capacities of literary form and language in relentless determination to imagine the reality of what it meant to be alive in a given place and time and to invent other lives that were partly his own as their author and partly that which he could never fully inhabit. Faulkner created a Shakespearean cast of indelible, larger-than-life characters out of the family stories he heard, out of the local idiosyncrasies he observed, out of the wide variety of literature he read avidly, as well as purely out of his head. Locals in his hometown of Oxford, Mississippi, claimed they recognized this or that individual, this or that anecdote from the real life of the town, but Faulkner is actually one of the least directly autobiographical authors you will encounter. For all the personal material – subject matter as well as emotional and psychological experience – that Faulkner draws upon, his plots and characters are largely composites and layered inventions.[1] To forge a way to see those individual characters in motion, against the backdrop of their common history, Faulkner experimented with narrative form and style in ways that extended the methods other modernists were also developing to record the whirlwind of modernization. Faulkner once compared writing a novel to building a henhouse in a hurricane, and readers who respond to his artistry are often spellbound by the extensive rearrangement of chronology in his plots, which cut quickly between scenes, flash backward without warning, alternate between parallel narratives, and offer conflicting versions of events.

Yet Faulkner's admirers testify most ardently to the seductiveness of his style. Its technique of easing unhurriedly into the evocation of a place, for example, which requires minute notation of sounds, sights, and the feel of things, nudges Faulkner's sentences into motion, barely, reluctantly (think of the image of Rosa Coldfield in her father's office that develops slowly in the opening pages of *Absalom, Absalom!*, like an old-fashioned photograph, or the hardly discernible movement of a mule-drawn wagon making its way uphill toward the patiently waiting Lena Grove at the outset of *Light in August*). Sometimes they gather momentum as they describe, correct, re-describe – distinctions proliferating with nearly every assertion. In Faulkner, the sentence becomes the measure of the world. Faulkner comments, "This I think accounts for what people call the obscurity, the involved formless 'style', endless sentences. I'm trying to say it all in one sentence, between one Cap and one period."[2] Frequently, a narrator's underlying anxiety, rage, desire, or terror unmoors the sentences, and a torrent of emotion carries words beyond syntax, beyond manageable units of thought, even beyond reason, to the almost unimaginable extension of prose style as the very stuff of self. Faulkner understood the extreme demands he placed on literary language: "The aim of every artist is to arrest motion, which is life, by artificial means and hold it fixed so that 100 years later when a stranger looks at it, it moves again since it is life" (*LG* 253). When the contemporary French African author Tierno Monénembo was growing up in Guinea, he came across a ragged book with missing pages on the shelf of his village store. "Stunned by the unfurling of sentences, dazed by the flood of images and adjectives," he recalls, "I did not immediately pay attention to the title and the author's name. Nor did I understand the importance of my discovery when I realized a few days later that it was *The Sound and the Fury*."³ As an author from a country with a past of colonialism and slavery, Monénembo would later process Faulkner's writing in historical terms supplied by another post-colonial writer, Édouard Glissant. But at the moment of Monénembo's personal discovery, it was Faulkner's sheer artistry that entranced.

The central features of Faulkner's writing that contribute to its endurance and influence – probably of any literature that lasts – are the depth and subtlety of its portrayal of humans interacting with circumstance, and its transcendent realization of form and style. Yet one must also acknowledge that Faulkner persists because he is a *valuably* difficult writer, one who looms over succeeding generations because he wrestles so strenuously with what we recognize as still-urgent social and aesthetic problems. It's not just that the formal features of his writing require sustained attention, patient reading and rereading, trial and error, and a willingness to accept lingering confusion and irresolution even after the novel is over, amid the hangover of besotted reading; Faulkner also willingly put himself in awkward positions with respect to any number of popular attitudes and ideas. He was a white Southerner from a prominent (if declining) Mississippi family that included slave-owning ancestors. He made his home in the town of Oxford all his life, and wrote about the most horrid elements of Southern and national life: slavery, racism, lynching, segregation, desegregation, patriarchal misogyny, plantation evils, the destructiveness and destruction of his own civilization, the intolerability and intolerance of life in a poor rural world, the lethality of ignorance and bigotry, the contradictions of American democracy and capitalism. Faulkner's accomplishment as a modernist writer also involved the perversity of calling into question the very authority of the "literary" to convey worlds and render individual subjectivities. Haunting his texts is a deconstructive suspicion that what feel like the immediate realities of thought, consciousness, truth, and the real are fundamentally effects of discourse, of the way people construct reality with agreed-upon concepts and interpret it with words they must share. Such an uncompromising mistrust of the very artistic medium the novelist must so desperately trust reflects wider modernist doubts in philosophy, physics, psychology, and new mechanical recording media about the "presence" created by representation.

There's a lot of obstinacy to Faulkner. He admired mules and bred them on his farm. Faulkner reflexively refuses to compromise with readers, to endorse conventional wisdom, to side with history's winners or spare its losers, to side with history's losers or spare its winners, to accept the judgment of others, or to see only one side of an issue, no matter what question of justice or morality is involved. However enchanted, Faulkner's readers unavoidably must expect to be offended by his writing. That has been true since he began publishing wickedly perverse books, such as *Sanctuary*, as well as uncompromisingly demanding ones, such as *The Sound and the Fury*. Faulkner makes you uncomfortable (and in fact he often seemed unbearable to himself) as he asks everything of you in making sense of a puzzling world, in savoring the pleasures and agonies common to all human lives, in reveling with pure delight in the "miracle" of the written. That's how Vladimir Nabokov has one of his characters, a crazed scholar of literature, put it: "We are absurdly accustomed to the miracle of a few written signs being able to contain immortal imagery, involutions of thought, new worlds with live people, speaking, weeping, laughing."⁴ Nabokov in fact had no taste for what he considered Faulkner's stylistic vulgarity, yet he shared his willingness to make art a matter of outrage and scandal. Nabokov once makes fun of Faulkner's *Sanctuary*, a novel that tells the story of a young woman's horrific sexual assault by a gangster whose impotence leads him to use an implement to defile her, as one of the Southern author's "corn-cobby chronicles."⁵ Yet his own masterpiece, *Lolita*, defies readers to separate the utterly abhorrent (its narrator, a child kidnapper and molester) from the sublimely beautiful (who happens to write gorgeous prose). And *Lolita*, after all, perversely ends up mimicking *Sanctuary*, Faulkner's evil Popeye a mute anticipation of the florid Humbert Humbert, Lolita a prepubescent avatar of Temple Drake. The perverse, the difficult, the unwelcoming, the critical, the uncooperative, the unbelievable, the mad – these are all manifestations of the force of *negation* in Faulkner's writing, as in much great literature. Theodor Adorno describes the power of art to say "no" to life led unthinkingly, to life in which human evil proceeds untroubled from one unspeakable atrocity to the next. Writing in the wake of the Holocaust, Adorno develops a theory of modern art that emphasizes its powerfully critical or negative function. Literature stands apart from the world as we know it, even as it reproduces that world's ways, giving readers the opportunity for critical reflection.⁶ Optimistic affirmative "messages" belong to self-help books and moralistic literature. Faulkner's books provide little consolation, although they do suggest a kind of indefatigable capacity in humankind to "endure," and maybe even to "prevail." At least that's the bare hope Faulkner ventured in his Nobel Prize speech in 1950, delivered in the midst of the Cold War, as the writer's generation stared at the possibility of global nuclear holocaust. Faulkner's novels urge us today to cherish the passionate intricacy of literary art; to value prolonged stays in freely imagined worlds; to reflect on the interplay between individual will and the world's contingency; to be as concerned with what is hidden as with what is conspicuous; and to realize that the stories we tell about our lives are inseparable from the lives themselves.

The original *Cambridge Companion to William Faulkner* (1995), edited by Philip Weinstein, contained eight essays. Five were organized as studies of Faulkner's relation to principal cultural formations: American modernism, post-modernism, the culture industry, European modernists, and post-colonialism. Each of them dealt with a range of Faulkner texts, but they mainly crisscrossed through Faulkner's major novels: *The Sound and the Fury, Light in August, Absalom, Absalom!,* and *Go Down, Moses.* The second set of essays (entitled "The World in the Texts," complementing Part I's "The Texts in the World") offered sample critical readings by zeroing in on three of those novels and examining specialized topics important to Faulkner's fiction: the Great Migration; the Southern discourse of race; and plantation paternalism.

The first *Companion* attempted to represent "recent trends in Faulkner studies" by placing his work in the "critical practice of the 1990s." Twenty years later, our *New Companion* attempts to capture continuing developments and fresh directions in the ways scholars and teachers conceive of principal contexts for Faulkner's writing and in the methods advanced to study them. Readers familiar with the earlier version of the *Companion* will find continuities here with its interests, as well as important evolutions, fresh takes, and new additions. Modernist studies, for example, newly emphasizes transnational features: modernism's relation to anti-colonial cultural projects, the growth of the modern state, and the formation of sub-national cultural mentalities; its international modes of production and consumption; its mindfulness of concurrent developments in film and other electronic media; the submerged centrality of environmental history – to name just some. Formerly predominant analytical categories have been challenged, complicated, or replaced. For example, as useful as the concept of post-modernism has been for identifying the ontological skepticism and meta-narrative playfulness in Faulkner that anticipate the generation of John Barth or Thomas Pynchon, it might be helpful today to think about Faulkner's imaginative legacies more diversely and pluralistically – in the wider ambit of post-1945 fiction that he began to participate in himself during the later portion of his career.

Each essay in the *New Companion* reflects a disciplinary sub-field or methodological approach in which current broader thinking about literature – from new theoretical platforms to new paradigms in modern, American, or Southern studies – has advanced or transformed the questions critics bring to the study of Faulkner's writing. In some instances, a solid body of scholarship has already materialized; in others, a few notable pieces promise the emergence of a fresh line of inquiry into Faulkner. In addition to representing the precepts of its method, the main task of each chapter is to provide a strong piece of interpretation that warrants the approach taken. Our *New Cambridge Companion to William Faulkner* attempts to give readers at least a partial sense of the innovative ways Faulkner is being read in the twenty-first century and to bear witness to his continued importance as a world writer.

The opening chapter by Julian Murphet wonders what it meant for Faulkner to be writing at a time when new forms of mechanical recording technologies like the phonograph and film were making a broad impact on modern life. Murphet's approach is based on the premise that many forms of modernist experimentation in literary techniques were stimulated by competition with transformative developments in audio and visual reproduction. Within this "multimedia ecology" of modernism, novelists like Faulkner directly depicted novelties like "the graphophone" that appears in *As I Lay Dying*, exploring how the technological preservation, circulation, and broadcast of sound created new sensations of the divorce between body and voice, the living and the dead, the individual and disembodied communities. Murphet presents Faulkner as a pivotal figure in modernism's confrontation with the eclipse of received models of consciousness, of narrative as storytelling, of style as voice, of the "literary" itself under the pressure of the mechanical reproduction of voice and image – the appearance of new media provoking equivocal responses from modernist writing, of rejection and imitation, often simultaneously.

Peter Lurie pursues the implications of the graphic or textual nature of film's mechanical inscription of reality by taking up the way Faulkner's writing reflects the relation between early cinema and depictions of race. The surprising centrality of race in early American film was advanced by Michael Rogin in his essay on D. W. Griffith's masterpiece of racism, *The Birth of a Nation* (1915). Lurie shows how Faulkner, as a novelist deeply interested in race, writing at the moment of film's emergence, was particularly alert to Griffith's use of the medium to establish whiteness as the bedrock of national identity. Both modes, literature and film, betray how whiteness is the result of a process of projection (psychological as well as mechanical), structured by differential representation and compromised by representational instability and inadequacy. Lurie's premise is that film must be understood not as a transparent window on reality but as a coded representation of it, and that, in particular, *The Birth of a Nation*'s effort to depict races as visually distinct – a tendency shared by other early films – is compromised by the inseparability of black and white as they define each other. The impossibility of establishing absolute racial difference is replicated in the technical inseparability of black and white film images and process, a phenomenon that may be seen as an individual case of the general structure of writing, of textuality. Cinema is a kind of modern writing with light.

Aliyyah Abdur-Rahman addresses a Faulkner who must face a legacy of post-Reconstruction Southern dreams that a moribund white aristocracy might be resurrected, visions that informed wider racist fantasies about white solidarity and modern nationhood. She studies *Absalom, Absalom!* as demonstrating the exclusionary oblivion of Quentin's racist conditioning, seconded by Shreve's, and the multiple narratives' shared inability to imagine social and political futures in which African-Americans have gained full enfranchisement, let alone reparation. Abdur-Rahman's chapter shows how the modern South reproduced the moral blindness, ethical indifference, and social and economic violence demanded by an order of elite identity that does not understand itself to be already dead. This situation amounts to something like the newly dead memorializing the long dead. Abdur-Rahman's reading demonstrates the repeated, willful avoidance by Faulkner's privileged characters of realities that challenge fantasies of white supremacy: for example, Quentin Compson's cutting off Shreve in *Absalom, Absalom!* when he brings up the fact of West Virginia's statehood, since it recalls the South's internal divisions over the injustice of slavery. This is exactly the refusal of history one sees in *The Sound and the Fury* when Quentin daydreams during a lesson on Mississippi colonial history. *Absalom* exhibits how racist projection shapes the various tellings of Sutpen's saga, with Charles Bon taken to *signify* the sort of future Quentin finds unimaginable, unsurvivable, as opposed to who Charles Bon might actually *be*. Abdur-Rahman's reading for racial exclusion and projected unintelligibility intersects with Peter Lurie's treatment of race as textualized in film image and narrative.

Patricia Chu's chapter probes another facet of Faulkner's response to modernization: his concern with the growth of the modern state, and expressly its monopolistic production of biopower. Chu reverses the habit of reading Faulkner's South as an exception to national modernization by showing it as an epitome of modernity. In a richly contextualized close study of one of Faulkner's short stories about New Deal Southern farm reform, "The Tall Men" (1941), Chu illustrates how Faulkner dramatizes the perils not just of traditional Northern/national domination of the South but more broadly of the evolution of total modern state power – not just the U.S.

Government but "governmentality" itself. By framing Faulkner's story with modern developments in the scientific understanding of life-forms, with Georg Simmel's theorization of how modern urban life affects habits of perception, and with a genealogy of the modern state's control of biopolitics drawn from Michel Foucault, Chu's essay exemplifies how issues prominent in the so-called new modernist studies enable us to see Faulkner afresh.

The question of Faulkner's engagement with the modern transformation of the South also roots Susan Scott Parrish's chapter on the impact of the Mississippi River's "Great Flood" of 1927. Parrish's essay suggests how Faulkner's texts, and modernist literature more broadly, must be read for its "environmental unconscious." Focusing on *As I Lay Dying*, Parrish describes how this environmental trauma hides behind two crises more salient in the novel: World War I and the Great Depression. Parrish shows how Faulkner's modernist modes of representation engage with a thick substratum of local and regional history to represent the South attempting to deal with uprooting transformations associated with national modernization. The essay traces the catastrophe of the flood as experienced by the novel's characters to environmental degradations caused by the "second" modern industrial revolution, witnessed in the South roughly between 1880 and 1930. Leading to that moment is a long history of environmentally abusive hemispheric and regional plantation economies, exacerbated locally by federal (mis)management of the Mississippi Valley. Such a genealogy creates the conditions for the "natural" disasters depicted in Faulkner's flood novels (which include for Parrish *The Sound and the Fury* and *If I Forget Thee, Jerusalem*).

Greg Forter develops an account drawn from psychoanalytic theory to describe the overlapping phenomena of individual and collective trauma, exemplified by Parrish's study of the Bundren family. Forter distinguishes between trauma felt as an external impingement and trauma experienced as an internal problem of self-interpretation. Moving between the conceptual and textual levels, Forter shows how these contrasting models of trauma contribute to the struggle to render the formation of consciousness in Faulkner and how his style's rich surfaces embed trauma in their figurative language. In his reading of *Sanctuary*, Forter finds the expression of traumatic symptomology in varieties of formal delay or deferral (Nachträglichkeit) and shows the stylistic effects of psychoanalytic logic in the novel's imagery, which repeatedly overwhelms visual order with somatic excess. Forter's essay also raises an important question of ethics in trauma studies: how to distinguish trauma as suffered historically by certain people from the sort that is passed on to others.

Jaime Harker ranges widely across Faulkner's work to show the extent of transgressive sexuality explored in his fiction. Demonstrating how ubiquitous Faulkner's renegade sexual imagination is, Harker expands our comprehension of Faulkner as a writer of same-sex desire. Focusing on the subversive and often subliminal relations between women, the chapter patiently assembles a compelling argument from the plenitude of Faulkner's depiction of intimacy between women. Given the brutalities of heterosexual violence rife in the South that Faulkner portrays, Harker's illumination of dissenting relations between women and the counter-communities they form shows readers how to read across the grain of more expected behavior and relationships. Numerous fresh insights appear in the essay's systematic sweep across the expanse of heterosexism: one sample is the way that Temple's "refusal" to leave Miss Reba's brothel indicates not only that she is a victim of rape and a prisoner (a condition belatedly elucidated in the criticism by trauma studies approaches, as in Forter's chapter) but also that she herself embraces, horribly, a sexist caricature like "nymphomania" – played out in the scenes with her "lover" Red, for instance, and subscribed to further by the men in her world who seek paternalistically to protect her.

Melanie Benson Taylor takes up the consequences of the new Southern studies for reading Faulkner, both in its efforts to expand the conceptualization and material of "the South" and in the scholarly movement's unwitting perpetuation of longstanding preoccupations and blind spots. Taylor is especially interested in new opportunities to redress earlier neglect of Native American expression in accounts of Southern culture. In 2001, Houston A. Baker, Jr. and Dana D. Nelson co-edited a special issue of the journal *American Literature* in which they identified a new determination in studies of the U.S. South to understand its regional exceptionality as a projection of national needs to disavow responsibility for slavery, corporal violence, degradation of nature, commercial opportunism, and so forth. Baker and Nelson referred to this movement as the "new Southern Studies" and reported that their editorial maxim had become: "'The South' is the U.S. social, political, racial, economic, ethical, and everyday-life imaginary written as 'regionalism.'" Looking back at more than a decade of ensuing reconsiderations of the region, Taylor rehearses the overlapping, contradictory, uneven constitution of what has been meant by "the South." In doing so, she prepares for her reading of what Mikhail Bakhtin would call a heteroglot (or linguistically composite) South in Faulkner's heterodox depictions. One key Faulkner text for this chapter is *Requiem for a Nun,* in which Taylor delineates Faulkner's critique of national origins, with its resonances for U.S. democracy's Cold War embattlement. Her reading of this hybrid literary work prefaces her excavation of the problematic of the Native American for conceptions of national solidarity. The chapter suggests how the new Southern studies has inspired much innovative work on Native Americans while still lagging in fully reckoning with native presence in the formation of nation and region, particularly the South.

Martyn Bone lays out the burden of the Faulkner syndrome – the sense among Southern novelists who followed him that Faulkner's was an impossible achievement to match, coupled with the conviction that certain limitations of his vision rightly call for stratagems of creative revision, elusion, and complaint. Bone's chapter brings mainstays of contemporary U.S. fiction such as Cormac McCarthy and Richard Ford into focus as *Southern* writers, rarely the way either is classified, making clear what the stakes are for each in their desire to escape Faulkner-likeness. Bone's account of more expressly avowed Southern writers, such as Barry Hannah, who, having lived in Oxford, Mississippi, had to parody Faulkner to breathe, captures the agonistics of post-Faulkner Southern writing. The chapter's turn to African-American writing from, of, and about the South does not spare Faulkner from the disappointment and even rage that compel their engagement with his work. Such novelists as John Oliver Killens, twenty years younger than Faulkner, and Jesmyn Ward, a contemporary novelist from Mississippi, have their exemplary challenges to Faulkner compellingly set out in Bone's account.

Benjamin Widiss constructs another post-Faulknerian lineage by conjoining the projects of Gabriel García Márquez and Toni Morrison, two of the twentieth century's most prominent novelists, both of whom have acknowledged the importance of Faulkner's writing to their own. Although their departures from Faulkner are usually understood to be quite distinct – Márquez creating his Colombian version of a multi-generational plantation saga via the mode of magical realism, Morrison concentrating on the rendering of black subjectivity in the afterlife of U.S. slavery in twentieth century racism – Widiss's analysis lets us see how much these authors share as they explore the possibilities of post-realistic narrative. From Faulkner's admission that stories of the past often just "don't explain," to Márquez and other Latin American Boom writers' appreciation for the Faulknerian novel as the very genre that dramatizes the discrepancy between history and the individual's synthesis of time, to Morrison's incarnation of history in the very body of a lost child, Widiss charts a genealogy of commitment to the novel as a modern literary form. In the novels of contemporaries like Jeffrey Eugenides and Jonathan Safran Foer, Widiss locates a devotion to "alternative explanatory systems" that, rather than bemoan the failure of narrative authority bedeviling Faulkner's tellers, revels in the opportunity to fill such truth-gaps imaginatively.

Hugues Azérad consolidates and powerfully extends efforts to resituate Faulkner – as well as U.S. Southern literature and U.S. literature more broadly – in Caribbean and hemispheric contexts. Azérad's chapter recharges the value of thinking about the categories and traditions of "American" literature outside national perimeters. Azérad proceeds on a number of critical fronts. The introduction of Édouard Glissant's thinking early in the chapter does more than just set up the Martinican writer's "reading" of Faulkner, influential as that has been in Faulkner studies; Azérad establishes a *substantial* Glissant, one whose own hemispheric stature as poet, novelist, and critic authenticates his claims about the importance of equality and friendship across temporal and geographic borders discussed subsequently. Framing his chapter with discriminations between Antonio Benítez-Rojo and Glissant, Azérad also provides a sense of the particular colonial histories that determine the variety of Caribbean post-colonial theory; these histories dictate the questions, if not necessarily the shape of the answers, posed by the literature and analytical models originating in the hemisphere's "estuary" of colonized settlements. All this prepares for the presentation of Glissant's dialogue with Faulkner's texts. Glissant brings a post-colonial perspective to his account of Faulkner's poetics: Faulkner's formal habits of deferral and suspension, his preoccupation with the unknowable or the unrepresentable. The chapter widens to consider creative reverberations of the Caribbean Faulkner in Patrick Chamoiseau, Maryse Condé, and Jamaica Kincaid.

Ramón Saldívar and Sylvan Goldberg identify fundamental features of the global South that situate Faulkner's writing within the broadest terms of peripheral mentalities, colonial temporalities, and resistant or alternative aesthetic practices. Saldívar and Goldberg take up the question of postcolonial poetics by excavating their roots in the long history of human domination over nature, what has become known as the Anthropocene era. From this perspective, Faulkner's stylistic repetitiousness and the cyclical temporality of his narratives are manifestations of the rhythms of repeated human assaults on nature, obscured to any individual eye because of long trans-generational spans of time, and structuring Faulkner's texts as things felt but unknowable. This is a version of transatlantic modernism, but a Caribbean sort, rather than the more familiar Euro-American north Atlantic kind. Saldívar and Goldberg demonstrate Faulkner's mindfulness of ecological deep history in the tissue of his language, as it grapples with the incommensurability of individual experience and social history, with the palpability of effects but not causes, with cyclicality as the antithesis of progress but also its double. Saldívar and Goldberg's interests here intersect with those of Susan Scott Parrish's discussion of environmental history, parallel Hughes Azérad's discussion of Glissant's poetics of Caribbean post-colonialism, and reinforce Randy Boyagoda's view of a syncretic global post-colonialism.

Randy Boyagoda's chapter counsels wariness in constructing a one-size-fits-all post-colonial version of Faulkner's writing, demonstrating how fundamental material differences between ex-colonial and ex-colonized places cannot be left out of characterizations of the post-colonial. Boyagoda bases this critical position on politically sensitive and economically interested theorists of modernity such as Arjun Appadurai, Aijaz Ahmad, and ultimately Pankaj Mishra, a novelist and cultural critic who writes about the colonial history of subcontinental India. To discriminate Faulkner's post-colonial situation, Boyagoda draws on Walter Johnson's study of the antebellum U.S. South's Mississippi River Valley as a plantation economy wholly connected to an international network of speculation, labor, production, finance, and commerce. Johnson's view of an already-global U.S. South allows Boyagoda to illuminate why Faulkner today appeals to writers occupying quite different positions amid imperial world systems. Boyagoda finds Faulkner's late novel *A Fable* prescient in capturing Faulkner's skepticism about the United States' facile succession to western imperial domination during the so-called American Century after World War I. In Boyagoda's reading, the novel also foresees the United States' eventual comeuppance as a result of the insubordinate indifference of soon-to-be-ex-colonials such as the Senegalese guards ordered to defend their own conquerors. The chapter includes an exploration of *A New History of Torments* (1982), a novel by Zulfikar Ghose, a Pakistani writer who teaches in Texas and who sets much of his fiction in Latin America. In works like his, Boyagoda finds ample confirmation of the complexities of contemporary post-colonialism in the many-layered global South(s).

NOTES

1 Philip Weinstein's *Becoming Faulkner* (Oxford: Oxford University Press, 2009) considers key moments in Faulkner's life whose emotional impact gets transformed into situations and events but that do not show up directly in the fiction. Judith Wittenberg's *Faulkner: The Transfiguration of Biography* (Lincoln, NE: University of Nebraska Press, 1980) suggests how Faulkner more directly imported autobiographical material into his fiction while altering it significantly.

2 Malcolm Cowley, *The Faulkner-Cowley File: Letters and Memories 1944–1962* (New York: Viking Press, 1966), p. 14.

3 Tierno Monénembo, *Global Faulkner: Faulkner and Yoknapatawpha*, 2006, Annette Trefzer and Ann J. Abadie (eds.) (Jackson: University Press of Mississippi, 2009), p. 174.

4 Vladimir Nabokov, *Pale Fire* (New York: Vintage Books, 1989), p. 289.

5 *New York Times*, January 30, 1966, "Why Nabokov Detests Freud," excerpts from an interview the US National Educational Television network conducted with Vladimir Nabokov. Reprinted at http://www.nytimes.com/books/97/03/02/ lifetimes/nab-v-freud.html (accessed August 18, 2014).

6 Theodor Adorno, *Negative Dialectics*, trans. E. B. Ashton (London: Routledge, 1990). Originally published as *Negative Dialektik* (Frankfurt: Suhrkamp Verlag, 1966).

I

JULIAN MURPHET

New Media Ecology

The view from Balzac's *Comédie humaine* (with interrelated plots and characters appearing in numerous individual works) to Faulkner's Yoknapatawpha cycle (similarly with stories and families reappearing in its many novels) is, like the view from Everest to Kanchenjunga, distorted by the curvature of the earth. What associates these two monumental achievements in literary prose – their Himalayan endeavor to rear above and so disclose an entire way of life – is also what separates them, since not only do other colossal peaks intervene (James, Dostoevsky, Joyce, Proust), but the ceaseless tectonic realignments of literary space in the zone between make any clear view impossible. But what might it mean to say that the chief difference between Balzac and Faulkner is, precisely, "the media"? That the most fateful historical factor to have distinguished the first great multi-novel act of "world creation" from its most illustrious successor was the intervening appearance, over eighty years, of machines of representation, storage, and dissemination that threatened to take over the redoubtable institutions of literature – its imperturbable "storage monopoly"[1] – and sent the ominous depth charge of *obsolescence* deep into the spiritual substance of the West? Putting the matter this way has the advantage of spotlighting a materialist infrastructure lodged within or beneath literary history – the actual technologies of reproduction that can be appealed to so as to sidestep the persistent critical temptations toward facile speculation about Zeitgeist (the spirit of the times) or, still worse, the tedium of biographical explanation.

The "media" – as system and network – can then serve as explanatory key to the reversal of epistemological fortunes evident in the shift from the great narrative sequences of the *Comédie* to the baffled and tortuous opening pages of *The Sound and the Fury*. Any number of interpretive options is available to explain what Faulkner is doing here – from sabotaging the omniscience of a heroic bourgeoisie to staging the relativity of modern "selfhood"; or practicing the ideal of Flaubertian "pure" style; or toying with the decadent shadows of Naturalism – but the sensed looseness of these doubtless very worthy solutions is given a rude comeuppance by an alternative account of the transformation of the publishing industry itself, which now calls redoubled attention to the material form taken by Faulkner's text. In this approach, what strikes us most in Faulkner's extreme and wing-clipped parataxis (one simple statement after the next) is the stunted shape of the sentences themselves: their orphaned nominalism on the page, each suspended between the others like a crude link in a barbarous chain, folded over on itself and here and there broken, mended only with glue and string. Balzac's billowing syntax, meanwhile, is to be grasped as the product of a media ecology whose alpha and omega are publishing; a civilization of lively, circulating printed matters, of feuilletons, coffee shops, and what was called a "public sphere" or civil society. The sentences of a Balzac are supported, in their rhetorical modes of engagement, their figural insistences, their allusive and connotative breadth, by what Friedrich Kittler called a "discourse network" sustained across the innumerable institutional and material nodes of the Enlightenment.[2] After which, this:

> Roskus came with the milk buckets. He went on. Quentin wasn't coming with us. He was sitting on the kitchen steps. We went down to Versh's house. I liked to smell Versh's house. *There was a fire in it and T. P. squatting in his shirt tail in front of it, chunking it into a blaze.*
>
> Then I got up and T. P. dressed me and we went to the kitchen and ate. Dilsey was singing and I began to cry and she stopped. (*SF* 28)

One's immediate sense is of the utter implosion of Balzac's discourse network. Such a neutered style – in which assertion fails to engender significance – is the syntactical index to some absolute crisis in the way that literature functions socially: no longer the organic tissue of a national consciousness, but a torn motley of threads, a violently amputated impulse to connect. We feel the contraction of an entire industry, the straitening of an institution, a history of declining markets and the foreshortening of a privileged form. These uninflected indicative sentences stream together into what Faulkner called an "unbroken-surfaced confusion," where a dozen or more temporal planes are shuffled according to subliminal cues and an enigmatic spatial logic.[3] The formal decision to subtract the conventional transitional markers – adverbs, verb moods, shifts in tense – accords, to be sure, with a traumatized first-person psychological monad in which time has ceased to exist, but it accords as well with a transformed cultural environment whose new technological instruments (radio, cinema, phonographs) cast their audiences and spectators willy-nilly into an immediate present tense, devoid of the "deep time" available to Proustian or Jamesian prose.

That this is something more than an equivalent of the "continuous present" that Gertrude Stein had patented in her own reaction to the century of "cinema and series production"[4] is attested, however, by Faulkner's daydream that Benjy's chapter could be printed with different colored inks: "I wish publishing was advanced enough to use colored ink," he complained to his agent.[5] The temporal gearshifts were to be represented not grammatically but visually on the page, as so many patches of typographic color: a mediatic synesthesia now made good in The Folio Society's vulgarly literal edition. I take it that Faulkner's hope was never meant to be realized but was instead a kind of ideological symptom, produced by one of the most prodigious bursts of aesthetic energy in all of modernism, left on the living art of literature by a new media ecology profoundly competitive with it. The dream of a book enlivened by "special effects" not confined to the linguistic sphere is a dream of evolutionary advantage, akin to the contemporary pipe dream of Bob Brown's "readies" or the explosion of activity in the world of "artists' books."[6] To "do the Compsons in different voices," and then in different inks, is to ask the novel as a form to adjust its techniques to an environment of image-machines, sound-machines, and cultural distractions predicated on novelty and disposability. And yet the real evidence for such a competitive adaptation is to be found buried deep in the linguistic substance itself, where Faulkner truly did make literature "advanced enough" to tackle the Darwinian trials of the second machine age.

In this chapter we will take a brief survey of some of these effects, in order to give a sense of how saturated Faulkner's immense act of literary "world creation" is by the signs and rhythms of a post-literary media ecology. What we will want to know is how, under the accumulating pressure from new narrative media such as cinema and radio and new communicational media such as the telegraph and telephone, Faulkner obliged the art of prose narrative to adapt in order to survive. Our thesis is that the concerted attempt to do just that – to ensure the survival and aesthetic legitimacy of literature in a new media ecology – is one salient explanation for what we know as modernism more generally, which can be productively understood as a systemic mutation across all the established genres and modes in the light of rapid ecological change. As the newer mechanical and electronic media stole an increasingly greater share of the cultural marketplace over the first few decades of the twentieth century, those older, non-mechanical arts and media such as sculpture, dance, painting, chamber and symphonic music, and (more complicatedly) writing internalized the threat, not by turning backward in fits of nostalgic pique, but by homeopathically transferring this or that technical feature of the new media system into their own methods of representation.[7] Faulkner's place in that broader story is a pivotal one, and his most vivid stylistic traits are some of our best clues for solving a mystery that he was one of the first to have shrouded in a haze of disavowal and ideological opacity. His public antagonism toward the movies, as toward radio and television, fostered a myth of aloof indifference, whereas the truth was rather one of ingenious adaptation and transference. Let us see how.

Ecology

We are suggesting that, circa 1930, "the writer" is no longer the central load-bearing pillar of the cultural edifice that "he" once was, that the very possibility of a Balzac or a Dickens has been obviated by the march of technical progress, such that even though "he" carries about him the residual vatic airs of a vanished type, "the writer" has already been absorbed into media systems and discourse networks that make "his" labors look quaintly anachronistic, if not fully adapted to the cultural assembly line. In a story entitled "Artist at Home" (1933), Faulkner provides a satiric snapshot of the conditions under which writing must take place after *King Kong* and *Amos 'n' Andy*. The successful Southern writer based in rural Virginia is besieged by a modernity that makes its presence felt above all through various new media. Ambitious writers from the big cities announce their coming by telegram but arrive faster than the artist can collect their dispatches; rather than Balzac's ink and quill, the central technical presence in this house is the click-clack of the typewriter on which everything is written directly ("Bull market in typewriting, you might say" [CS 639]); meanwhile, the telephone rings constantly, with more news than the writer can properly accommodate. After informing us disparagingly of a minor tryst between a visiting poet and the author's wife, the narrator comments: "But that's not it. That can be seen in any movie. This is what it is, what is good" (636). And this infection from the terrain of mass culture, prompting such narrative disavowals, precipitates a situation where one's "whole life was a not very successful imitation of itself" (644). To be a writer, an artist, is henceforth to be a "writer" or "artist," a simulacrum of a Balzac, rather than the thing itself. It has become increasingly impossible to fashion an adequate literary signal – let alone a world synthesized out of them – in a situation of such dinning media noise.

Where Balzac would, as a matter of course, compare his characters and scenes to the great works of Western painting and sculpture to stabilize what Barthes called the "cultural code" of his post-Enlightenment discourse network,[8] Faulkner feels himself asphyxiated by the logic of the simulacrum to resort to such comparisons as: "his brow like that of children in daguerrotypes" (SF 274); "that dead and stereotyped transience of rooms in assignation houses" (*SF* 282); "as flat and without perspective as a painted cardboard set upon the ultimate edge of the flat earth" (*SF* 292); "the rigid gravity of a cigar-store Indian" (*AILD* 4); "that vicious depthless quality of stamped tin" (*S* 4); "all angles, like a modernist lampstand" (*S* 7); "like a [K]odak print emerging from the liquid" (*LA* 108); "like the Katzenjammer kids in the funny paper" (*LA* 353); and "exactly like when the needle is lifted from a phonograph record" (*LA* 371). The point of highlighting this infinitely illustratable tendency in Faulkner is to underscore the place of a new media system within the novelistic imagination itself. Where once the treasured masterpieces of humanistic art served as the civilized medium for all verbal descriptions that thought of themselves as *literary*, now the flattened stereotypes of cinema, gramophone, and photograph are the go-to vocabulary for comparison in the age of "mechanical reproduction."

This is how the media ecology was felt by practicing artists at the time. Faulkner's own stake in it was perplexed and conflicted. Discovering that it was impossible to make a good living writing what he knew to be his best, novelistic work, Faulkner participated of necessity not only in the motion picture industry as a salaried writer but also in the market for short stories in magazines – both relatively new media outlets for otherwise serious writers who (unlike Gertrude Stein, but like Fitzgerald and Hemingway) were without sufficient independent means to float their more uncompromising efforts – writing no fewer than seventy stories and working on dozens of screenplays and treatments between the years 1922 and 1936 alone, his peak years as a novelist. Even the novels themselves, especially in the early years, are not to be construed outside of a media ecology driven by commercial imperatives of concision, efficiency, and pace, which is how Faulkner's first fully mature work, *Flags in the Dust*, came to be *Sartoris*: a vastly reduced, streamlined version that Faulkner essentially handed over to his agent to manage. It is not uninteresting to note that, at the very same time that Ben Wasson was hacking away a full quarter of the bulk of *Flags* to satisfy the publishers, Faulkner himself was composing *The Sound and the Fury*: a work therefore to be understood as emerging under the sign of cultural Fordism; a work so condensed, so fat-free and sprung with modernity as to make everything written previously look Victorian and antiquated. The short stories are adapted to an already existing market of short and "readable" fiction; *The Sound and the Fury* is adapted, as it were, to a market that does not exist but whose tastes and expectations are governed by a principle of concentration minted by the speeds of mass production.

The *locus classicus* of our usual attention to this evolutionary "adaptation" in Faulkner's work is of course *Sanctuary*, that book caught halfway between potboiler and art novel, an unholy synthesis that pleased nobody at the time, least of all Faulkner, who reacted to the page proofs with the verdict that "it was so badly written" and "cheaply approached." His shame still hovered over the preface he wrote to a second edition of the book in 1931, where he confessed "it was deliberately conceived to make money" (vi). But the critical interest lies in attending to how this overt act of novelistic capitulation to a mass market bears the scars of that noble form's subjection to a ruthless campaign of deterritorialization by the triumphant powers of the new media. It is, indeed, precisely through the cynical act of abandoning the novel to the market that the form confesses, formally, to its traumatic destiny within a media ecology whose central position it has lost. The famous opening comparison of Popeye's apparition to "that vicious depthless quality of stamped tin" establishes a convention whereby former novelistic duties are shifted onto a technological apparatus that operates by two-dimensional cliché and mechanical reproduction. Popeye is less a novelistic being than a cinematic one, patched into the text to baffle and derange the usual procedures for long-form storytelling.[9] Horace Benbow's focalized consciousness gamely attempts to resituate the encounter within a novelistic economy: "He smells black … like that black stuff that ran out of Bovary's mouth and down upon her bridal veil when they raised her head" (7). But what hope is there for such rallying around the literary in a social space whose every cultural signal is now amplified, mechanical, electronic?

> The sunny air was filled with competitive radios and phonographs in the doors of drug- and music-stores. Before these doors a throng stood all day, listening. The pieces which moved them were ballads simple in melody and theme, of bereavement and retribution and repentance metallically sung, blurred, emphasised by static or needle – disembodied voices blaring from imitation wood cabinets or pebble-grain horn-mouths above the rapt faces, the gnarled slow hands long shaped to the imperious earth, lugubrious, harsh, and sad. (112)

Even so fundamental a literary category as gender has been coopted by the newer waves and radiation: "It was as though femininity were a current running through a wire along which a certain number of identical bulbs were hung" (120). Where once figures might have emerged from the textual space with a salience earned purely through discursive effort, now they have a habit of borrowing their salience, a kind of secondhand trick of depth rather than the thing itself: "a fat man in a dirty apron with a toothpick in his mouth, stood for an instant out of the gloom with an effect as of a sinister and meaningless photograph poorly made" (142). At one point, Horace is obliged to communicate with Virgil Snopes over the telephone. Not only is Snopes's voice broken down into electrical values, propagated at light speed along untold miles of line, and recombined into passing verisimilitude by a speaker output, but it is scattered "across a remote blaring of victrola or radio music," such that it finally arrives speaking "in a guarded, tomblike tone" (202). In this post-human technological space, the novel has nowhere to go but against the back wall of the media morgue.

Is the sanctuary being sought by this book not finally a Utopian one, lodged far away from the tinny toy-symphony of these mechanical media? There is a definite formal recoil at work here, a perverse last stand of the written word, overlaid with the irony that this is a potboiler written for cash. *Sanctuary* obeys the (narrative, sensational) dictates of the forces it (ideologically) excoriates. It is, as a novel, a complex resistance mechanism, pitted against radio, victrola, jazz band music, cinema, telephone, magazine, all the forces mechanizing human passion and activity, yet the plot itself is in the grip of these same enemy forces, above which the style and invisible hand of the author must rise in reflexive distaste and condemnation, a reflux that is a displacement and reification of the book's own self-disgust.

What we are calling the media ecology is just this radically transformed cultural terrain whose new technologies of mediation are doing the critical work of transmission, communication, dissemination, and entertainment at speeds and levels of efficiency undreamed of by literature in its nineteenth-century heyday. It is an environment where literary prose has no serious option but to meditate formally and discursively on the newfound redundancy of its own procedures. One productive way of reading Faulkner is to grasp his oeuvre as a lifelong allegory of literature's own agonized self-consciousness as the outraged anachronism of the new media ecology. It is a situation he could present acerbically:

> News passes Blizzard about four times before it ever lights. News happens in Pittsburgh, say. All right. It gets radioed, passing right over us to Los Angeles or Frisco. All right. They put the Los Angeles and Frisco papers into the airplane and they pass right over us, going east now to Phoenix. Then they put the papers onto the fast train and the news passes us again, going west at sixty miles an hour at two A. M. And then the papers come back east on the local, and we get a chance to read them. ("Idyll in the Desert," *US* 410)

This figure of stranded, village-like anachronism is an apt one for an institution like literature, lost amid modernity's unprecedented communicational velocities. But it is "all right" because such stubborn turgidity fosters a protective shell in which, to borrow a phrase, the "news stays news." Literature, like Blizzard, may be somewhere that the news never visits directly, but its thrice-bypassed, de-linked place far off the informational grid is what allows it to gather the news into a form that endures, while the buzz of gossip and hearsay leaves fading vapor trails across the television skies.

That, I think, is the proper context in which to comprehend some of the most prototypical of Faulkner's stylistic effects, such as the painstaking rhetorical elaboration of speeds that could not possibly register on any other recording device:

> Though the mules plod in a steady and unflagging hypnosis, the vehicle does not seem to progress. It seems to hang suspended in the middle distance forever and forever, so infinitesimal in its progress, like a shabby bead upon the mild red string of road. So much so is this that in the watching of it the eye loses it as sight and sense drowsily merge and blend, like the road itself, with all the peaceful and monotonous changes between darkness and day, like already measured thread being rewound onto a spool. So that at last, as though out of some trivial and unimportant region beyond even distance, the sound of it seems to come slow and terrific and without meaning, as though it were a ghost travelling a half mile ahead of its own shape. (LA 8)

This is an extraordinary effort, in prose, to mark out some territory appropriate to a medium consigned to the outer edges of the media ecology. Literature, unable to keep pace with the irresistible mechanical seduction of the senses abroad in the national culture, suddenly discovers an astonishing capacity to say a great deal about nothing at all, about what *does not* happen, what *cannot* be sensed, what has *no place* in the streamlined cognitive cartography of the present. Its meticulous attention to these micro-fluctuations in the climate of the Nothing, its fanatical interest in notating some "motion so soporific, so dreamlike as to be uninferent of progress, as though time and not space were decreasing between us and it" (AILD 107–8) makes this prose style supremely adapted to a place within the cultural ecosystem not yet colonized by the aggressively territorial newcomers – a place that Faulkner called Yoknapatawpha, where the new media system's coercive "distribution of the sensible" has left its inevitable rejectamenta strewn across a forgotten back lot, for the act of writing to pick over like a beachcomber after the storm.[10]

Time, Tense, and Event

Fredric Jameson's remarkable new theorization of the novel as a cultural institution in which two opposed tendencies are negotiated and transformed across the arc of modernity is particularly useful in coming to terms with Faulkner's artistry as a progressive response to a rapidly evolving media ecology. Those two tendencies – the narrative impulse and affectivity – Jameson argues, are simultaneously the presence in the text of the intellect's mastery over the past and a destabilizing immersion in the body's present, and of the very tension between "meaning" and "experience." The emergence of Realism is a matter, it is argued, of the irresistible rise of "affect" – of the existential present – from within the cracks and fissures of that creaking sense of narrative order inherited from the neo-classical and feudal past. Where narrativity thrives on the stringing together of known and named emotional nodes, affectivity consists instead of unpredictable upsurgings of unquantifiable intensities – sudden coloristic loomings, vertiginous sensory apprehensions, singular outcroppings of mood – that interrupt and disable narrative drive.[11]

Although modernism is not part of Jameson's analysis here, it can readily be seen how the "balance" reached between these two forces during the great period of Realism is subsequently thrown off by the later period's relative neglect of the narrative impulse and the final ascendency of affect as such – in Proust, in Woolf, in Kafka, in Musil, in Joyce's epiphanies, and most curiously in Faulkner himself. And the key determinant here may well have been the emergence, after Realism, of mechanical narrative media, whose prodigious capacity to refashion narrative time within the technical dimension of fixed durations left the novel floating relatively free in an existential present cut adrift from Bergson's hated "cinematographic" modes of perception.[12] For the cinema, as for radio in a distinct manner, time is a fixed and reproducible quantity into which narrative materials can be squeezed; narrative in these media is felt as a steady mounting of tensions within given technical limits. The forcing of these media, by commercial interests, into lucrative narrative forms thereby left to that lumbering titan of narrativization, the novel, the function of dwelling instead within the "affective" or existential present to an extent unimaginable in any previous epoch. So it is, perhaps, that Jean-Paul Sartre could detect in Faulkner's early novels "a frozen speed at the very heart of things"[13] – his famous reading fixes on this most curious of Faulknerian affects, the suspension of narrative event and the horror of a temporality freed from the "death" of mechanical time. "Because Father said clocks slay time. He said time is dead as long as it is being clicked off by little wheels; only when the clock stops does time come to life" (*SF* 85). As it is with clocks, so it is with gramophone motors and the cinematic apparatus: little wheels clicking off known intervals, arranging modern temporality into repetitive narrative shapes: lunch hour; the arrival of stock reports; the post-lunch rush; suppertime. But in Faulkner's texts, composed as it were on the wreckage of these broken wheels, "frozen speed" is the key to a bewildering new dominion of affect for their reader: "At every moment, formless shadows, flickerings, faint tremblings and patches of light rise up either side of him, and only afterward, when he has a little perspective, do they become trees and men and cars."[14]

What is then most astonishing and paradoxical about Faulkner's procedure, his modes of access to this new dominion, is how he retrofits the new media themselves as allegorical figures of the very matter at issue. So a story that seems to want precisely to *narrate* the heroism and glory of young pilots in the Great War leaves us finally with this flare-gun of an *affect*, to deliver the impact no narrative could:

> And that's all. That's it. The courage, the recklessness, call it what you will, is the flash, the instant of sublimation; then flick! the old darkness again. That's why. It's too strong for a steady diet. And if it were a steady diet, it would not be a flash, a glare. And so, being momentary, it can be preserved and prolonged only on paper: a picture, a few written words that any match, a minute and harmless flame that any child can engender, can obliterate in an instant. A one-inch sliver of sulphur-tipped wood is longer than memory or grief; a flame no larger than a sixpence is fiercer than courage or despair.
>
> ("All the Dead Pilots," CS 531)

Affect, what is "too strong for a steady diet," is what subsists in the unknowable moment, the instant unmoored from narrative steadiness; which is why its most fitting medium is perhaps a photograph, whose preserved "instant of sublimation" is finally as inflammable and frail as the printed page itself. Writing discovers a sibling medium in that now-ageing apparatus of paper-printed still photography, whose technique has been absorbed into cinematography but which lurks there still as the "frozen speed at the very heart of things" in the form of the photogram itself.[15] What Jacques Derrida called "the past resources of paper … its *previously* multimedia vectors,"[16] are here brought to the surface – literature regarding photography as a *brother in paper* in order to sidestep the narrative compulsions of cinema and short story both, to offer an allegorical, affective *punctum* against the *studium* of narrative temporality, all wrapped up in the melancholy accents of medial mortality.

Faulkner's prose artistry is full of these remarkable suspensions of narrative time and pocketed by affective intensities "frozen" at the heart of conventional novelistic incident. If we can learn to read them as the scar tissue left behind by a bruising encounter between a once-dominant narrative medium and the twentieth century's new storytelling machines, we can begin to attend properly to what is at stake in Faulkner's tactical dismantling of the very tissues of narration – its transitions, its logic, its arcs – and his exploitation of that freshly turned ground for the raising of new crops of affectivity. To take a minute example, there is a moment in *As I Lay*

Dying when the tenanted coffin is being lugged by Jewel so precipitously that it "begins to rush away from me and slip down the air like a sled upon invisible snow, smoothly evacuating atmosphere in which the sense of it is still shaped" (98). Note that the incident does not actually happen here, it "begins" to happen but is usurped by a simile of snow and sled, and then just as quickly we are delivered to a grammatically off-kilter clause that dwells upon the space "evacuated" by the coffin's rushing away. This is, I take it, what affect in Faulkner looks like; it is the tremulous wake left by an event that will not be told directly; the residual trace of what never happens as such but has always already happened. Affect is the atmospheric "shape" of a determinate absence, the bleeding gum of a ripped tooth; and only literature has the appropriate registration devices to transcribe this inscrutable meteorology, while the newer media are fixated on incident and known emotions to the exclusion of all else.

In a truly agonizing degree of self-consciousness, it is not as if "literature," or at least printed narrative matter, can be exculpated here either. Joe Christmas's experience with "a magazine of that type whose covers bear either pictures of young women in underclothes or pictures of men in the act of shooting one another with pistols" (110), bears close scrutiny in this regard. The magazine is a factory of "story," one straight after another in mechanical succession, a profusion that brushes at its outer extremity against the very institution here being adapted to the media ecology engulfing it: "He had previously read but one story, he began now upon the second one, reading the magazine straight through as though it were a novel" (111). Novels in this media-ecological space are scarcely to be distinguished from the magazines that order their narrative units sequentially rather than "polyphonically"; they are simply what is read "straight through," the way an express train bypasses the smaller stations. But once again, Faulkner is interested in the capacities latent even in this most unpromising and pessimistic of scenarios for a genuine affective "stasis," and it is not slow in coming:

> Then he read again. He turned the pages in steady progression, though now and then he would seem to linger upon one page, one line, perhaps one word. He would not look up then. He would not move, apparently arrested and held immobile by a single word which had perhaps not yet impacted, his whole being suspended by the single trivial combination of letters in quiet and sunny space, so that hanging motionless and without physical weight he seemed to watch the slow flowing of time beneath him.   (112)

This truly extraordinary moment crystallizes the logic of Faulknerian affect with precision. The units of narrative organization – the book or volume as such, the plot, the various "stories," the chapters, the pages, the paragraphs, the sentences, the lines, the words, and, within those, finally, the letters – are progressively broken down into their component parts by a reading experience that here and there catches on some unquantifiable intensity; finally, at the lowermost molecular level, where the letters and phonograms in their "trivial combination" seem to suspend the reader in an atemporal "quiet and sunny space," we hit upon the perdurable thing itself – *affect* in a pure state, whose peculiar perspectival effect is to enable us to "watch the slow flowing of time" itself. There is perhaps no more strikingly allegorical illustration of the contradiction between narrative and affect in modern fiction, and it is particularly telling that it comes to focus in a meta-textual meditation on the fate of the novel in a second machine-age media ecology whose reifications of the printed word disorder the very pulse and flow of novelistic prose.

Voices, Voices

"She speaks in the same dead, level tone: the two voices in monotonous strophe and antistrophe: two bodiless voices recounting dreamily something performed in a region without dimension by people without blood" (*LA* 376). We turn, finally, to one of the more unsettling and uncanny of Faulkner's many weird idiosyncrasies as an author – his experimentations with the category of "voice" in the novel and his veritable obsession with its *undeath,* or spectral otherness, speaking into the novelistic present from a beyond whose sources we can perhaps now draw into view. This description of the bloodless voice of Mrs. Hines in "antistrophe" to the monotony of Byron Bunch's address, taken from a crucial backstory chapter late in *Light in August,* assumes a position within a chain of insistent vocal figurations. First, her husband:

> He talks clearly, just a little jerkily…. His voice ceases; his tone does not drop at all. His voice just stops, exactly like when the needle is lifted from a phonograph record by the hand of someone who is not listening to the record.
>
> (371)

And next, herself:

> Then she begins to speak again, without moving, almost without lipmovement, as if she were a puppet and the voice that of a ventriloquist in the next room.
>
> (379)

What is happening here? Why has a novel, and particularly so confident and masterful a one as this, taken to categorizing its constituent voices as so many disembodied, raspy, mechanical acts of inhuman ventriloquism? It is perverse indeed for a form, stitched together out of what Bakhtin called the "heteroglot, multi-voiced, multi-styled and often multi-languaged elements" that comprise the novel's social raw material, to afflict its own wellsprings with a figuration so unequivocally posthumous, even post-human.[17] And yet, it begins to make sense if we step back to consider what has been happening to "voice" in the Republic in the age of mechanical reproduction. No doubt Alessandro Portelli is correct to dwell on the insistent haunting of American literature's "vocality" – its anti-grammatological pseudo-*orality* in mode and diction – by a certain "ghost or specter" that whispers in the intervals between text and imaginary voice.[18] But how much the more will the spectrality associated with "the effects of the voice on the materiality of the real" have been exacerbated by the introduction of media specifically invented to carry the voice at speeds, and across distances, unthinkable for merely physical speech, let alone literary mediation?[19] Faulkner's career as a novelist is coeval with the rise of one of the most astonishing cultural events in any nation's history: the present-tense linking up of American cities from coast to coast, thanks to syndication and electromagnetic propagation, through voices speaking into living rooms and office spaces "out of the air" and directly into the resonant chambers of the soul. Adorno wrote in his *Current of Music*,

> The very fact that they are confronted by 'voices,' without being able to argue with the person who is speaking, or even may feel somewhat in the dark about who is speaking – the machine or the man – may help to establish the authority of the tool. The absence of visible persons makes the 'radio voice' appear more objective and infallible than a live voice; and the mystery of a machine which can speak may be felt in atavistic layers of our psychical life.[20]

On the one hand, the immense regional variations that preserve the "heteroglot" differentiations of accent, idiom and pitch across the vast landmass of the United States are imperilled at their root by a new national "voice" disseminated monologically from who knows where; on the other, the invisibility of the radio voice's origins introduces a new degree of uncanniness in the mechanization of human sense organs speaking *for* those who, thanks to the logic of the medium, cannot speak back. Throughout the culture, "'fantastic' accounts of oceanic wireless presented an increasingly uncertain world, one populated by citizens cut loose from previous social ties and now suffused with electro-magnetic waves set free from tributaries of cable and wire. Although most accounts of wireless celebrated communities increasingly interconnected by the technology, these other tales brooded instead over lives and souls transmuted and dispersed into the enveloping ether."[21]

When the related and often rival institution of the phonograph industry is added to the sonic picture, this is a rich context indeed in which to consider Faulkner's bleak portrayals of voices like Mrs. Compson's, calling Dilsey's name "with machinelike regularity" (*SF* 270); like that reverberating in "Pennsylvania Station" "with a quality methodical, monotonous, and implacable" (*CS* 624); or like the voices undergoing their eerie dislocation at chez Bundren:

> Tilting a little down the hill, as our house does, a breeze draws through the hall all the time, upslanting. A feather dropped near the front door will rise and brush along the ceiling, slanting backward, until it reaches the down-turning current at the back door: so with voices. As you enter the hall, they sound as though they were speaking out of the air about your head. (*AILD* 19–20)

What matters in Faulkner is how the art of the novel is adapted, in a state of emergency, to absorb these new, disembodied voices of radio and gramophone, not as alien impositions on the living speech and dialogic richness of an expanding nation but precisely as the transfiguration through mechanical mediation of all that dynamic vitality into corporate and institutional death-masks of the *polis*. Faulkner does not repel the "radio voice" so much as he admits it into the inner sanctum of compositional method. Those "disembodied voices blaring from imitation wood cabinets or pebble-grain horn-mouths" are placed exactly where they ought to be: in the middle of Jefferson's town square, because "radio [is] a symptom of an entire network of social processes."[22] In the radio, the nation comes home – as a vampire. The individual is no such thing; the voice is not one; the novel's polyphony is to be woven, therefore, not of the inalienable voices of living individuals but of the impersonal forces that manufacture "personality" out of slogans, price-tags, and mail-order sales campaigns.

> And then I see that the grip she was carrying was one of them little graphophones. It was for a fact, all shut up as pretty as a picture, and every-time a new record would come from the mail order and us setting in the house in the winter, listening to it, I would think what a shame Darl couldn't be to enjoy it too. But it is better so for him. This world is not his world; this life his life. (*AILD* 261)

NOTES

1 See Friedrich Kittler, "Introduction," *Gramophone, Film, Typewriter*, Geoffrey Winthrop-Young and Michael Wutz (trans.) (Stanford, CA: Stanford University Press, 1999), pp. 1–19.
2 Kittler, *Discourse Networks 1800/1900*, Michael Metteer and Chris Cullens (trans.) (Stanford, CA: Stanford University Press, 1990).

3 Letter to Ben Wasson, July 1929, quoted in Joseph Blotner, *Faulkner: A Biography* (Jackson: University Press of Mississippi, 1974), p. 244.

4 See Gertrude Stein, "Lectures in America: Portraits and Repetition," in *Writings 1932–1946*, Catharine R. Stimpson and Harriet Chessman (eds.) (New York: Library of America, 1998), p. 177.

5 Letter to Ben Wasson, July 1929, quoted in Blotner, *Faulkner: A Biography*, p. 244.

6 See, on the "readies," Michael North, *Camera Works: Photography and the Twentieth-Century Word* (Oxford: Oxford University Press, 2005), chapter 2, pp. 61–82.

7 See Julian Murphet, *Multimedia Modernism: Literature and the Anglo-American Avant-Garde* (Cambridge: Cambridge University Press, 2009).

8 Roland Barthes, *S/Z*, Richard Miller (trans.) (Oxford: Basil Blackwell, 1990), pp. 54–6 and 97–8.

9 See here Peter Lurie's extended discussion in *Vision's Immanence: Faulkner, Film, and the Popular Imagination* (Baltimore and London: Johns Hopkins University Press, 2004), pp. 25–67.

10 For an account of the "distribution of the sensible," see Jacques Rancière, *The Politics of Aesthetics*, Gabriel Rockhill (trans.) (London and New York: Continuum, 2004), pp. 7–46.

11 Fredric Jameson, *The Antinomies of Realism* (London and New York: Verso, 2013), esp. pp. 15–44.

12 Henri Bergson, *Creative Evolution*, Arthur Mitchell (trans.) (New York: Henry Holt, 1911), pp. 306–47.

13 Jean-Paul Sartre, *Literary and Philosophical Essays*, Annette Michelson (trans.) (London: Hutchinson, 1968), p. 81.

14 Ibid., p. 82.

15 On this, see Garrett Stewart's *Between Film and Screen: Modernism's Photo Synthesis* (Chicago: University of Chicago Press, 1999).

16 Jacques Derrida, *Paper Machine*, Rachel Bowlby (trans.) (Stanford, CA: Stanford University Press, 2005), p. 47.

17 Mikhail Bakhtin, *The Dialogic Imagination: Four Essays*, Caryl Emerson and Michael Holquist (trans.), Michael Holquist (ed.) (Austin: University of Texas Press, 1981), p. 265.

18 Alessandro Portelli, "The Sign of the Voice: Orality and Writing in the United States," *The Novel: Volume 1, History, Geography, and Culture*, Franco Moretti (ed.) (Princeton, NJ: Princeton University Press, 2006), p. 533.

19 Ibid, p. 533.

20 Theodor Adorno, *Current of Music*, Robert Hullot-Kentor (trans. and ed.) (Cambridge: Polity, 2009), p. 47.

21 Jeffrey Sconce, *Haunted Media: Electronic Presence from Telegraphy to Television* (Durham, NC: Duke University Press, 2000), pp. 63–4.

22 David Jenemann, *Adorno in America* (Minneapolis: University of Minnesota Press, 2007), p. 54.

2

PETER LURIE

History's Dark Markings: Faulkner and Film's Racial Representation

> how can I say things that are pictures
> – Toni Morrison[1]

When Toni Morrison recalls the Middle Passage in *Beloved*, her titular character memorably refers to the ship's white sailors as "men without skin."[2] Describing Europeans from an African perspective that recalls the history of interracial contact in the Americas, Beloved notes a quality of absence to her captors; unlike herself and her fellow Africans onboard the ship, these men are "there" yet, oddly, in her account, dispossessed of something that ordinarily and, in the case of her dark complexion (and in her view), establishes visibility and hence presence, agency, being.

In the cinema, the opposite is true of skin color. African-American or otherwise dark-complected actors do not radiate light in the way white actors do; a result is that they fail to register as fully, or at least as readily on the surface of the film's image. Richard Dyer refers to this phenomenon in *White*, his book-length study of the broad cultural practice of depicting whiteness as presence or even something beyond physical being: a "transcendent" quality that attaches to light. Dyer details the way in which visual media such as photography and film adapted technologies that racially favored the requirements for representing whiteness but not blackness on screen. As he puts it, "Movie lighting discriminates against non-white people because it is used in a cinema and a culture that finds it hard to recognise them as appropriate subjects for such lighting, that is, as individuals."[3]

This seeming difficulty, or markedness, of blackness is also evident in fiction. In Faulkner's case, we can trace not only his effort to show black skin but also his white characters' efforts (and his own authorial efforts) to "see" blackness in, and through, writing. As with the visual media Dyer mentions, there are particular difficulties associated with depicting race that trouble the writerly surface or "image." Such anomalies are instructive. For what they reveal are the strains not only on writing but also on characters' thinking and thus on broader social understandings of racial difference. In ways that we will see are important to understanding how Faulkner confronts the representational "problem" of blackness, it is important to note Dyer's corollary point about whiteness. Visual culture such as film has no trouble depicting white characters because technical features of the media are tuned to whiteness, the consequence of the cultural attitudes that subtend them.[4] Whiteness can presume a social presence and identity, that is, but black presence is always marked – and remarked upon. That denoting is the marking of difference, one that manifests itself in an insistent but problematic embodiedness, unlike white associations with an "extra-bodily" or metaphysical realm.[5] Writing when he did, and confronting both the violence of Southern social reality and particular cultural representations of it, Faulkner adopted a way of writing that, like the images he had seen in film, bears the material trace of the near-impossible task of representing a negative, a no-thing within the aegis of dominant Southern racist thought and social practice: blackness, as well as his white characters' sense of this "phenomenon."

In *Playing in the Dark* Toni Morrison describes American writers' habits of presenting blackness as an absence. The literary, in such instances, betrays a particular strain in depicting difference, a difference that marks the surfaces of both texts and bodies. As she puts it, "Even, and especially, when American texts are not 'about' Africanist presences or characters or narrative or idiom, the shadow [of race] hovers in implication, in sign, in line of demarcation."[6] Earlier in her discussion, Morrison makes a passing but important reference to Poe's novel *The Narrative of Arthur Gordon Pym* and the appearance at the book's end (in a highly imaginary South pole) of a mysterious and ethereal figure, "very far larger in its proportions than any dweller among men. And the hue of the skin of the figure was of the perfect whiteness of the snow."[7] Such imagery here in *Pym* and elsewhere, Morrison contends, "functions as both antidote for and meditation on the shadow that is companion to this whiteness – a dark and abiding presence that moves the hearts and texts of American literature with fear and longing."[8] We will see how in Faulkner an Africanist presence is both absent and present at the same time, his fiction confirming the phenomenon Morrison identifies in its indication of blackness through the use of "idiom" or as a "hover[ing]" "shadow" and a literal "line of demarcation." But, as we will see, such "playing" in Faulkner operates productively differently from the writers Morrison mentions.

We will turn to Faulkner and the ways his fiction contends with this "dark and abiding presence" shortly. We would do well first, though, to note the appositeness of Morrison's remarks to an understanding of early film as well as to American literature, and in particular to two watershed movies of film history. In her discussion of the white imaginary, Morrison refers to the dynamic of projection, a process that allowed whiteness to define itself negatively and against a constructed blackness of the sort that her examples of Poe and other writers demonstrate. "Black slavery enriched the country's creative possibilities," she observes. "For in that construction of blackness *and* enslavement could be found not only the not-free but also, with the dramatic polarity created by skin color, the projection of the not-me."[9] In the same context, she refers to the ways blackness provided all Americans, including the country's immigrant population, the opportunity to sharpen their identity as white. "It is no accident and no mistake that immigrant populations (and much immigration literature) understood their 'Americanness' as an opposition to the resident black population.... American," Morrison succinctly puts it, "means white."[10]

This formulation is precisely what critics have attributed to several key works of cinema, films that, in their only indirect depiction of blackness, define Americanness as white. The cultural work of blackface in films like *The Birth of a Nation* (1915), directed by D. W. Griffith, and *The Jazz Singer* (1915), starring the white Russian immigrant Al Jolson, are notable examples. In each case, performers' "blacking up" allowed audiences to project stereotypical behavior on a non-white Other and, by way of such projection, to secure their own hold on a white identity that corresponded to a national citizenship. This is the nation that Griffith's film invokes and envisions through a national reconciliation of North and South after the Civil War, one that thoroughly excludes blackness. (The film's solution to the "problem" of freed blacks is re-disenfranchisement and the Ku Klux Klan.) Michael Rogin refers to the fact that Griffith located the origins of the "modern" postbellum state in the rise of the Klan and its enforcement of a white nationhood, one that his film's reception supported. "Asked why he called his film *The Birth of a Nation*," Rogin offers, "Griffith replied 'Because it is.... The birth of a nation began ... with the Ku Klux Klan, and we have shown that.'"[11] Subscribing to the movie's mythologizing of the Klan and its romantic vision of the Old South, as its enthusiastic embrace by national as well as Southern audiences demonstrated, viewers on a genuinely mass scale embraced as well a way of thinking about race and the South set out in the popular fiction of Thomas Nelson Page and Thomas Dixon, the latter of whom wrote the novels on which *Birth* was based. Watching the film and being swept up into its revisionist rhetoric contributed for many Americans to a new collective national identity.[12]

Birth also trafficked in a particular kind of image or mode of vision vis-à-vis race that is unique to film but that, as we will see, Faulkner's writing both practices and criticizes. Referring to Griffith's conviction – one he shared with many in the silent era – that film constituted a "universal language," Rogin suggests that a film such as *Birth* "replace[s] history by film. Presented as a transparent representation of history (more transparent than language could ever be), movies actually aimed to emancipate the representation from its referent and draw the viewer out of history into film."[13] Despite the stunning success of Griffith's picture, however, its claims to historicity foundered on precisely the terms Griffith set for it. For this very transparency, the putatively "universal language" at play in (the) film, was occluded by particular practices and in ways that Faulkner's notably dense, productively non-transparent writing about race helps reveal.

While *Birth* includes several actual African-Americans, its most visible "black" presence is the image of whites masquerading as mulattoes or black slaves. The actors playing Gus, Silas Lynch, and Austin Stoneman's housekeeper/mistress, Lydia, all feature centrally in the movie's story; each of these characters, however, is played by a white actor in blackface. As such, their blackness operates as far *more* visibly and distinctly problematic than otherwise, and certainly more than that of any of the African-American actors who appear in marginal roles. Jolson's *The Jazz Singer* reveals this same dynamic, and as pointedly. It depicts an ethnic immigrant – the son of a Jewish cantor – who seeks to assimilate into a non-Jewish, secular "white" culture; he does so in part by donning blackface and using his vocal skills to sing plantation ditties such as "Mammy." For both Griffith and Jolson, we find a version of what Morrison attributes to earlier examples of U.S. fiction: the process whereby white readers (or here viewers) "understood their 'Americanness' as an opposition to the resident black population" – or to a blackness that is both imaginary and, as these examples amply demonstrate, textual.

Films such as these, however, raise thorny issues about how they represent blackness. For example, Griffith's *The Birth of a Nation* has somewhat paradoxically been celebrated for its realism. In addition to using actual Civil War uniforms and weaponry for both its Confederate and its Union troops in the film's battle sequences, Griffith was scrupulous about all costumes, manners, and the often-noted historical "facsimiles" that appear throughout the film [sequences purportedly based on photographs of the South Carolina legislature, for instance, or the Ford Theater for the scene of Lincoln's assassination]. Despite such concerns over historical fidelity, however, *Birth* notably – though we should also say, tellingly – falters in depicting its more prominent black or mixed-race characters. In line with Rogin's assertions about the film displacing history with representation, Mary Ann Doane comments on blackface's notable rupture of the film's rigorously maintained surface realism. As she puts it, "[b]lackface and white robes [the film's Klan costumes] both potentially destabilize the fetishized reality effect of the classical Hollywood cinema (and, in particular, of the historical genre which *Birth* strives to epitomize)."[14] This troublesome aspect of *Birth* is true, of course, in all cases of blackface. As a cultural practice, blackface in Griffith's film, as it did in *The Jazz Singer* and had for years before either movie in American minstrelsy, patently falsifies the image of blackness is proffers. An important difference in *Birth* is the fact that Griffith claimed to want to represent blackness "truthfully," in a manner that served his efforts to depict history accurately.[15] Yet, as every instance of these characters' appearance on screen reveals, such truthfulness is shadowed, darkened we might say – as Morrison does say – by its opposite, a cancelling of realism by the very substance of the text: its materiality, signifier, or, following the racial logic of Griffith's cinema, the movie's (and the characters') "skin."[16] What viewers thus see on the screen, rather than a representation of reality, is blackness as a conspicuous marker of artifice.

These representational problems are not limited to cinema's early phases, and in fact even afflict progressive films released well after Faulkner's lifetime. The technical and formal qualities of a film such as *In the Heat of the Night*, for example, bear on the issue of representing race in ways that Faulkner's writing had already anticipated. Released in 1967 at the height of the Civil Rights movement, *Heat* was notable for depicting its African-American protagonist on equal footing with his white partner. Starring the barrier-breaking Sydney Poitier, the first black performer to win the Academy Award for best actor (for his role in the 1963 *Lilies of the Field*), in one shocking sequence for contemporary viewers, *Heat* has Poitier vigorously slap a white man who has struck him. Here, the film seems to place its African-American protagonist on equal footing with its white characters. Yet, as Dyer notes, when Poitier's black character, Virgil Tibbs, and his white partner Gillespie, appear in one important scene together, the subdued half-light produces discrepant effects – a more recessive image of Tibbs, which contributes to his character's "emblematic," transcendentally heroic stature; and a starker, more individualized Gillespie, one more recognizably present or "real."[17]

The Birth of a Nation and *In the Heat of the Night*, appearing at key moments in social and film history that were separated by half a century, offer testimony to the persistent ways that cinema's textual surface effects a social-racial signification or "language" that is over-determined. And this practice continues. Even a recent film such as James Cameron's *Avatar*

(2009) – like *Birth* upon its release, a movie heralded for its radical technical advances in the film medium – manifests a problematic racial aspect as a part of its innovation. *Avatar* is a movie in which, as Morrison avers about her literary examples, silences about race allow us to see again how depicting racial otherness disturbs the text's surface. The film's celebrated use of 3D and motion-capture is not necessarily keyed to its mode of representing race. Yet the way the film imagines – and *images* – its futuristic world draws on a rich (and problematic) history of racial stereotyping. Its blue-skinned Na'vi characters combine elements of Asian, African, and Native American cinematic depictions, including long hair, bodily markings and face paint, costume (a loin cloth), ornamentation such as neck rings, and martial implements (the bow and arrow), and Cameron presents this "othered" presence in a text that foregrounds, one might even say insists on its putative materiality – the illusion of depth and a tactile three-dimensionality that further "embodies" or corporealizes its non-white characters.[18]

While there is no definitive record of Faulkner's having watched either Griffith's epic or the Al Jolson vehicle, it is hard to imagine that, as an avid moviegoer, he would have missed two of the most heralded events in film history, particularly given that both touched on matters of race and, in the case of *Birth*, on a region and a history of which Faulkner was painfully aware.[19] For one critic, Faulkner's most important modernist discovery was informed by the same phenomenon of racial "ventriloquism" as the blackface Jolson's character exhibits in *The Jazz Singer*. John T. Matthews relays the complex dynamic of disavowal and enabling associated with blackface, minstrelsy, and, as in other examples of literary modernism, Faulkner's use of dialect in *The Sound and the Fury*, and he suggests that Faulkner's discovery of a radical means of storytelling in his fourth novel owed itself to his identifying as a marginal figure in Southern culture and social reality.[20] Matthews uses the fact that Quentin sounds to the boys he meets walking by the Charles River " 'like a colored man' " " 'from the minstrel show' " (*SF* 120) to suggest that "When Faulkner finds his voice [in *The Sound and the Fury*] the year after *The Jazz Singer*, he discovers it to be black, too."[21]

In addition to this emphasis on vocality, race, and sound, I wish to stress the manner in which race and racial difference in Faulkner – as in film – is *seen*. By this I mean the visual emphasis in a racial system of categorizing that relies largely on the outward markings of skin color.[22] Considered thus, it is not only cultural history like *Birth* or *The Jazz Singer* to which Faulkner's texts refer or that they recall; it is the same effort of early film and of cultural history generally to depict racial otherness that troubles the process of signification and the text itself. Such an endeavor amounts to an attempt on Faulkner's part to write what Jacques Derrida calls *différance*, to write that which cannot be signified, an insuperable contrast or the "negative" of what a word (the signifier) means to denote: its only imaginary, and thus absent, presence, the signified.[23] This linguistic system of negatives or opposites, of course, has its corollary in a Southern racial "language" that insisted on its own "true," full meaning: the absolute difference between black and white subjecthood.

That Faulkner confronts this only seeming truth is everywhere evident, but particularly in novels like *Light in August*, which pivots in its entirety on a visual recognition or "reading" of race (exemplified by Doc Hines's persistent *watching* of Joe Christmas, like everyone else's in the novel).[24] This trope is epitomized in the oft-cited description of Joe turning white "like a kodak print emerging from the liquid" on the road one night, caught in the headlights of a car (108). Here Joe's bodily presence is marked as white, and emphatically not black. The simile is telling, however, for, like the Kodak negative Joe's skin resembles, whiteness here defines itself against its visual opposite – such whiteness as Joe sees, that is, calls forth the very blackness that haunts him, as well as the entire white South. The image that Faulkner's narrator describes is not a photographic print of Joe as white but rather whiteness's opposite, its "negative" – the exposed film seen here in the process of developing. Like Morrison's account of early U.S. writing, the "white" film negative is always "shadowed," but also defined, by its opposite.

Faulkner's next novel to grapple in a full-bodied way with race, and, like *Light in August*, with the difficulties and pain of racial crossing, is *Absalom, Absalom!*, a book often seen as notable above all else for its formal and stylistic difficulties. From *Absalom*'s first sentence and its extended syntax, through Rosa's tortured prose and memory, to particular instances of strained dialect such as "*Air you Rosie Coldfield?*" (69, 106), uttered by a character whose racial status (or skin) is indeterminate ("Wash" Jones, whose visible whiteness retains a trace of the economic blackness that muddles him and other Faulkner poor whites),[25] through what Gilles Deleuze would call Quentin's riven, *schizomatic* utterance in the novel's final lines (*I don't. I don't! I dont hate it* [the South]! *I dont hate it!* [303]), we find a novel whose textuality is marked repeatedly and thus visually.[26] Jim Bond's howl extends beyond the book's ending, offering another case of a racial marking that is auditory, like dialect in *The Sound and the Fury*. The same figure of Bond, though, also suggests its own visual tension or strain. In the novel's close, Shreve confronts Quentin with the linking of black and white that Bond represents, telling him that with time such blackness as exists in Sutpen's family – in the South's "family" – will fade. "Of course it wont quite be in our time," he prods, "and of course as they spread toward the poles they will bleach out again ... so they wont show up so sharp against the snow. But," Shreve then taunts, "it will still be Jim Bond; and so in a few thousand years, I who regard you will have sprung from the loins of African kings" (302). Like other examples, these instances or figures (black or mixed-race characters; Faulkner's striking figures on the page) offer a provisional answer to what Morrison's Beloved asks in my epigraph: "how can i say things that are pictures[?]" In light of such patterns or turns, we might say that writing as differential play of the sort Faulkner produces may augur a new social world, one that inverts the permanence of racial identities on which film – and much Southern thought about race – depends.

Such material-visual density is perhaps nowhere more prominent in Faulkner than in *Go Down, Moses*. Shortly I shall elaborate on the ways in which such properties mark or "darken" the surface of Faulkner's text in a manner similar to how we've seen blackness affect the film image. In the challenging section four of the pivotal story "The Bear," which compresses and highlights the textual and racial "playing" I have been attributing to earlier Faulkner and to film, there appears a supremely telling textual detail. It arises in the context of a highly reflexive section of the novel: Ike reading the commissary ledgers that, with him, we read too. The ledgers that Ike has read and reread are notable for several things, above all the secret of his family's racial history, which the entries both reveal and obscure. Related to this is the fact that the entries are also striking in their appearance, shorthand references to the plantation's events, such as the purchase and birth of the McCaslin slaves, that are also particularly conspicuous as writing, an impression conveyed by glaring mistakes in spelling, capitalization, and punctuation, or to their idiosyncratic abbreviations ("@" for "and," for example). The most significant of these entries refers to Tomey's death in childbirth, a fact that follows her mother's suicide six months earlier, and to the birth of her son. Faulkner offsets these entries with Ike's speculation about Eunice's drowning or, more properly, his uncle's account of it.

> Why did Uncle Buddy think she had drowned herself? finding, beginning to find on the next succeeding page what he knew already he would find, only this was still not it because he already knew this:
>
> *Tomasina called Tomy Daughter of Thucydus @ Eunice*
> *Born 1810 dide in Child bed June 1833 and Burd. Yrs stars fell*
>
> nor the next:
>
> *Turl son of Thucydus @ Eunice Tomy born Jun 1833 yr stars*
> *fell Fathers will* (257)

The McCaslin brothers' nearly illegible handwriting misreports the facts of Eunice's daughter's and her grandson's paternity, a hidden fact that Ike's perspicacious reading penetrates, but not without considerable deciphering of the ledgers' difficulty. Yet, despite these traceable errors – or, I will suggest, because of them – Ike achieves a particularly forceful envisioning of the events in the ledgers' recording. These include the doings of the slave Thucydides, visualized so vividly "it would seem to the boy that he could actually see the black man" (255). Earlier the whole line of McCaslin slaves similarly materialize: "Roscius and Phoebe and Thucydides and Eunice and their descendants, and Sam Fathers and his mother … [who] took substance and even a sort of shadowy life with their passions and complexities too as page followed page and year year" (252–4).

In the midst of these powerfully visual, we might even say cinematic evocations, with their emphasis on the play of light and moving "shadows," two entries include the key textual detail I mentioned earlier. In the passage that relays Eunice's suicide, Faulkner has the McCaslin brothers twice include a cosmic notation, "*yr stars fell,*" one that neither Ike nor the authorial narrator directly addresses but that reveals a great deal about the novel's historical and epistemological workings. While this reference might denote a nocturnal celestial display, or a fact of astronomy in 1832, it is equally notable for its figurative significance. The falling stars connote an extinguishing of their light, a darkening of the skies that attends Ike's greatest and most shocking moment of discovery. This extinguishing conveys Ike's state of mind upon learning of his family's history of incest and its interracial lineage, a kind of cataclysm that, the novel suggests, is akin to a hail of shooting – hence, dying – stars. Paradoxically, that "dark" event occurs concurrently with Ike's profound enlightening about what the ledgers hold.

Maurice Blanchot's theory of language can help us understand this seeming paradox, and in ways that will shed further light on Faulkner's affinity with film. Faulkner's reference to the "*yr stars fell*" shares Blanchot's formulation in *The Writing of the Disaster* and elsewhere of a use of language that, through its very failings and displacements of meaning, conveys the general difficulty of writing to capture reality, as well as, more specifically, the particular difficulty of representing painful events such as slavery, war, or genocide – the whole sequence of "disasters" that constitute history. Blanchot downgrades the value of writerly "clarity" and grounds his philosophy of language instead on the ineffable nature of much that writers, particularly writers of literature, mean to convey – the sense that, as Addie Bundren puts it in *As I Lay Dying*, "words dont ever fit even what they are trying to say at" (171). One French word for star, "*astre,*" which comprises the Latinate "disaster" in both French (*désastre*) and English, figures in Blanchot's sense of a language that founders on its very effort to "elucidate" or enlighten, as would any effort to write – or to read – disasters of the sort Ike envisages.[27] Literary language thus understood becomes something like an enactment of the failure of language to represent reality.

What passages from the ledgers such as these and their manner of working have in common with film, and particularly with the film of Faulkner's period that treats race, is their shared quality of being strongly marked as *texts*. In addition to their Blanchotian overtones, the ledgers' renderings, as we have seen, are notable for their emphatic textuality, the ways in which, through various tics or irregularities, the entries draw attention to themselves. The markings of Faulkner's figures – as well as his figurations – are "dark," then, in several ways. We have noted the ways in which Ike's vision and light are "put out" upon his discovery of his grandfather's actions ("*yr stars fell*"). In drawing attention to the ledgers' textuality as he does, Faulkner also emphasizes the play of characters – letters, written words – on the page. Writing such as that which appears in "The Bear," as elsewhere in Faulkner, is not transparent or a clear window onto the content it means to convey. Additionally, the words that the McCaslin brothers write deliberately obfuscate their father's doings, lying, as they do, about the births of Eunice's daughter, Thomasina, and "Tomey"'s son, Turl (attributing them to Eunice and Thucydides) and deliberately misleading readers of the ledgers about certain events.

Film theory offers a useful variation on this idea of the invisibility of bodies. Describing a general effect of film, one I take as especially relevant to the representation of race, Gilles Deleuze refers to the absence of the body in cinema (in contrast, say, to the theater, where an actor's live body is always present). In terms that recall the oddities of film blackface, he asserts, "If cinema does not give us the presence of the body and cannot give it to us, this is perhaps because it sets itself a different objective: it ... affects the visible with a fundamental disturbance, and the world with a suspension, which contradicts all natural perception."[28] Film as an "affect" of the visible disturbs the assumption that race can be declared openly by the appearance of bodies. Yet Deleuze also makes clear that such a powerful disturbance is important for what it enables of thought. This is so because the cinema models a way of conceiving our relationship to reality, or even, for Deleuze, a version of philosophy. As he puts it, "What it [the cinema] produces in this way is the genesis of an 'unknown' body which we have in the back of our heads, like the unthought in thought, the birth of the visible which is still hidden from view."[29]

The "unknown body" in Faulkner's world is, of course, the black body. And, while obviously his novels are not films, in them we see repeatedly a dynamic of bodily presence and absence that pivots on the matter of race and in which occurs a dawning awareness, "the genesis of an 'unknown' body" that white characters and readers "have in the back of [their] heads" and for which Faulkner seeks adequate means of representation. The opening story of *Go Down, Moses*, "Was," demonstrates this well; in it, Faulkner offers a comic version of the misplaced black body, Tomey's Turl, whom his owners seek to reclaim. Yet, like the cinema as Deleuze conceives it – and in quite serious ways – Faulkner's fiction also reveals the only partly unknown or unacknowledged body at the heart of the plantation system and Jim Crow. Charles Bon, Joe Christmas, Lucas Beauchamp, Tennie's Jim (or his grand-daughter) – such mixed-race characters in Faulkner's novels trouble white characters such as Doc Hines, Ike McCaslin, Thomas Supten, and Quentin Compson, and serve to remind them (and us) of the body *within* whiteness that the South would wish to deny. Faulkner's attention to racial crossing is in this respect both different from Griffith's cinematic anxiety over it, in that Faulkner shows the effects of strain (on language, on individual characters' psyches) that racial difference (and its suppression) produces, and similar, in that the mixed-race figure proves a powerfully destabilizing effect that is also *textual*.[30] White actors in blackface, in this sense, operate like the "markings" of the ledgers, replete with their own displacements of trans-parency; they are figures that contradict the seemingly natural relationship between signifier and signified.

Such markings offer another important way to connect Faulkner's writing to film. For what this aspect of Griffith's cinema (for Deleuze, an aspect of all of cinema) reveals and that Faulkner's fiction shares is the indexical quality of "skin" in both film and writing. Filmic indexicality – the idea that what appears on screen points to the realness of the things shown – meant some-thing quite specific for theorists of realism such as André Bazin, who went to extraordinary lengths to demonstrate that in its physical record of light rays on the surface of a photographic and film negative, something of the original subject is actually preserved.[31] While Bazin's theories resonate with notions of filmic realism, their relevance to a patently false depiction of real-ity is also meaningful. For of *Birth*, as of other examples like *The Jazz Singer, In The Heat of the Night*, or even *Avatar*, we might say that we have another kind of filmic indexicality. The image of white actors in blackface, like the sequence in *Birth* at the South Carolina legislature that depicts "shifty" elected officials – all of them black – drinking in the capitol and eating fried chicken, is a visual record, not of light and its momentary interaction with objects or bodies, but of the very ways in which cinematic representation here patently *fails* to convey the real, instead offering up a contrived "affect" of reality. As we have also seen, each of these other films, celebrated for their timeliness in film history and notable for their particularly cinematic racial renderings, reveals how American movies have often foundered in depicting blackness "realistically." Yet this representational foundering is important, as it is in Faulkner's writing. For what Faulkner's work demonstrates and what it shares with theories of language like Blanchot's is the way in which writing, like the film image, is often a screen for its own envisionings.

The visual dissonance of films like *Birth* returns in Faulkner's work as a verbal or textual *difficulty*. That very "mark" on the text, though, has the productive quality of pointing up the contradictions of racial discourse and the problem of representing race. Ike's straining with the ledgers is all the more relevant in this context. The very troubles of the ledgers' writing, their indexical marking of the dehumanization of slavery, suggested by the simultaneous darkening and revelation of entries like "*yr stars fell*" and the errors of Uncle Buck and Uncle Buddy's inscriptions, show the capacity of Faulkner's writing to register the enormity of what his fiction countenances and what perhaps no language can represent directly. In an opposite way, Griffith's racist imagery also fails to represent race as transparently real. Such paradoxes animate Faulkner's challenge to the representational codes of language as they obtain in Southern racial narrative and in film more generally. Unlike Griffith, to be sure, Faulkner poses such challenges deliberately as part of his ongoing effort to "*Tell about the South*" (AA 142) and, thus, to "write" race meaningfully.

The cultural history that surrounded and informed Faulkner's modernism includes films such as *The Birth of a Nation* and *The Jazz Singer* as well as modes like minstrelsy and models from earlier fiction (as in the example of dialect). This comparison is all the more important in the contemporary context of the digital age, one that is at an even further remove from the events of Faulkner's fiction and of films such as *The Birth of a Nation*. This is true in terms of film history, as we have seen; yet it is also true technically, in the sense that digital media do not possess the same visual or, arguably, textual density or "grain" of either analogue film or of certain kinds of writing like Faulkner's. Thus we may say in closing that the indexical aspect of Faulkner and of film is worth emphasizing in the face of what may be said to threaten both: a genuine historical erasure and an attendant forgetting of what such particularly marked forms as his fiction and film manifest and, thus, remember. So that we may too.

NOTES

1 Toni Morrison, *Beloved* (New York: Vintage, 1987), p. 210.
2 Ibid., p. 215.

3 Richard Dyer, *White: Essays on Race and Culture* (London: Routledge, 1992), p. 102.

4 Dyer, *White*, p. 39.

5 These suppositions have come under increasing critical attention and questioning recently through critical race studies and, particularly, whiteness studies. For a consideration of them in relation to Faulkner, see *Faulkner and Whiteness*, Jay Watson (ed.) (Jackson: University Press of Mississippi, 2004). Ted Atkinson in fact shows Faulkner reversing these terms for visuality and perception in a recent article, "The Impenetrable Lightness of Being: Miscegenation Imagery and the Anxiety of Whiteness in *Go Down, Moses*," *Faulkner and Formalism: The Returns of the Text*, Annette Trefzer and Ann J. Abadie (eds.) (Jackson: University Press of Mississippi, 2012).

6 Toni Morrison, *Playing in the Dark: Whiteness and the Literary Imagination* (New York: Vintage, 1992), pp. 46–7.

7 Ibid., p. 32. Quotation from Edgar Allan Poe, *The Narrative of Arthur Gordon Pym of Nantucket, and Other Related Tales*, Gerald J. Kennedy (ed.) (New York: Oxford World Classics: 1998 [1838]), p. 175.

8 Ibid., p. 33.

9 Ibid., p. 38.

10 Ibid., pp. 47.

11 Griffith quoted in Michael Rogin, "'The Sword Became a Flashing Vision': D.W. Griffith's *The Birth of a Nation*," *The Birth of a Nation: D.W. Griffith, Director*, Robert Lang (ed.) (New Brunswick, NJ: Rutgers University Press, 1994), p. 252.

12 Rogin suggests that this newly national view of racial and ethnic conflict was, in part, a result of the early twentieth-century influx of immigrants to Northern cities. "When the Southern race problem became national, the national problem was displaced back onto the South in a way that made the South not a defeated part of the American past but a prophecy of its future" (Ibid., pp. 255).

13 Ibid., p. 287.

14 Mary Ann Doane, *Femmes Fatales: Feminism, Film Theory, Psychoanalysis* (New York: Routledge, 1991), p. 228.

15 One such contemporary audience member who subscribed to Griffith's view was no less than the sitting president, Woodrow Wilson, who in 1915 famously described the movie as "like writing history in lightning" after a screening of it at the White House. Wilson quoted in Michael Rogin, "D.W. Griffith's *The Birth of a Nation*," p. 251.

16 I have described this quality of film and of Faulkner's prose in relation to it elsewhere. See my "Introduction" to *Faulkner and Film: Faulkner and Yoknapatawpha 2010*, Peter Lurie and Ann J. Abadie (eds.) (Jackson: University Press of Mississippi, 2014). There I also refer to several examples of cinema scholarship that addresses the idea of film as possessing a tactile, "haptic" property, such as Laura Marks's *The Skin of the Film: Intercultural Cinema, Embodiment, and the Senses* (Durham, NC: Duke University Press, 2000) and Jennifer Barker, *The Tactile Eye: Touch and the Cinematic Experience* (Berkeley: University of California Press, 2001). For an earlier account of these and similar arguments, see also Thomas Elsaesser and Matle Hagener, "Cinema as Skin and Touch," *Film Theory: An Introduction Through the Senses* (New York: Routledge, 2010).

17 Dyer, *White*, p. 99. The film's narrative trajectory enhances this sequence's visual effect. Over the course of the story, Gillespie emerges as the fuller character, one whose transformation from bigotry to greater open-mindedness about race is far more pronounced than Tibbs's own character "arc." The latter remains dignified and noble – but static compared to Gillespie's more flawed but "human" development.

18 This is, again, a variation on Dyer's point about non-white actors or characters being marked, or remarked-upon, whereas whiteness in film is not.

19 See Faulkner's brother's account of his and William's moviegoing, in which Murry Falkner stated that he and "Bill" went to the movies in Oxford regularly, often twice a week (*The Falkners of Mississippi: A Memoir* [Baton Rouge: Louisiana State Press, 1967], p. 49–51).

20 Matthews refers to Faulkner's appearance in *Mosquitoes* as "a little black man" and to his article for *Ebony* magazine, "If I Were a Negro," to suggest this identifying with African-Americanness ("Whose America? Faulkner, Modernism, and National Identity," *Faulkner at 100: Retrospect and Prospect*, Donald M. Kartiganer and Ann J. Abadie (eds.), [Jackson: University Press of Mississippi, 2000], p. 80). For another example of modernist dialect, he points to Joseph Conrad as an earlier writer who, like Faulkner, animated his novels with a non-standard English that drew on black vernacular speech. For a similar discussion of Conrad, specifically *The Nigger of the "Narcissus"* and American writers, see Michael North, *The Dialect of Modernism: Race, Language, and Twentieth Century Literature* (New York: Oxford University Press, 1994).

21 Matthews, "Whose America?" p. 73, p. 80.

22 Novels such as *Light in August* and *Absalom, Absalom!*, like fiction by Kate Chopin, Nella Larsen, and others, attest to the fact that skin color is a highly unreliable marker of racial identity. Commensurately, Faulkner scholars pay considerable attention to the "one drop rule," the idea common in the South that "blood," more than skin, determined racial identity. Nevertheless, the emphasis on visuality in plantation life and Southern social reality is a powerful nexus that determined many aspects of daily experience, including the acts of looking (or not looking) at others, visual gestures of politeness or deferral, and symbolic acts and spectacles – such as lynching.

23 Jacques Derrida, "Différance," *Margins of Philosophy*, Alan Bass (trans.) (Chicago and London: Chicago University Press, 1982).

24 Others have read *Light in August* as one of Faulkner's particularly visualized novels, including its reliance on a "cinematic" gaze that seems mesmerized by the visual and epistemological puzzle Christmas offers. For an account of the various characters' perusing of Joe and the ways it recalls a pattern that is unique to film, see Peter Lurie, "Cinematic Fascination in *Light in August*," *The Blackwell Companion to Faulkner*, Robert Hamblin and Charles Peek (eds.) (Oxford and New York: Blackwell, 2001), pp. 284–300). Thadious Davis has recently followed this interpretive line in "Visualizing Race in *Light in August*," *Faulkner and Formalism: The Returns of the Text*, Annette Trefzer and Ann J. Abadie (eds.) (Jackson: University Press of Mississippi, 2012); she finds in Joe Christmas and Lena Grove characters whose movements derive from film (and, for Davis, from the animated movies of Faulkner's era) and that mark both characters in others' visual perceptions.

25 Abner Snopes voices an embittered but pointed recognition of this racial overlap in "Barn Burning." Referring to Major de Spain's white mansion, he declares to his son Sarty that it was made with "nigger sweat" but offers that "it ain't white enough yet to suit him [de Spain]. Maybe he wants to mix some white sweat with it" (*CS* 12).

26 For Deleuze's account of this idea about a "split" language, see *Anti-Oedipus*, with Felix Guattari, Robert Hurley, Mark Seem, and Helen R. Lane (trans.) (Minneapolis: University of Minnesota Press, 1983) and "Life and Literature," *Essays: Critical and Clinical* (Minneapolis: University of Minnesota Press, 1997), pp. 2–5.

27 Maurice Blanchot, *The Writing of the Disaster*, Ann Smock (trans.) (Lincoln: University of Nebraska Press, 1986). See Martin Jay, *Downcast Eyes: The Denigration of Vision in Twentieth-Century French Thought* (Berkeley: University of California Press, 1994), for a gloss on this aspect of Blanchot's thinking about writing and vision (pp. 552–4). See also Blanchot's *The Space of Literature*, Ann Smock (trans.) (Lincoln: University of Nebraska Press, 1982) and his essays "The Gaze of Orpheus" and "Literature and the Right to Death" in *The Gaze of Orpheus and Other Essays*, P. Adams Sitney (ed.), Ann Smock (trans.) (Barrytown, NY: Station Hill Press, 1981).

28 Gilles Deleuze, *Cinema 2: The Time-Image*, Hugh Tomlinson (trans.) (Minneapolis: University of Minnesota Press, 1989), 201.

29 Ibid., p. 201.

30 Thadious Davis offers a variation on this approach in her monograph on *Go Down, Moses*. As she puts it, "The games marking [the novel] as contest and contested site also mark Tomey's Turl as the trope, the embodiment, the represented contest and contested site, that necessarily refocuses attention on the text" (*Games of Property: Law, Race, Gender, and Faulkner's Go Down, Moses* [Durham, NC: Duke University Press, 2003], p. 15).

31 André Bazin, "The Ontology of the Photographic Image," *What Is Cinema?* Hugh Gray (trans.) (Berkeley: University of California Press, 1967).

3

ALIYYAH I. ABDUR-RAHMAN

"What Moves at the Margin": William Faulkner and Race

Tell us ... what moves at the margin. What it is to have no home in this place. To be set adrift from the one you knew. What it is to live at the edge of a town that cannot bear your company.

Toni Morrison[1]

Perhaps it is the reality of a future as durable and far-reaching as the past, a future that will be shaped by those who have been pressed to the margins, by those who have been dismissed as irrelevant surplus, by those who have been cloaked with the demon's cape.

Toni Morrison[2]

Toni Morrison opens her lecture upon receiving the 1993 Nobel Prize in Literature with a parable and a meditation. A blind guru is consulted by a group of young men who question her about the contents of one member's hand: is he carrying a live bird or one that has died? The question is meant to shame the interrogated, to publicly undermine her credibility as a clair-voyant, to make her physiological blindness stand in for and reveal a larger metaphysical one. The guru sidesteps the performance of disparate power, stating simply that the responsibility for the bird's life or death belongs to those who have taken hold of it. Taking the bird for words, Morrison pro-ceeds to contemplate the properties of language, what words can and must do, where language inevitably fails, and the overarching ethical dimensions of the literary enterprise.[3] For Morrison, survival is bound up with words; subjects either dwell in language or are dwarfed by it.

The essay that follows analyzes the voluminous and intricate *Absalom, Absalom!* as a novel of southern masculine defeat and renewal in the three decades immediately following Reconstruction, a period typically referred to as the nadir of black experience. I approach William Faulkner, the mod-ernist southern writer seemingly obsessed with the shape and status of things no longer fixed in time, place, ideology, or memory, in the way that has often felt most effective – and perhaps most comfortable – for me as a student and a scholar of African-American literature. I come to him by way of Toni Morrison, with a preoccupation with the narrativization of U.S. racial history, a will to know the significances of those figures in black, and a critical entry from the (under)side. What I am after ultimately in this analysis is a working theory of differential racialization in the decades following the emancipation and enfranchisement of enslaved people and the struggle in *Absalom, Absalom!* to make sense of the psychic, symbolic, and sociopolitical upheaval in the South occasioned by the conversion of slaves into compatriots – the transformation, that is, of serviceable others into qualified members in the fraternal order of national citizenship. I take for granted that Thomas Sutpen's attempt at dynastic creation may be read as an allegory of U.S. nation-building – through (ad)ventures in imperialism, land theft and mass murder, the forced migration and enslavement of black people, and the deft deployment of tropes of heteropatriarchy in white plantation homes. I investigate how black figures signify – as in make meaning – in this novel, given that for the most part they do not speak and thus do not indicate specific processes of black subjectivization.

For most of its history, the critical consensus about *Absalom, Absalom!* has been that Jim Bond, a black man and Sutpen's (purported) sole descendant, who essentially concludes the novel, emblematizes the devolution of his line and the failure of Sutpen's bids for both civilization and empire. Christopher J. Cunningham, for example, completes his analysis of the novel asserting: "Sutpen ... leaves behind a legacy of two sets of reproductions: A dynastic design which ends in incomprehensible howling and apocalypse, and a narrative genealogy which insistently and consistently reiterates this very failure."[4] Similarly, James Guetti asserts, "Bond represents the entire story: he is potential meaning, always just out of reach, but asserting in his idiot howling the negation of meaning.... For Sutpen, Bond would have been the final symbol of nothingness, the last failure, and he thus embodies the defeat of both narrator and the character."[5] While I appreciate Guetti's grasp of Jim Bond's fundamental significance in both the life-world of the text and its overspun narrative approximation, I am cautious of the assumptions that subtend the meaning that he, and many other critics, assign to Jim Bond – that figurative blackness signals negation, nothingness, defeat. This interpretation risks reinforcing racial logics that take for granted that there is a scale of human becoming and that black people occupy its bottom, that rather than embodying the promises of U.S. national citizenship, the black (whether enslaved or emancipated) reflects only its defining limits and that when the wail does not eventuate in a word, human intelligence and sentience are not in evidence.[6] I move against this reading and those incumbent assumptions by approaching *Absalom, Absalom!* not simply as the densely commingled narrative of Thomas Sutpen's life and tragic end but, equally important, as the history, the genealogy of Jim Bond, the howling rem(a)inder of Sutpen's dynasty – the last man standing, that is – in order to make a claim about the importance of *hearing* the unspeaking black figures in this novel and why, in Faulkner's imaginings of national redemption, even eighty years later, we must do so.[7]

I

At the heart of *Absalom, Absalom!* is failure, thematized in the failure of Sutpen's design and textualized in the overwrought, interwoven, and largely speculative narrative that fails to make sense of it. In this section, I show that the central failure with which the novel is preoccupied is that of national redemption. I argue, further, that, rather than Jim Bond, Quentin Compson is the figure who shares Thomas Sutpen's lack of purchase on the (national) future. The novel begins rather close to its climax. Quentin Compson, the novel's organizing intelligence, does not know the purpose for which he is summoned to Rosa Coldfield's home, but, once the narrative of her life and its frustrated entwinement with Thomas Sutpen's has begun, Quentin surmises that his purpose that September mid-afternoon in 1909 is not simply to listen to the narrative she is spinning but to help her spin it. She has called him, in other words, to serve not simply as audience or witness to her testimony but to involve him in the collaborative process of narrative transmission because, as he surmises, "she wants it told" (5). Quentin notes that, outside of his discursive manufacture, Thomas Sutpen does not exist. Long dead, without meaningful material trace (a home, inheritable wealth, or socially recognizable heirs), and, like all slaveholders, from a bygone era, Sutpen takes up residence in the narratives that conjure him, "where a more fortunate [ghost] would have had a house," that testify that he once *was* there (4).

As if summoned by incantation, Thomas Sutpen appears in Rosa's words, as he supposedly appeared that day in Mississippi in 1833, upon a horse, entering the one hundred acres of land that he would call Sutpen's Hundred prior even to building the home that would in stature and design resemble a courthouse, before marrying the respectable white wife who would guarantee the safe and legitimate transfer of his accumulated wealth, before fathering a single proper heir; he arrived "with grouped behind him his wild band of niggers like beasts half tamed to walk upright like men" (4). Evident in this initial description, or pictorialization, of Thomas Sutpen is the way in which racial difference, both its conceptual logics and its visual deployments, support white ascendancy. The promise of Sutpen's design – specifically, his successful iteration of established nineteenth-century ideals of white manhood – is indicated in that storied arrival. Sutpen appears, notably, prior to having accumulated the necessary symbols of wealth, acculturation, and civic standing that would affirm his worldly promise. The swindled land on which he stands and the black people whom he has forced into unpaid, captive labor are the most salient and significant symbols of his (white, masculine) becoming. The asymmetric accruals of privilege and the unfair distribution of rights and resources that whiteness systemically produced (and which account for its persistent desirability) are signaled by the black men who arrive with Sutpen, standing barely upright.

The central dilemma of *Absalom, Absalom!*, then, is how to restore both content and coherence to white masculinity given that it was founded on fallible, racist logic and the institutionalization of racial slavery. In the now of the novel, the white masculine has languished under the pressures of Civil War defeat, the transformation of the plantation economy into an industrial one, and the legal emancipation of formerly owned black men and women. As the mediating consciousness of the novel, the one who undertakes the journey and makes the climactic discoveries, the one who analyzes letters and gravestones, the one who attempts to make it all cohere in unfolding conversations with his expat Harvard roommate Shreve, Quentin is tasked with redefining and restoring white manhood one decade into the new century. It is his job, in other words, to wake the dead:

> Quentin had grown up with that; the mere names were interchangeable and almost myriad. His childhood was full of them; his very body was an empty hall echoing with sonorous defeated names; he was not a being, an entity, he was a commonwealth. He was a barracks filled with stubborn back-looking ghosts still recovering, even forty-three years afterward, from the fever which had cured the disease ... weak from the fever yet free from the disease and not even aware that the freedom was that of impotence. (7)

Quentin's subjectivity is emptied of its own individuating content, as is Sutpen's. In the image of Thomas Sutpen and the legend that enfleshes it, Quentin discovers himself, not in the typical sense of ethnic belonging or of group descent or even of having been shaped by the same set of external circumstances that combine to create a shared social location. Instead, Quentin sees himself, his very body, as a mausoleum where the remains of the dead are stored for practices of mourning and memorialization, and where memorialization eventuates in resurrection. Sutpen's life and the South's loss, as invoked by Rosa Coldfield, expanded and reworked by Quentin's father and grandfather, and embellished by Quentin's and Shreve's own imagination, form the interwoven myths of collective pre-Civil War white male identity, of which Quentin is both heir and archivist. Like Thomas Sutpen, he is abstracted into the historical collective, made to serve as sign and surrogate for a social position rendered obsolete by the arrival of northern troops and abrogation of the right to hold slaves.

It is noteworthy that, despite his signification, despite being tasked with the work of regional recovery, and despite his ultimate knowledge that "freedom was that of impotence" and that redemption was to be found only in accepting the losses, Quentin is unable to manage a workable future; his suicide is foretold seven years earlier.[8] Only Jim Bond can rescue the future from the irremediable past, but I will get to that later. Quentin's failure to embody the hope of national redemption (despite leaving the South) or to produce a vision of sustainable collective futurity is caused by his inability to imagine an interracial national polis in which black men and women are regarded as equals in sociopolitical, juridical, economic, and humanistic terms. As Chandan Reddy astutely puts it, "It is precisely [the] loss of national identity through black racialization, an uprooting from the national landscape, that dialectically opens up a new set of possibilities."[9] To be sure, U.S. national futurity is not securable through adherence to racist ideology or the de facto reinstallation of slavery's structural design.

The failure with which both Sutpen and Quentin must contend is the national failure epitomized in the post-bellum period. After the departure of the federal troops from the South in 1877, the country turned its attention to the reunification of the fractured union after the Civil War. Rather than ensure that newly enfranchised black people and nascent free black communities were given necessary economic, juridical, educational, and political supports to thrive, the government conceded to the South, granting southern states the sovereignty to preserve or to develop racist legislation in every arena of political and social life. These included voting procedures, property laws, miscegenation laws, and hiring practices. States were granted the right to provide separate accommodations for white and black people in transportation, public facilities, and other significant sites of civic existence. The *Plessy vs. Ferguson* ruling of 1896, preceded in 1883 by the repeal of the Civil Rights Act of 1875, not only legalized racial discrimination in every arena of civic life but mandated repeated enactments of that discrimination each time a black person appeared in public. By legalizing the race-based division of public spaces, the Supreme Court barred black people from fully enfranchised civic inclusion. In the period of Quentin's birth, the will to white supremacy was encoded in rampant lynchings and in Jim Crow segregation, which converted every instance of African-American participation in the ordinary, everyday behaviors and movements that characterize civic belonging (purchasing and selling goods; traveling; attending places of work, worship, and learning, etc.) into ritualized iterations of racial subordination and civic exclusion: into, in other words, repetitive stagings of racial harm.

Quentin misreads racial difference, mistaking whiteness for a racial category, intrinsically superior to all others, when in the United States it is, in fact, the organizing apparatus of privilege. His misapprehension of racial logics and the symbolic and structural hierarchies they uphold is discernable in a minor argument he and Shreve have about Sutpen's place of birth.

> "Because he was born in West Virginia, in the mountains where –" ("Not in West Virginia," Shreve said. "–What?" Quentin said. "Not in West Virginia," Shreve said. "Because if he was twenty-five years old in Mississippi in 1833, he was born in 1808. And there wasn't any West Virginia in 1808 because–" "All right," Quentin said. "–West Virginia wasn't admitted–" "All right all right," Quentin said. "–into the United States until–" "All right all right all right," Quentin said.) (179)

Though a seemingly minor oversight that Quentin grants and then quickly dismisses, the narrative interruption signaled by the parenthetical break asks us to linger.[10] 1808 was the year in which the United States banned the capture, importation, and enslavement of black people via the international slave trade. For slavery's continued growth, slave-owners had to contend with reduced methods of procuring captive labor and the regional reconfiguration of the slave population. Even as it delegitimizes his particular slave-owning and renders him a criminal, Sutpen's importation of slaves from Haiti, already a sovereign black country for a decade and a half prior to his arrival, reenacts (and indicts the United States for) the international crimes of invading black nations and of kidnapping and enslaving their populations.[11] That he was born into a territory not yet formally recognized as a distinct state in the U.S. geopolitical sphere suggests that Sutpen is a partial outsider who is similar to, or will at least undertake the journey of, those early white immigrants/slave-holders who shaped white male subjectivity and established the (propertied, economic, juridical) qualities of national citizenship. The discursive and legal production of racial hierarchy under the regime of slavery granted heft to the early logic of whiteness and undergirded the conceptual, sociopolitical, capitalist, and legal machinery of white supremacy. In the nascent U.S. republic, composed of dislocated Europeans from varied countries, racial slavery supplied the delineating contours for the emergence and consolidation of whiteness as a necessary component of (individual and national) identity and as the essential basis for group claims to privileges as both coherent subjects and New World citizens.

Quentin's main failure is one of future-oriented looking. It is he who imagines and then refutes the possibility of interracial fraternity, and by extension of a racially unified nation. In her excellent essay "'The Direction of the Howling': Nationalism and the Color Line in *Absalom, Absalom!*" Barbara Ladd summarizes adroitly the shifting characterizations of Charles Bon according to the varying narrators.

> At first, we know only that Charles Bon is a mysterious French Creole, but as Quentin's story unfolds, Bon is transformed from colonialist creole into Thomas Sutpen's elder son into "the nigger that's going to sleep with your sister." In other words, Quentin's narrative transforms Charles Bon from a man who had, at a prior stage of history (Jason Compson's), some – albeit negligible – claim upon the white estate (a claim to assimilation) into someone who cannot possibly, according to the conventional logic of American radical racism, sustain any such claims.[12]

In his construction of the relationship between Sutpen's legitimate heir, Henry, and his purported first-born son, Charles Bon, Faulkner thematizes many things: fraternal competition, miscegenation, the contest over lineage and inheritance, homoeroticism, incest, the (white) family post-slavery. Rather than take up any of these thematic foci exclusively, I treat them here as interwoven tropes aimed at working through the implications of an integrated U.S. polity, in which the properties of personhood and the entitlements of citizenship are equally accessible to white and black Americans alike.

The earliest mention of Bon's secret, Henry's upset discovery of the secret, and the potential disqualification of Bon for marriage to Judith as a result of that secret casts Charles Bon as a white man, not unlike Thomas Sutpen:

> [Bon] must have known that Sutpen now knew his secret – if Bon, until he saw Sutpen's reaction to it, ever looked upon it as cause for secrecy, certainly not as a valid objection to marriage with a white woman – a situation which all his contemporaries who could afford it were likewise involved and which ... would no more have occurred to him to mention to his bride or wife or to her family than he would have told them the secrets of a fraternal organization he had joined before he married. In fact, the manner in which his intended bride's family reacted to the discovery ... was doubtless the first and last time when the Sutpen family ever surprised him.... He came into that isolated puritan country household almost like Sutpen himself came into Jefferson: apparently complete, without background or past or childhood. (73–4)

Like Thomas Sutpen, prior to his arrival in Jefferson, Bon married an "octoroon" woman, with whom he has a son. His surprise in this passage reflects his sense that given the illegality of the marriage ceremony, it is not to be regarded seriously. Moreover, he feels that his sexual access to black women is a standard privilege of white masculinity. He asserts, "We – the thousand, the white men – made them [biracial women], created and produced them; we even made the laws which declare that one eighth of a specified kind of blood shall outweigh seven eighths of another kind" (91). Bon's invocation of law and its quantification of blood to determine racial status speak more to post-emancipation legislation than the predominant law of enslavement, *partus sequitur ventrem*, which determined slave status according to matrilineage. This point is critical in that it makes clear that the novel is less concerned with the era of racial slavery, which it mythologizes, than with the period of post-emancipation, with which it actually contends.

In the post-bellum period, Jim Crow segregation and anti-miscegenation laws reinvigorated archaic legal systems in which "the blood of the attainted person was held to be corrupt, so that he could not transmit his estate to his heirs, nor could they inherit."[13] The discourse of blood, thereby, established race as a legal category that could be mobilized to maintain the racial order of citizen-subjects in the absence of legible racial demarcation – the case of Homer Plessy powerfully exemplifies this. As Colin Dayan argues astutely, "The degrees of blood, distinguished through the dubious means of observation, rumor, and reputation, reinforced the law's legitimation of whiteness.... As a metaphysical attribute, blood provided a pseudorational system for the distribution of a mythical essence: blood = race."[14] Whereas racial slavery established the legal category of the slave in relation to an identifiable and specified matrilineal line of descent (enslaved persons could sue for freedom on the basis of having a mother who had not been born into slavery), post-bellum laws that limited African-American civic participation – including Jim Crow segregation, anti-miscegenation legislation, and voting (dis)qualifications – established racial blackness as a legal category of second-class citizenship characterized in part by the absence of meaningful kinship ties or group membership. As the irrational and unscientific discourse of blood had the power to divest even phenotypically white persons (like Plessy, like Bon) of legal whiteness, racial blackness was fixed in culture and law as a permanent site of – and referent for – natal alienation, cultural illegibility, and disenfranchised personhood.

Prior to Quentin's reinvention, Bon was a self-identified white man (a Sutpen surrogate, but not his descendant) guilty of miscegenation, cast in this instance as the mere expression of white male sexual license, and potentially of bigamy. In Quentin's imaginative retelling, Bon is transmogrified into Sutpen's abandoned son, arrived to avenge his forsaken "octoroon" mother. By attempting to marry Judith, Quentin's Bon is guilty of the outlawed form of miscegenation, the one that provided the predominant justification for the rampant ritualized killing of black men during the post-bellum period through the first half of the twentieth century. In the moment before killing Bon, the tortured Henry cries "– *You are my brother*" (286). Henry proclaims a filial tie to Bon, establishing for Bon a delegitimized place within the familial network, the mixed-race brother who is potentially guilty of incest. Bon disavows the possibility of even partial, problematic belonging: "*No I'm not. I'm the nigger that's going to sleep with your sister*" (286). In the aftermath of racial slavery, miscegenation posed a threat to whiteness in that it impeded the continuous propagation of white generations and, thus, violated the unity/integrity of the white family as the basic unit of capital acquisition and consolidation in the U.S. political economy. Bon is not a "brother" but a "nigger" in the metaphorical national house. And as a "nigger," that is, having putatively "black blood," Bon would defile Judith and corrupt Sutpen's line. After all, Sutpen "just wanted a grandson," who would confirm his generational mastery (176). The inheritance that Quentin's narrative ultimately denies Bon is not in the arena of specified material wealth (especially considering that Sutpen claims to have provided abundantly for his first wife and child, and Charles Bon is wealthy) but the more important inheritance of legal whiteness, the right of normative abstraction into the "unmarked" body of the citizenry. It is his commitment, then, to the ideology of whiteness and the incumbent cultural, juridical, political practices of white hegemony that ultimately prevents Quentin from fulfilling – or even envisioning – the promise of national redemption and sustainable U.S. national futurity.

2

Before Jim Bond is seen, he is heard. Unlike the other embodied black figures in *Absalom, Absalom!*, whose representative location and meaning in the racial schema of both the life-world of the text and the lived experience of the nineteenth-century South is indicated by a highly visible, unchronicled, subordinate, immobile, and mute material essence, Jim Bond is both spectral and mobile. Embodying black sound and movement, he exists in the novel as the emblem of what *might be*, or as the invocation of the possible. Centralizing the figure of Jim Bond, the current section pursues two critical motives: first, an analysis of the figures in black that populate *Absalom, Absalom!* in which I attempt to theorize what blackness is and offers (other than the supposed specified content of racial alterity) and, second, an argument about the redemptive potentiality of black noise, defined for my purposes here as the sound(ing) of racial injury and the cry for national remediation.[15]

As I demonstrate in the opening discussion of Thomas Sutpen's storied arrival, blackness structures, through conceptual and ocular logics of negation, the contours of personhood and rights-bearing citizenship in the United States. In her illustrious treatise on what she calls the pervasive "Africanist" presence in American literature, Toni Morrison argues that figurative blackness constitutes a creative shorthand, or textual symbology, for the depiction of and meditation on themes that have come to define U.S. literature, along with national narratives about U.S. identity and exceptionalism: freedom, innocence, individualism, morality, and so on. She writes:

> The slave population, it could be and was assumed, offered itself up as surrogate selves for meditation on problems of human freedom, its lure and its elusiveness. The black population was available for meditations on terror – the terror or European outcasts, their dread of failure, powerlessness, Nature without limits, natal loneliness, internal aggression, evil, sin, greed. In other words, the slave population was understood to have offered itself up for reflections on human freedom in terms other than the abstraction of human potential and the rights of man.... Black slavery enriched the country's creative possibilities. For in that construction of blackness and enslavement could be found not only the not-free but also, with the dramatic polarity created by skin color, the not-me.[16]

Morrison contends that the black figure in early American literature signified the underbelly of societal endeavor and structure. At stake in those representations were the very aspirations, principles, and collective longings that defined New World formation. The figurative black – captive, embodied, enslaved – was assigned the features and made to inhabit the social position that was most detested and feared in the collective imaginary.

It is important to emphasize that figurative blackness did not and does not bespeak the individual interiority of self-identified and/or embodied black people. Nor is racial difference the exclusive province of the racialized figure; blackness emerges, rather, as the method and measure of an embedded and asymmetric sociopolitical dynamic. As Huey Copeland eloquently describes:

> Blackness functions ... as both a free-floating trace unmoored from individual subjects and as a concrete index of power relations that reveals the deep structure of modernity's modes of visualization, the despotism on which they rely, and the ways that they might be contested in the present. At once abstract and bodily, literal and metaphorical, the ultimate sign of aesthetic negation and the prime marker of the socially negated, blackness marks those historical forces that continue to differentially engender subjects and objects in the modern world, everywhere shaping a cultural unconsciousness in which the individual

effects of racialization assume a shifting texture despite the unyielding ruth-
lessness of their overarching logic.[17]

In the nineteenth century, the black was conceptualized as primitive, wild,
sexually rapacious, mentally and morally deficient, unfree and so forth
because the white was purportedly and precisely not these things or, in other
words, "not-black." Blackness was incorporated and negated within the
symbolic and social system in which whiteness – as legalized and literalized
mastery – took shape. In *Absalom, Absalom!*, Thomas Sutpen's ascendancy
is presented as a series of encounters with the black – or repeated stagings of color-coded homosocial primal scenes – in which Sutpen overcomes
or overthrows the black masculine. This happens in bare-chested wrestling
matches, during a plantation revolt in Haiti, in taming the acres that comprise Sutpen's Hundred, in the swampy pursuit of the escaped architect, in
building Sutpen's courthouse-like plantation mansion. Defeating and over-
coming black figures is portrayed in these various scenes as the subjection
of brute Nature, the seed-work of Sutpen's becoming, the ultimate test of
his masculinity, and the index of his qualification for the status at the heart
of his design: that of the white master citizen-subject. Notably, in all except
one encounter, Sutpen is victorious. The exceptional circumstance occurs
when one black man exceeds his own static and dense material signification
by opening his mouth to speak.

When he was a boy, Sutpen was destitute. He and his family lived in such
abject poverty that they saw enslaved black people who were better clothed,
housed, and fed than they. Sutpen was unbothered by this. He knew somehow that an uncontested claim to whiteness held more proprietary promise,
would yield in time more cultural dividends, than any and all possessions a
black person might claim.[18] The decently attired and enslaved butler, coach,
and manservant to the local wealthy plantation owner were mere "mon-
keys," "monkey-dressed niggers" to Sutpen's understanding (187). Even as a
young adolescent boy, Sutpen perceived the racial schema and witnessed the
appallingly low value placed on black life. He overheard tales of black men
who were taken and tortured by white mobs: "the torch-disturbed darkness
among the trees, the fierce hysterical faces of the white men, the balloon
face of the nigger. Maybe the nigger's hands would be tied or held but that
would be all right because they were not the hands with which the balloon
face would struggle and writhe for freedom, not the balloon face" (187).
The balloon face, the black, was a grotesque form without human essence or
individual interiority. The insinuation here is that, by law and by the logics
of racial slavery, the enslaved black was mere bodily material to be animated
and manipulated by the external will of the white.

When Sutpen was approximately twelve years old, he was sent by his father to a wealthy plantation on an errand. The purpose of the errand remains throughout the text undisclosed and unremembered due the trauma of what followed:

> And now he stood before that white door with the monkey nigger barring it and looking down at him in his patched made-over jeans clothes and no shoes and I dont reckon he had even ever experimented with a comb because that would be one of the things his sisters would keep hidden good – who had never thought about his own hair or clothes or anybody else's hair or clothes until he saw that monkey nigger, who through no doing of his own happened to have had the felicity of being housebred in Richmond maybe, looking ... at them and he never even remembered what the nigger said, how it was the nigger told him, even before he had had time to say what he came for, never to come to that front door again but to go around to the back. (188)

Thomas Sutpen, located in that transitional moment between boyhood and manhood, was shocked by the movement and by the speech act of the black. This scene is particularly resonant in a novel that is concerned with how the abolition of racial slavery, which may be understood as granting black people social membership in the metaphorical national house, impacts white masculinity. The enslaved black man first barred Sutpen's entry into the home. That is, he used his body in a way that did not reflect the disciplined shape of servitude.[19] He shaped his body, rather, in a gesture of imposition and dismissal. In so doing, the enslaved black butler performed his right/rite of belonging, as he refused the white boy entry into the plantation household. Moreover, the black figure spoke; he used his voice to evidence his interiority and, in this instance, his authority. Possessed of the power of illocution, the black man told and, thereby, made the white boy move. So terrorized and terrified by the possibility of his domestic exclusion in favor of the black, Sutpen fled to Haiti to take up what would become his life's obsession: white generational mastery.

Sutpen is, alas, unable to fulfill his dynastic hopes of white mastery, given the new era of (at least formal) black freedom. Nor is Quentin, the heir and archivist of triumphal white masculinity, able to resuscitate it. The new decade of the new century is nearly complete when Shreve reminds Quentin: "You've got one nigger left. One nigger Sutpen left. Of course you cant catch him and you dont even always see him and you never will be able to use him. But you've got him there still. You still hear him at night sometimes" (302). By now, Sutpen's house has burned to the ground, and not a single heir who carries his name lives. Jim Bond is the only one left, and his name signals the collective position of the formerly enslaved; the durable tie, forged in the intimate violences of the slave plantation, that binds all American futures, and the reparative debt still owed to African-Americans for the modern atrocity of racial slavery.

Unlike the black (balloon face) of Thomas Sutpen's understanding, Jim Bond is a "living creature, living flesh to feel pain and writhe and cry out" (187). Jim Bond's howl is the sound of liminality, the vocal expression of nominal freedom, the hope and the frustration of inhabiting in time and place the line between enslavement and emancipation. Stephen Best and Saidiya Hartman describe such expression as caught "between grievance and grief; between the necessity of legal remedy and the impossibility of redress ... between the unavoidable form of the 'appeal' and its ultimate illegibility and insufficiency ... between the complaint that is audible ... and the extralinguistic mode of black noise that exists outside the parameters of any strategy or plan for remedy."[20] Jim Bond's wail is the sonic registration of grief, of internality, of sentience, of righteous opposition.

Moving indefatigably at the margins, Jim Bond critiques, revises, and unfinishes the dead past. His failure – or refusal – to form words, to create a narrative of historical harm that results in both the grievance and the basis for contemporary black identity, may be understood here as resistance to discursive cooptation. Like the blind guru in the parable that opens this essay, he sidesteps public enactments of disparate power. By disappearing behind the haunting cry, Jim Bond absents himself from both the conceptual and the visual logics of racial othering. He is not caught, that is, not captive. He is not stationary, that is, not made to occupy the gestures, shapes, and practices of racist subjugation. He is not available for use; that is, he is self-possessed, nearly free. Understanding Jim Bond this way, as both the novel and the nation's redemptive promise, sheds necessary light on the conclusion to *Absalom, Absalom!*: when Shreve prophesies that, "the Jim Bonds are going to conquer the western hemisphere," it is not a lament; it is a prayer (302).

NOTES

1 Toni Morrison, "Nobel Lecture in Literature," *What Moves at the Margin*, Carolyn C. Denard (ed.), Jackson: University Press of Mississippi, 2008, p. 206.

2 Toni Morrison, "The Future of Time: Literature and Diminished Expectations," *What Moves at the Margin*, Carolyn C. Denard (ed.), Jackson: University Press of Mississippi, 2008, p. 186.

3 Morrison makes clear that certain atrocities may never be adequately revealed or recorded in words. Even as she calls our attention to the uses of language and the necessity of its constant use, expansion, and revision, she alerts us to its limits.

In the case of world-historical violence, such as racial slavery and genocide, language only allows us to approximate its effects.

4 Christopher Cunningham, "Sutpen's Designs: Masculine Reproduction and The Unmaking of the Self-Made Man in *Absalom, Absalom!*," *Mississippi Quarterly* 49.3 (1996), 563.

5 James Guetti, "*Absalom, Absalom!*: The Extended Simile," *William Faulkner's Absalom, Absalom!: A Critical Casebook*, Elizabeth Muhlenfeld (ed.) (London: Garland, 1984), p. 86.

6 For more on this point, see Michelle M. Wright, *Becoming Black: Creating Identity in the African Diaspora* (Durham, NC: Duke University Press, 2004).

7 My understanding of Thomas Sutpen's design as an allegory of U.S. nation-building follows the seminal work of important scholars of Faulkner's writing, race, and processes of racialization in the southern context. I am indebted in particular to Thadious Davis, Eric Sundquist, and Erik Dussere for critical revisionist work, which foregrounded racial difference, slavery, and national mythmaking in William Faulkner's writing.

8 Quentin's suicide is foretold in *The Sound and the Fury*.

9 Chandan Reddy, *Freedom with Violence: Race, Sexuality, and the U.S. State*, Durham, NC: Duke University Press, 2011, p. 73.

10 Quentin's quick dismissal of Shreve's correction indicates his own refusal to seriously ponder the ramifications of the Civil War. West Virginia seceded from Virginia in opposition to the secession efforts and the perpetuation of slavery. Its formal recognition as a state was one victory of the North in the Civil War, as it evidenced the regional reconfiguration of the South and the legal abolition of slavery.

11 For more on the depiction of Haiti and its significance in Faulkner's novels, see John T. Matthews, "Recalling the West Indies: From Yoknapatawpha to Haiti and Back," *American Literary History* 16.2 (2004), 238–62

12 Barbara Ladd, "'The Direction of the Howling': Nationalism and the Color Line in *Absalom, Absalom!*," *American Literature* 66.3 (1994), p. 544.

13 Colin Dayan, "Legal Slaves and Civil Bodies," *Materializing Democracy: Toward a Revitalized Cultural Politics*, edited by Dana Nelson and Russ Castronovo (Durham, NC: Duke University Press, 2002) p. 58.

14 Ibid., p. 64.

15 Fred Moten (*In The Break: The Aesthetics Of The Black Radical Tradition*, [University of Minnesota Press, 1993]) and Tricia Rose (*Black Noise: Rap Music and Black Culture in Contemporary America* [Wesleyan University Press, 1994]) are important theorists of the sound(ing) of black resistance and sonic radicality.

16 Toni Morrison, *Playing in the Dark* (New York: Vintage, 1993), pp. 37–8.

17 Huey Copeland, *Bound to Appear: Art, Slavery, and the Site of Blackness in Multicultural America* (Chicago: University of Chicago Press, 2013), p. 11.

18 My thinking about the proprietary value of whiteness is informed by the seminal work of Cheryl Harris on the intersection of whiteness, property, and law. See Cheryl Harris, "Whiteness as Property," *Harvard Law Review* 106.8 (1993), 1707–91.

19 Harvey Young deftly theorizes phenomenological blackness, arguing, "The black body, whether on the auction block, the American plantation, hanged from a lightpole as art of a lynching ritual, attacked by police dogs within the Civil

Rights era, or staged as a 'criminal body' by contemporary law enforcement and judicial systems, is a body that has been forced into the public spotlight and given a compulsory visibility.... This awareness of one's status as the seen/scene structures behavior" (*Embodying Black Experience: Stillness, Critical Memory, and the Black Body*, Ann Arbor: University of Michigan Press, 2010, p. 12).

20 Stephen Best and Saidiya Hartman, "Fugitive Justice," *Representations* 92.1 (2005), p. 3.

4

PATRICIA E. CHU

Faulkner and Biopolitics

One of the major developments in Faulkner criticism has been to set his work
in terms of contemporary history: exploring his negotiations with specific
political discourses that emerged from representations of fascism, the policies of the New Deal, the experience of the Great Depression in the South,
the incorporation of the South into the national economy in the 1930s and
1940s, American imperial policy, and the artist's place in the political (or
the federally funded) sector. But it seems to me that even with this change,
Faulkner's work is still persistently understood in the terms that his famous
character Quentin understands himself: "his very body was an empty hall
echoing with sonorous defeated names; he was not a being, an entity, he
was a commonwealth. He was a barracks filled with stubborn back-looking
ghosts" (*AA* 7). That is to say, even when Faulkner is read as an aesthetically
modern(ist) author, it is very often in terms of how this literary modernity
is "back-looking," using the modernist shattering of linear chronology and
objective time to make a point of how regional understandings of time and
history clash with national/federal time. He is interpreted somewhat in isolation from "non-regional" modernists, indeed, despite the subject matter of
his oeuvre and the facts of his biography, and also in isolation from broader
modernist thematics. In this essay I reconceive Faulkner's modernity in
terms of biopolitics to set him in the context of other modernist authors
who addressed the management of lives and bodies, a context that became
manifestly visible in the case of the modern soldier of the world wars and
that was extended into everyday life after the war more subtly. I argue that
we may read Faulkner as anxious not only about Southern autonomy and
subjectivity but as part of an Anglo-American modernist movement that
collectively (if not always accurately) expressed anxiety about the targets of
the new state strategies of governance. By example, I will reread one of his
stories, "The Tall Men," contrary to its usual interpretation as Faulkner's
assertion of Southern local character over federal bureaucracy.

As we see in Georg Simmel's words, even at the most elite positions of society, anxiety over retaining agency in the face of modernization was expressed quite dramatically:

> The individual has become a mere cog in an enormous organization of things and powers which tear from his hands all progress, spirituality, and value in order to transform them from their subjective form into the form of a purely objective life.... The metropolis is the genuine arena of this culture which outgrows all personal life. Here in buildings and educational institutions, in the wonders and comforts of space conquering technology, in the formations of community life, and in the visible institutions of the state, is offered such an overwhelming fullness of crystallized and impersonalized spirit that the personality, so to speak, cannot maintain itself under its impact.[1]

Simmel describes urbanization as central to a general threat to the individual personality. Americans were also to experience their own rise of the metropolis as the population shifted from primarily rural to primarily urban, starting at the turn of the century and with increasing speed during the interwar years. Industrialized, mechanized, standardized, centralized, socially isolated, and consumerist metropolitan life seemed to have become American life. Describing the "Americanization" of the South – the shift from traditional, small-scale, local production to capital-intensive and mechanized agricultural business that could be incorporated into an international cash-crop economy – became a way for all Americans to map the contours of what it meant to be a citizen in the modernizing American political economy. That is to say, Faulkner's "Southern" modernism may well be simply modernism.[2]

"The Tall Men" describes federal inspector Pearson's attempt to serve a warrant on two brothers, Anse and Lucius McCallum, who have not registered for Selective Service during World War II. The local marshal, Gombault, takes him to the family home, where they and their uncles are gathered at their father Buddy's bedside as he waits for a doctor to amputate the leg he has injured in an accident on the farm that day. Buddy tells the boys to leave for Memphis and register; when Pearson protests that it is too late, since a warrant for arrest for failure to register has already been issued, everyone ignores him and the boys depart. The marshal refuses to pursue them, forcing the inspector to wait until the amputation is complete and he has buried the leg in the family graveyard, lecturing the inspector all the while.

Ted Atkinson has argued that although "Faulkner had kept his distance from regionalists who romanticized the Southern way of life, 'The Tall Men' represents an affiliation with the brand of defiance that emerged in *I'll Take My Stand* and progressed through the thirties as an alternative to leftist programs of social and economic reform." He reads the story as "an explicit warning against an intrusive Federal government ... intent on manipulating rural folk and folkways through social engineering."[3] My argument here is not against this claim but rather for an additional layer to it, a broader sense of Faulkner's unease – about governmentality rather than "the Government" – and about state subjectivity as something beyond what a homogenized federalized North imposes on a more authentic South.

The overdetermined object at the center of this story is Buddy McCallum's leg. He does not actually lose the leg in military service, but its loss is juxtaposed with his service in World War I and his father's service in the Confederate Army. The amputated leg metonymically presents Buddy's body as a national resource; burying the leg puts bodies in national service in a material and local context. The leg is also biological matter. As such, it could invoke the Gothicism so often claimed for Faulkner and implicitly associated with, again, the "back-look." What I am interested in, though, is how Faulkner interarticulates modern biology's new view of organic life as subject to human manipulation as a result of the rise of new techniques of governance.

A significant hallmark of modern biology is that it no longer distinguished sharply between animate and inanimate matter based on the presence of a vital or life force. Instead, life was understood in terms of its chemical and physical properties. Matter is "biological" not because of a "property peculiar to the living" but according to "chemical and physical phenomena that can be measured."[4] The study of life came to include the ways in which it was plastic and open to human intervention. As Hannah Landecker puts it, beginning in the twentieth century, the "human relationship to living matter ... [became] one structured by the concept of life as technology."[5]

Similarly, philosopher of science François Dagognet describes twentieth-century work in the life sciences as facilitating, encouraging, and accelerating the unfurling of a natural life of infinite and plastic combinations, rather than making a static account of forms as they developed by chance in "nature."[6] In 1907, Ross Harrison grew a nerve cell without a body using amphibian embryonic tissue. The new ability of scientists to sustain life that would actually move, grow, and differentiate outside the body, the ability to observe processes of the internal body outside the body, and the idea that cellular life was autonomous reverberated far beyond the scientific community. This was a fundamental shift, and even those within the scientific community saw it as a philosophical and cultural disturbance. Harrison himself wrote that it forced a realization that "each one of us may be resolved into myriads of cellular units with some definite structure and with autonomous powers."[7] An illustrative popular description of Harrison's work from 1912 reads in part: "Each of the elements ... of our bodies lives without doubt a little for us, but they live above all for themselves."[8] This is a view of biological organisms as composed of separable and alienable units, susceptible to a hyper-individuation at the cellular level that allows for more and more effective manipulation of the whole organism.

These apprehensions of the paradigm shift in biological science echo Simmel's, T. S. Eliot's, and Max Weber's diverse descriptions of the modern man as threatened by a loss of agency stemming from attacks on individual autonomy. The men living in Simmel's metropolis who form Eliot's crowd flowing over London Bridge to the financial district, each "fix[ing] his eyes before his feet," are on their way to Weber's bureaucratic organization.[9] Once there, they will work with "precision, speed, unambiguity, knowledge of the files, continuity, discretion, unity, strict subordination, reduction of friction and of material and personal costs."[10] Where Harrison's experiment suggested that humans might be nothing but administered masses of cellular units, the modernists feared themselves to be nothing but cogs in a larger machinery fully susceptible to manipulation beyond their knowing. In fact, the social sciences, rational design, regional planning, large-scale economic management, and modern wartime mobilization all practiced social management on the level of the individual to yield large-scale results. The two together form the paradigm of biopower and the infamous alienation of modernism, experienced alike by elite Northerner, European sociologist, and Southern Agrarian.

In Faulkner's story about "the Government," the local marshal Gombault employs words akin to those used to describe Harrison's experiment and others like it that received popular media coverage:

> We have come to be like critters doctor folks might have created in laboratories, that have learned how to slip off their bones and guts and still live, still be kept alive indefinite and forever maybe even without even knowing the bones and the guts are gone. We have slipped our backbone; we have about decided a man don't need a backbone anymore; to have one is old-fashioned.
>
> ("The Tall Men," CS 59)

There is a decidedly modern edge to the marshal's Southern folksiness about "critters" and "having a backbone" that should belie a solely "locals/South versus federals/North" interpretation. The backbone as an image here connects modern biological revisions of the understanding of life with a metaphor for asserting the individual self. The anxiety expressed here is not merely about modern loss of free will, agency, and authority but about whether it is possible to recognize fully the loss of these ("be kept alive indefinite and forever maybe even without even knowing the bones and the guts are gone").

We might understand the burial of Buddy's amputated leg as a modernist meditation on life matter, on bodies and parts, on autonomy and administration and biopower. The marshal refuses to let the investigator leave until Buddy's leg is buried. While waiting for the amputation to be completed, Gombault tells Pearson the story of the McCallum family men, their military service and their refusal to cooperate with federal efforts to manage farm production on a national scale. He then takes Pearson outside with the leg and estimates where Buddy will someday be buried. "After the boys was born Jackson and Stuart was to come up here by their pa and ma so Buddy could move up some and make room. So he will be about here.... Yes, sir. We done forgot about folks. Life has done got cheap, and life ain't cheap. Life's a pretty durn valuable thing. I don't mean just getting along from one WPA relief check to the next" (60). Readings of Gombault's speech as anti-welfare state are certainly valid, but I would like to add another, historically and geographically broader, element to this.

As Foucault has taught us, modern political power emerges from the management of all the aspects of the life of a population in the name of the well-being of that population. Managing the well-being of the population is done by managing individual behavior that adds up to everything from ideal production levels in agriculture to family arrangements to the eradication of polio. To return briefly to the laboratory, the culturing of life outside of whole bodies to be "plastic," that is, susceptible to manipulation and engineering apart from its original whole organic existence, parallels the way the individual is viewed in biopolitical terms as manipulable for a larger effect. But a side effect of this is that even as increasing life in terms of population relies on valuing life highly, individual life can become "cheap."[11] As Gombault explains to Pearson, the McCallums never understood why the government wants to manage how much cotton they grow, gin, and sell. They cannot see themselves as merely part of a large group growing an optimal amount of cotton for the nation as a whole any more than Gombault would want to be reduced to his parts as an unknowing critter in a laboratory.

Thus, as the marshal and the inspector stand in the McCallum family plot, the act of burying Buddy's leg turns into a temporary reversal of the processes of atomization, hollowing out, and fragmentation so many modernists describe as the experience of living in the first half of the twentieth century. Marshal Gombault's lectures to Inspector Pearson constitute a funeral oratory that both underscores and challenges calculations of life in parts (what Foucault calls "the statization of biology") by (re)attaching the leg not only to a man but to a family *and* insisting that the leg is fully dead. The concern with the burial of biological matter as told in the story can on the one hand be read as regional local color verging on the comic, or, on the other hand, that concern can be set in the context of modernists such as Frazer, Eliot, D. H. Lawrence, H. D., and others who invoke the Osiris myth in a contrary way. That is, while Faulkner does not directly reference the myth, we might find in this scene a similar interrogation of modern atomization and a (failed) turn to anthropologically described traditional "whole cultures." Faulkner's connection of this to the modern laboratory modernizes and politicizes the myth anew.

During the modernist period, modern biology shifted from *in vivo* practice to *in vitro* practice.[12] Heretofore, scientists studying life processes had to end the process at intervals and extrapolate what had gone on in-between. At each interval, the scientist would "kill, stain and fix." The organism and the parts and processes of its organic life were inseparable, and the processes took place inside an opaque container that had to be opened. But with the advent of tissue culture, cells and tissues (including those of humans) could live outside bodies, with a new transparency to the investigative and monitory gaze.[13] In the context of laboratory biology, the burial of the part resists the notion of life outside the body and asserts the fundamental nature of the whole. Buddy's leg will have no life of its own; young Anse and Lucius are instructed not to forget their name.

This is a political apprehension of a radical change that goes far beyond the "for or against" politics of specific policies of the emerging welfare state in the American South that may comprise the first layer of this story. Rather, it addresses an all-encompassing change. The Anglo-American modernist period, approximately 1890 to 1945, coincides with a marked new era in biopower, as modern states began to identify, track, and regulate their populations in new ways. The second wave of industrialization meant a radical rise in systematized factory production, which sparked urbanization and broke families and communities into separable wage laborers who moved transnationally to where capital was concentrated. The great powers were industrializing nations competing for imperial territory in the years before World War I because the new basis of global power was modernization and expansion of production. Managing this production meant managing the individuals on whose labor and boundless tractability the nation's carefully coordinated economies of scale relied.[14]

Thus although, as many critics have noted, *individualism* was a catchword for Faulkner and for anti-leftists after the Depression, it seems obvious that both had some inkling that the *individuation* necessary to the workings of the modern biological laboratory and to state biopower was something quite different. To "govern" now meant to shape the behaviors of citizens in ways that would be experienced as choices, which would in their turn produce particular social objectives.[15] For "tractability," then, we might use a term from the twentieth-century laboratory Gombault evokes: "plasticity." Landecker summarizes this as follows:

> Plasticity is the ability of living things to go on living, synthesizing proteins, moving, reproducing, and so on despite catastrophic interference in their constitution, environment or form.... Although living things can be radically manipulated, part of the particularity of biological plasticity is that biological matter may change or react to intervention in totally unexpected ways.... [Plasticity] is not just the inherent ability of living matter to adapt flexibly and to live through shock and rearrangement but also its capacity to *be* changed by humans. (10)

Plasticity enables exploitation. This ideal of plasticity even has built into it something like a possibility for cooptation of creativity/rebellion: unexpected results, as with the theory of evolution, simply provide resources for development. Efficiency, managed economies, and rational design, the equivalents of plasticity outside the laboratory, demand detachment from whole cultures and whole bodies so that individuals may be constantly changed and redeployed. We might understand the much-analyzed modernist sense of alienation as stemming from wondering whether one has been cut out to live *in vitro* as an unknowing cog in the machine, or in this case, a critter in the state laboratory.

"The Tall Men" participates in a thread of international modernism concerned with the nature of modern subjectivity as managed subjectivity under regimes of biopower, specifically, a massive conscription and deployment of men during World War I amid skepticism about the war being the result of international business practices. In their novels about the World War I soldier, Virginia Woolf (*Mrs. Dalloway* and *Jacob's Room*) and Rebecca West (*The Return of the Soldier*) depict the ways that national narratives of masculine agency obscured the machinations of a state treating men as resources for the trenches.

Significantly, neither the McCallums nor Gombault completely refuse national attachment or state incorporation. A large portion of Gombault's lecture to Pearson establishes the family's record of military service – Anse, Sr. in the Confederate Army and his son Buddy in World War I. Significantly, he refers to World War I as "the other war": "Buddy come along late, late enough to be in the other war, in France in it.... He brought back two medals, an American medal and a French one" (55). This phrasing puts the two wars *affectively* on the same level and in the same mode of American history.

That is to say, although one of those wars was fought against America, that is not its chief characteristic here. Faulkner is not writing this family as Southern throwbacks still fighting the Northern federals but as men who desire to be part of the larger nation. Buddy tells Lucius and Anse, (deliberately?) misunderstanding the warrant and the process of Selective Service registration:

> You will have uniforms in a day or two.... I'd like for you to enlist into the old Sixth Infantry, where I used to be. But I reckon that's too much to hope, and you'll just have to chance where they send you. But it likely won't matter, once you are in. The Government done right by me in my day, and it will do right by you. You just enlist wherever they want to send you, need you, and obey your sergeants and officers until you find out how to be soldiers. Obey them, but remember your name and don't take nothing from no man.   (52–3)

This is hardly anti-government language, and Buddy is telling them not to pack because they will be donning the federal uniform, which ought to be anathema to a Confederate. The repetition of the phrase "The Government" here echoes Gombault's earlier description of the McCallums's use of the word as one that should have meant protection.

> It was like they still couldn't believe it, still believed in the freedom and liberty to make or break according to a man's fitness and will to work, guaranteed by the Government that old Anse had tried to tear in two once and failed, and admitted in good faith he had failed and taken the consequences, and that had give Buddy a medal and taken care of him when he was far away from home in a strange land and hurt.   (56)

There is a narrative gap here. Buddy, after all, did not accidentally wander into France. We see that what Gombault and Buddy erase here is the link between (the illusion of) requited national desire and the state prerogatives that reduce men to biological resources. Akin to Virginia Woolf's World War I soldier Septimus Smith, who "was one of the first to volunteer" and who goes to France "to save an England which consisted almost entirely of Shakespeare's plays and Miss Isabel Pole walking in a square," these men believe in a nurturing nation.[16] Even Anse, Sr.'s Confederate service does not preclude a national embrace. The Southern Confederacy is not the center of contention here. But, like Septimus, the McCallums confront the state that deploys national affect to get voluntary and unknowing compliance but will make sure "Holmes is on" the individual who cannot be atomized and plasticized, whose interior will not yield to outside exploitation.[17] For Woolf, navigating this rift between the nation and the state requires either repression or schizophrenia and ends for Septimus in suicide; Faulkner's "tall men" choose the first. Buddy's instructions to Anse and Lucius firmly refuse to recognize the state prerogative and instead focus on the national relationship. His words to them are a correction to Pearson but not, on the level of the reader, a conclusive one. By telling the boys to go register and get uniforms, and by observing that they will not be bringing the truck back (when the truth is that registration is not the same as being called up), he asserts that the family is responding to the nation, not the state. Telling his sons that they must respond when the Government needs them, as he did in World War I, but ignoring the actual statutory violation, Buddy denies the right of the government to *manage* its citizens, to track and imagine them as atomized bits of life in a larger population. If the McCallums serve, he insists, it will be as whole men with volition, not as plastic or unknowing state resources. (Anse and Lucius have violated the Selective Training and Service Act of 1940, the first conscription act in the United States that called up men for service during peacetime, that is, when the government should not "need" them.)

Accordingly, Buddy represses his own conscription as well. Trapped in the discourse of national heroism that his medals impose, receiving medical care he can compare to triage field medicine decades ago, injured in a way that belies a modernizing national embrace of the small regional farmer, Buddy is unable to respond. Imagining his sons serving in his old unit and being treated in the same way he (imagines he) was treated is an attempt to construct affective channels of connection to the nation that are based on traditional biological views of life: patriarchal (as if the father is still the material model of political power to tell them when to go), and *in vivo* (life as a property inseparable from its manifestation in a natural organic body). Most notable to Gombault in his description of how Buddy's father enlisted in the Confederate army is that "he walked all the way to Virginia to get into it. He could have enlisted and fought right here at home, but his ma was a Carter so wouldn't nothing do him but to go all the way back to Virginia to do his fighting" (54). In these kinds of constructions, attachment to the nation is routed through the family, making personal biology (and *in vivo* biology) primary. This is not necessarily oppositional to the state, of course. As Benedict Anderson explains it, this strategy is fundamental to the historical instantiation of nationalism as a natural(ized) and requited identity that can then be mobilized as official (state) nationalism.[18]

Nonetheless, when Anse, Sr. subjected himself to the Confederacy and to a war on behalf of an elite class to which he did not belong by imagining his service through a biological family line – "his mother was a Carter" – such a species of subjection worked by reinforcing a sense of agency with regard to national attachment. But for the next generations, soldiers of the modern world wars and of internationally scaled economies, this is precisely the kind of agency that is denied. Much has been written about the experience of the World War I soldier as a trench combatant moving by inches and emasculated in the fetal position under a barrage of shells from an unseen enemy, in contrast to earlier wars in which battles were the occasion for the claiming of masculine agency over life. To assert *in vivo* biology in this context is, Faulkner shows in this comparison, ineffectual. Like Woolf's Septimus Smith and Rebecca West's Chris Baldry, World War I soldiers who can only escape understanding their status as state resources by retreating to the depths of their minds (breakdown/suicide and amnesia), Gombault and the McCallums willfully forget and misunderstand the difference between the pre- and post-twentieth-century wars. The laboratory violence underlying "an interior set of life processes that had been extracted, distributed and persuaded to live outside the body, glass-enclosed but always in full view"[19] parallels psychological treatment of the soldiers in Woolf and West's novels by doctors who try to return them to a "plastic" state in which their interior processes (what we might call the idea of the autonomous self) are kept manipulable. Making the interior exterior will allow the state access to their military service or to their participation in the economic recovery after the war. Faulkner has here recontextualized what we tend to think of as the stubborn Southern "back-look" into a semi-heroic though ultimately futile denial similar to those of Woolf and West. Thus, Buddy's overdetermined amputated leg also stands in for his being cut off from understanding how he is used in the war and after. What he thinks he knows is only the first layer.

Another reason to treat this story as a meditation on the larger parameters of modern power rather than as strictly an Agrarian account of the story of the struggle between the South and the North is that Faulkner also marks the McCallums as having, as critic Paul Bové's Gramscian reading of the Agrarians puts it, started the process of becoming attached to the hegemonic extended state, of becoming "new agricultural men." The McCallums refuse to accept payment for reducing their crops according to government specifications and do not file the papers that would allow them to sell the portion of crop they would have been permitted to grow. Lucius and Anse neglect to register with Selective Service. But Lucius and Anse also, the marshal repeats twice in his tale, "went to the agricultural college for a year to learn more about whiteface cattle" (55). This is not a trivial detail. As Gombault tells it, the McCallums quixotically ginned twenty-two bales of unsellable cotton and then defiantly decided to get out of farming if the Government was going to be in it. But, and Faulkner surely knew this, going to agricultural college was no way to remain independent of the government.

Paul Bové's larger argument about the Agrarian intellectuals tracks their "nationalization" from marginalized, regionalized political opposition to the center of state-sponsored academe, where they laid out the tenets of New Criticism and critiques of capitalist state apparatuses within a site contained by the state. Key to their transformation and most relevant to my purposes here is the rise of agriculture as a new administered part of the Gramscian extended state, "the entire complex of practical and theoretical activities with which the ruling class not only justifies and maintains its dominance but manages to win the active consent of those whom it rules."[20] Bové argues that the South at this time is perhaps most notable not for its resistance to hegemonic incorporation but for the way its elite negotiated "the South's entry into the national hegemony on different terms than that hegemony was offering."[21] Gombault may rail about the debased "alphabets" of the Government, "AAA and WPA and a dozen other three-letter reasons for a man not to work"[22] as something the Government does to manhood, but the state is not limited to the government (CS 58). In fact, one of the significant aspects of the development of twentieth-century governance is how, in the first half of the twentieth century, private philanthropic social reform initiatives targeting the management of social life became enmeshed with government initiatives such that penetration into the social and state administrative techniques and information combined, giving the social organizations more power and facilitating the exercise of state powers in a way that did not come directly through government initiative.[23] Going to college for a year to learn about whiteface cattle takes Lucius and Anse, perhaps even more so than registering for Selective Service, out of the freehold of independent farmers and puts them in the hands of the extended state:

> There had been farmers in the nineteenth century, but when they began to organize corporately rather than act politically in a populist struggle ... 'agriculture' came into existence as a political weight within the state apparatus.... Although a 'private' institution, the Farm Bureau acted as an extension of the state.... The national organization ... through local branches and in cooperation with extension services and land-grant colleges educates farmers in the leading technical innovations in intensive farming and orchestrates the farmers' relationships to markets in the United States and abroad.[24]

Foundational both to Gramsci's concept of the extended state and to Foucault's concept of biopower is that subjects do not understand themselves *as* subject. This third McCallum generation conforms precisely to production requirements of a national economy of scale (less cotton, more whiteface cattle) while allowing the family as a whole to feel that they are acting autonomously, even defiantly.

The key to the debate between Gombault and Pearson, then, is not the individual versus the Government or the Jeffersonian yeoman versus the WPA check recipient. Nor is it the local versus the federal. Gombault and Pearson engage on the issue of what it means to be "bonded" to the United States. Pearson first uses the word as a reference to their shared position when he realizes that Gombault will not help him execute the warrant: "Have you forgotten that you are under a bond yourself?" (45). Each describes the meaning of such a bond in affective terms. Pearson draws a picture of a "suffering and threatened government" that has given "these people" everything and asks merely for "one thing simply": registration for Selective Service (46). Gombault, as we have seen earlier, describes the government nurturing Buddy when he was "far away from home in a strange land and hurt." Each imagines that he must convince the other of the proper way to imagine connection to the nation-state in a way that also implies community through the state between themselves; where Pearson reminds Gombault of a "bond" similar to the one he himself has, Gombault says kindly to Pearson, using syntax that slides from the accusatory second person to the shared position first person plural: "you mean all right. You just went and got yourself all fogged up with rules and regulations. That's our trouble. We done invented ourselves so many alphabets and rules" (59).

Thus, the apparent extreme difference between Pearson's bureaucratese ("if the situation were controlled, it would devolve upon him to control it … if their departure with their prisoners were expedited, it must be himself and not the old marshal who would expedite it" [48]) and Gombault's folksiness does not represent the irreconcilability of the South and the state but modern citizen-subjects' common position under bond. If the inspector falls silent, it is not because Faulkner stages Gombault's overrun of his narrative control, but because they both "do the police in different voices."

What does taking careful note of the modern laboratory and biological understanding in "The Tall Men" do for Faulkner texts that have heretofore acted as the epitome of the regional past defying the federalist future? Considerations of space require me to enter the realm of critical speculation here, but we might begin with adding a layer to interpretations of Faulkner's narratives of white dispossession.

The ghostliness of Quentin and of the ladies his father describes as having been made into ghosts, and the bitter comparison the senior Jason Compson makes between people in the past and people in the present could, in other words, also index the position of any twentieth-century state subject rather than only a Southerner for whom it is too late to join the Confederate army. When Jason says "victims of a different circumstance, simpler and therefore, integer for integer, larger, more heroic and the figures therefore more heroic too, not dwarfed and involved but distinct, uncomplex who had the gift of loving once or dying once instead of being diffused and scattered creatures drawn blindly limb from limb from a grab bag and assembled" (*AA* 71), he echoes Georg Simmel in his feeling that possibilities for a distinct "personality" have been overwhelmed by a larger order that deprives him of subjective value and transforms him into a "cog" in the "metropolis." He echoes Max Weber and T. S. Eliot in their assessments of modern men as empty bureaucratic administrators. Inevitably, this sense of loss, which I claim elsewhere is as international as globalizing post-World War I capital, was imagined and discursively figured differently depending on cultural and geographical location. We might understand regionalization in modernism as precisely this difference, so that Simmel's "metropolis" with its "visible institutions of state" is substantively similar to (if less abstractly figured in) discourses of the South colonized by the federal government and of the agrarian ideal replaced by professional agriculture administered according to the demands of a centralized national market economy.

None of this is meant to claim that white supremacist actions did not deploy devastating power against black people in the modernist period. As is well known, elite modernists' *feelings* did not necessarily reflect their actual material reality, and expectations of agency were likely rather higher for men of that class and race, leading to greater disbelieving angst. Rather, I am arguing that these discourses may not be as specific to the South as we tend to assume when reading Faulkner. White supremacy of course was not only national but international. And the unions in the North were as unsympathetic to the black working class as white tenant farmers in the South were to black tenant farmers. When we look at the "dispossession" of white heirs like the Compson sons or the populist roots of Faulkner's white farmers, we should look not only to what they imagine they could have expected as white men living in the South pre-Civil War but to the loss of what, in the Anglo-American tradition, would have made them men of agency in the twentieth century and which was described as loss by elite men who were urban, Northern, even European. Certainly race provides a vocabulary to articulate the loss of authority or autonomy in many texts other than Southern ones.

Shreve and Quentin are not simply avatars of Confederates Bon and Henry but contemporaries of Woolf's Septimus and Jacob, West's Chris, Hemingway's Krebs, and so on. Where the Great War is understood as a watershed for many of the themes and aesthetics of canonical modernist writing, Faulkner studies has been looking for altogether different kinds of ghosts. It is very seldom, for instance, that anyone notes that had Quentin stayed "in time and hearing the watch," he would have had his war (*SF* 76).

Shreve, after all, will eventually serve four years in the Medical Corps of the Canadian Expeditionary Services. Their ratiocination as roommates at Harvard, their playing soldier marks, perhaps, their slow comprehension of how they will be like Buddy, not like Anse, Sr. Elsewhere, I focus on the figure of the zombie as an avatar for the modern self that elite modernists feared they might already have become after personality had collapsed under this "overwhelming fullness" that Simmel describes as the condition of modern life and a new apprehension of the individual's relationship to the nation. More specific to Faulkner's South, might it not be the case that that avatar is often a black person, tying race and racial figurations more tightly in some of his works to the psychology of the white modern democratic subject rather than to the defeated plantation owner? Is it possible that the "back-look" actually inscribes the twentieth century onto the Confederate experience of defeat rather than the other way around?

NOTES

1 Georg Simmel, "The Metropolis and Mental Life," *Simmel on Culture: Selected Writings*, David Frisby and Mike Featherstone (eds.) (London: Sage Publications, 1997), p. 184.
2 For examples of more detailed explorations of the U.S. south and modernism that depart from a center-periphery model, see Leigh Anne Duck, *The Nation's Region: Southern Modernism, Segregation, and U.S. Nationalism* (Athens: University of Georgia Press, 2006) and the collection edited by Jon Smith and Deborah Cohn, *Look Away! The U.S. South and New World Studies* (Durham, NC: Duke University Press, 2004).
3 Ted Atkinson, *Faulkner and the Great Depression: Aesthetics, Ideology, and Cultural Politics* (Athens: University of Georgia Press, 2006), p. 215.
4 François Jacob, *The Logic of Life: A History of Heredity*, Betty E. Spillman (trans.) (Princeton, NJ: Princeton University Press, 1993 [1970]), pp. 181–3.
5 Hannah Landecker, *Culturing Life: How Cells Became Technologies* (Cambridge, MA: Harvard University Press, 2007), p. 1.
6 Cited in Paul Rabinow, *Essays on the Anthropology of Reason* (Princeton, NJ: Princeton University Press, 1996), p. 108.
7 Landecker, *Culturing Life*, p. 61.
8 Ibid., p. 29.
9 T.S. Eliot, *The Waste Land* (New York: Norton Critical Editions, 2000 [1922]), l. 65.
10 Max Weber, "Bureaucracy," *Max Weber: Essays in Sociology*, H. H. Gerth and C. Wright Mills (eds.) (Oxford: Oxford University Press, 1946), p. 214.
11 Valuing the life of the population as a whole can also make cheap the lives of racialized or ethnicized populations within a general population (see Michel Foucault, *'Society Must Be Defended': Lectures at the Collège de France* [New York: Picador, 1997], p. 255; Etienne Balibar, "Class Racism," *Race,*

Nation, Class: Ambiguous Identities, Etienne Balibar and Immanuel Wallerstein [eds.], [London: Verso, 1991], pp. 204–16).

12 Landecker, *Culturing Life*, p. 14.

13 Ibid., pp. 60–7.

14 For some overviews of this phenomenon from various angles, see Eric Hobsbawm, *The Age of Extremes: A History of the World, 1914–1991* (New York: Random House, 1994); Nikolas Rose and Peter Miller, "Political Power beyond the State: Problematics of Government," *British Journal of Sociology* 43:2 (1992), 181–2; Patrick J. McGrath, *Scientists, Businesses and the State, 1890–1960* (Chapel Hill: University of North Carolina Press, 1984), pp. 10–11.

15 Rose and Miller, "Political Power Beyond the State," p. 175.

16 Virginia Woolf, *Mrs. Dalloway* (New York: Harcourt Brace Jovanovich, 1981 [1925]), p. 86.

17 Ibid., p. 92.

18 Benedict Anderson, *Imagined Communities: Reflections on the Origin and Spread of Nationalism* (London: Verso, 1993), pp. 144–5.

19 Landecker, *Culturing Life*, p. 33.

20 Paul Bové, "Agriculture and Academe: The Southern Question," *Mastering Discourse: The Politics of Intellectual Culture* (Durham, NC: Duke University Press, 1992), p. 119.

21 Ibid., p. 122.

22 Agricultural Adjustment Acts (1933 and 1938) and the New Deal's Works Progress Administration.

23 See Lauren Goodlad, "Beyond the Panopticon: Victorian Britain and the Critical Imagination," *PMLA* 118.3 (2003), 539–40; Stuart Hall, "The State in Question," *The Idea of the Modern State*, Gregor McLennan, David Held, and Stuart Hall (eds.) (Milton Keynes: Open University Press, 1984), pp. 10–11; Rose and Miller, "Political Power Beyond the State," pp. 181–2.

24 Bové, *Mastering Discourse*, pp. 124–5.

5

SUSAN SCOTT PARRISH

As I Lay Dying and the Modern Aesthetics of Ecological Crisis

Two far-off crises patter softly and suggestively at the edges of *As I Lay Dying*. One crisis the reader knows nothing of until the novel's final pages when Darl, beside himself, lets us in on the fact that "Darl" has been "in France at the war" (254). Somewhat like Virginia Woolf containing the world-historical colossus of the Great War within a parenthesis in her 1927 novel *To The Lighthouse*, Faulkner lets you in on *the big news* so off-handedly as if to let you know that you should have known it all along. The second crisis, which marks the other chronological boundary of the novel, never actually makes it into printer's ink. Only readers with visual access to Faulkner's manuscript of the novel can glimpse the date "October 25, 1929" in the upper corner of its first page.[1] The 25th was the day after the Wall Street panic erupted, signaling the collapse of the U.S. financial system. Faulkner thus began to write – or wanted posterity to think he had begun to write – as this crash reverberated around the world. Registering the greater importance of these crises to the novel than Faulkner was explicitly willing to do, critics have read *As I Lay Dying* as both a World War I novel and a novel that inaugurates the fiction of the Great Depression.[2] I concur that these two crises provided for Faulkner in 1929 the bookend occurrences of the book's modern world and that he deeply interested himself in how – as John Dewey put it – "forces so vast, so remote in initiation, so far-reaching in scope and so complexly indirect in operation" could be "felt" and "suffered" by people in apparent peripheries but not "known."[3] And yet there is a third event, one at the novel's very center, which, though also "remote in initiation," Faulkner saw to be the South's most proximate modern disaster. That was the Mississippi Flood of 1927, an event that Faulkner's metropolitan paper, *The Commercial Appeal*, called "the greatest disaster that ever afflicted our country."[4]

This protracted event actually began in August 1926, as extreme weather moved across the center of North America, inaugurating an exceptional series of storms that lasted through the winter. Flooding occurred in the

74

Figure 5.1. "Columbus Understands an Appeal Like This," *The Columbus Dispatch*, May 5, 1927.

Mississippi's western and eastern tributaries in the fall and winter; extreme flooding south of Cairo commenced in March 1927 and did not subside until the summer's end. Refugees were still returning to Delta plantations as late as the spring of 1928.⁵ Though slow-moving and long-enduring, this flood quickly became an intimate, virtual occurrence in homes around the nation as fund-raising drives, communicated via radio, movie houses, newspapers, and magazines, enlisted those outside the South to become an "army of rescuers."⁶ Cartoons like this one from Ohio's *Columbus Dispatch* represented "THE DISTRESSED SOUTHLAND" as a broken white family in need of northern salvation (Figure 5.1). Secretary of Commerce Herbert Hoover, the

Figure 5.2. "Poor Business," *Memphis Commercial Appeal*, June 10, 1927, 1.

man in charge of rescue and relief, borrowed the newly established national radio system twice to broadcast his insistence that "We of the North have the right and duty to bind their wounds," to help "this great army of unfortunate people."[7] Such a campaign, playing as it did on a romance of white sectional reunion, obscured the fact that the majority of the hundreds dead, and the 637,000 displaced, were African American.[8]

The cotton and sugar planters of the Delta region were major economic sufferers though, and they made it their point to communicate their understanding of the catastrophe as resulting directly from northern environmental practices and Federal policy neglect. This June 10th cartoon from the *Commercial Appeal* is typical of a slew of southern images that represent the high water as decidedly Yankee water, here figuratively flowing out of the nation's capital (Figure 5.2). Other southern commentators, pointing to northern industrial-scale deforestation, wetlands drainage, monoculture farming, and the federal levees-only policy, quipped: "We then wonder just whose water this is that comes pouring down upon us from the sheds of thirty states."[9] And a Louisiana planter remarked in a *National Geographic* article: "Up North of us they build levees that turn lots of marshes into farms; but, when high water comes, this system often turns a lot of our farms into marshes."[10] The fact that a major Red Cross camp was situated on the Confederate cemetery at Vicksburg, where Grant had overwhelmed southern forces in a water-born assault in the late spring of 1863, stamped with certainty the southern reading of this flood as a kind of biological reenactment of the "War of Northern Aggression." Faulkner was clear-eyed enough to see that Delta planters and governments, in concert with outside investors, had likewise compromised their own segment of the watershed in the fifty years leading up to 1927 by turning a swampy forested lowland into drained, leveed, and denuded New South cotton and sugar kingdoms.[11]

This flood provided the *environmental unconscious* of Faulkner's first major novel, *The Sound and the Fury*, written in the months following the catastrophe.[12] In *As I Lay Dying*, written a year later, he transforms the flood from a metaphorical into a material force. Placed at the very center of the novel, these river scenes comprise one sixth of the book. Though Faulkner saw the 1927 flood as the South's most proximate and catastrophic brush with modernization to date, he also understood its place in a looping series of crises, between World War I and the stock market collapse, brought on by the machine age, reckless resource extraction, and speculative capitalism. To John Limon's claim, then, that "the Great War explains *As I Lay Dying*," I would answer, only in part. And to his rhetorical question, what else is "the reason for the sheer muddiness of [the novel], which is perhaps the muddiest book in all literature?", I would answer that, while the mud in the novel *is* French and Belgian, while it *is* the mud of European trench warfare, it is *also* the mud of the estranged Mississippi watershed.[13] It represents the mud made when water, mechanistically shunted from northern soils and corralled into four-story high levees, broke like a cataract onto the Delta.

Journalists reporting on the Great Flood who had covered the Great War in Europe, like Mississippian Harris Dickson, a nationally syndicated columnist, were quick to make the comparison of this Delta muck to that wartime mire. As a way to raise the problem of how in 1927 to represent, and how to incite identification with, "a mud-bespattered mass of human beings" in the Lower Valley, Dickson brings up the analogous vision of "10,000 mangled bodies, grotesquely strewn along a battlefield."[14] For Dickson, though, this Mississippi muck was worse; describing his view from an airplane, he wrote: "The solitude above which we soar appals [sic] imagination. A water-conquered country, a dead, dumb, silent country, far lonelier than the hell-swept fields of France."[15] L. C. Speers of *The New York Times* reported likewise on the "desolation, absolute and complete" he found in Melville, Louisiana: "It's water, slime, sand, mosquitoes and sand flies for all four points of the compass."[16]

Faulkner's flood novels – *The Sound and the Fury* (1929), *As I Lay Dying* (1930), and *The Wild Palms* (1939) – allow us to see that one of his signal contributions to global Modernism was his engagement with human-caused environmental catastrophe as a major symptom of modernization. Though floods are an inherent feature of a river's "disturbance regime,"[17] and though man-made disasters are themselves of ancient origin, it was the period between 1881 and 1928 in the United States, roughly corresponding with the Second Industrial Revolution, that represented the nation's deadliest period of disasters, comprising 938 events.[18] Moreover, these disasters were distinctly modern because of the virtual ways in which they were brought to public consciousness and because of the increasingly governmental management of displaced mass populations.[19] Before he reckoned then, in *Absalom, Absalom!* (1936) and *Go Down, Moses* (1942), with how the southern and Caribbean slave-based plantation complex had "outraged the land" (beginning in the early modern period),[20] he first mused upon his own period's *national* "ecohistorical formation,"[21] in which modern federal engineering, as well as agriculture and silviculture throughout the Valley, all coalesced in their misapprehension of the complex behavior of the continent's major watershed. In this formation, Southerners appear not so much as the central culprits but as improvident colonial dependents collaborating with highly capitalized outsiders.[22]

Attending to this subject in Faulkner helps us to see that historians of Modernism have yet to adequately gauge how much environmental degradation and ensuing disasters were crucial to the period – its sense of altered embodiment, perception, strategies of representation, and even ontology. If, as Limon argues, Faulkner began his career writing war fiction with *Soldiers' Pay* (1926) "on the assumption that coming to terms with the Great War was the first obligation of the novelist,"[23] I would argue that Faulkner arrived at his great fiction once he decided that coming to terms with the land use practices of global capitalism – and how they were locally felt – was an equal obligation.[24] *As I Lay Dying*, narrated mainly by a character who experiences the Great Flood through a visual, psychic, and epistemological apparatus deeply affected by the World War and its art forms, gives us a singular opportunity to watch Faulkner realize that crises do not occur as distinct historical nodes in a "diminishing line" but instead accrete and double "like a looping string" (*AILD* 146).

That Spy-Glass

Faulkner's shorthand for describing the mental apparatus Darl got "in France at the War" is to say that he acquired a certain "spy-glass" (254). When Darl was a boy, Anse tells us, his eyes were "full of the land all the time" (36). Darl "was alright" because "the land laid up-and-down ways then," but once "that ere road come and switched the land around longways" and the law "threaten[ed] me out of him," Darl acquired a pair of eyes that nature had "run out of" (36–7). In other words, Darl was sane before he was drafted and sent to Europe. Importantly though, Anse also ties Darl's loss of sanity to shifts in land use from a local subsistence economy to one controlled by global commodity and financial markets. Once he possesses the "spy-glass," nature does not rule his mode of seeing, for Darl has abandoned the viewing habits fostered by painterly naturalism for the visual estrangements of the avant-garde. As Watson Branch and others have noted, Darl turns his surroundings into startling art objects – like abstracted landscapes viewed simultaneously from multiple perspectives – that seem to suggest a special kinship with Cubism.[25] Faulkner himself when in Paris in 1925 had viewed the work of Cubist painter André Lhote, but he had also visited a "very very modernist exhibition ... futurist and vorticist"[26] as well as other galleries exhibiting "numberless young and struggling moderns" (*SL* 13, 24). The Vorticists, in their heyday just before the war, had emulated the designs of machines as a way to perceive the fundamentals of Nature – in order, as Wyndham Lewis said, "to get deeply enough immersed in material life to experience the shaping power amongst its vibrations."[27] Faulkner came to interest himself not so much in mechanization's "shaping power" but in how natural things had been turned into odd, colossal machines capable less of "shaping" than of violently disintegrating and recombining its own *biota*.

During and just after wartime, it was especially the Dadaists, developing in the separate metropoles of Zurich, Berlin, Cologne, New York, and Paris, who, witnessing a machine, war, and consumer age that had brought on a kind of disastrous "exploded mimicry"[28] of familiar forms, drew attention to this process by cognate acts of representational shock.[29] I imagine Darl, when in France, being drawn to such a movement and being reminded a decade later, once he tumbles into flood waters, that no other way of seeing makes quite so much sense. In one manifesto, Tristan Tzara pronounced that Dada was "a furious wind, tearing the dirty linen of clouds and prayers, preparing the great spectacle of disaster, fire, decomposition."[30] Dadaists responded in an "*occasional*" and spontaneous manner to use art to redirect the world toward "*something else.*"[31] The practitioners' visual tactics included abstraction, collage, and montage as well as processes involving chance and automatization.[32] Naturalism, or "any imitation of nature, however concealed," was, in the words of Richard Huelsenbeck, "a lie" that linked itself with bourgeois morality and tired art traditions.[33] Though Dada, in mimicking the war's splicing of "the human" with so much considered un-human, sought to expose that "Nature" was just an Enlightenment invention that policed its own fondest polarities (human/animal, human/machine, man/woman, reason/unreason), it rarely addressed the environmental effects of modernization as such. What I see Faulkner doing in *As I Lay Dying* is asserting that an "imitation of nature" would not be "a lie" as long as it acknowledged how strange nature had become. For Faulkner, being a Modernist of the rural South meant that his "exploded mimicry" would first and foremost take its cue from imitating the neo-nature around him. He would call *As I Lay Dying* a deliberate "tour-de-force" because, as he said, he "took this family and subjected them to the two greatest catastrophes which man can suffer – flood and fire" (*FU* 87). Darl, possessed of that Tzara-like, "furious" mode of seeing, has the "queer eyes" to connect Dada's "disaster, fire, decomposition" with what lies before him in Mississippi.

Land Use

Doctor Peabody, the expert diagnostician who arrives from town too late to do any good, doesn't ever tell us much about Addie's body but does give us discomfiting information about the topography of the Bundrens's land and the area's history of logging. With Peabody's arrival, we come to see the terrain as dramatically vertical: the house perches atop a "bluff," a "durn wall" (42), indeed, a "damn mountain" that cannot be scaled without a rope to "haul" a body up and down it (43). That Anse offers a "plowline" (42) to do the hauling makes the connection between the practice of plowing and the perilous verticality of the topography. The environing, apocalyptic weather also makes Peabody see the "black cloud" on high as a "topheavy mountain range, like a load of cinders dumped" (42). This image of a mountain range reduced to cinders then leads Peabody to reflect on "a worry about this country being deforested someday" (42). In short, what Peabody has conjured before our eyes is a vision of the Bundren land as a nearly tree-less and over-plowed terrain in which the soil has been subjected to ever more dramatic gullying and a vulnerability to extreme weather events.

In the early twentieth century, "the hill lands of the north Mississippi Loess Plains ... were among the most severely eroded in the United States," explains Charles S. Aiken, due in part to "careless tillage practices," practices that led one commentator as early as 1860, only thirty years after white settlement, to comment that this land was "in danger of going, in the most literal sense, '*down hill.*' "[34] Peabody sees the supine body before him, already "dead these ten days" (43), not as a human, but as a "tenement or a town" (44), "a bundle of rotten sticks," a rubber "hose," "lamps" nearly empty of oil, and a "pack-horse" (45). In other words, he sees the cadaver before him as a humanly settled, severely worked, commodified, and "wor[n] out" place (41).[35] Again, it is not a woman all this causes him to muse on but instead "our rivers, our land ... shaping and creating the life of man in its implacable and brooding image" (45). Having catalogued the human power to harm the land, with this statement he completes the thought, attesting to the ongoing power of an altered nature to "shap[e]" the "life of man." Indeed, though the object of his diagnosis is already "dead," it still has the power to express itself "harsh and strong" (46). The ensuing flood is testimony, in this story, to how a deadened nature speaks.

That Peabody's patient is not a woman so much as a place suggests that Faulkner was inviting his readers to read the novel not only as a familial but also as a regional chronicle, allegorically rendered. At this scale, the central female characters are made to embody the southern region and its resources. Addie, as many have noted, is associated with "new earth" (169), water, trees, "wild geese," and "wild darkness," being "planted" (170), and also with "the dark land talking the voiceless speech" (175).[36] She has become, under humanity's, and especially patriarchy's, errant constructions, a "cyclone" (42), a "storm" (44), and "the red bitter flood boiling through the land" (174). In short, she is the wild, violated and now "harsh" environmental matrix of the South. Dewey Dell, her daughter, is associated likewise with the land at large – "the horizons and the valleys of the earth" (164) – but also quite specifically with cotton monoculture.[37] The burden she carries with her to town, trying to unload with various double-dealing middlemen along the way, is acquired because Lafe is, amid the rows of cotton, rather unscrupulously "picking into [her] sack" so that she "could not help" the condition she found herself in (27). What is suggested is that Lafayette County coerces its fields into reproduction and that market forces subject the yield to new forms of coercion.

More information about local logging practices emerges the closer we draw to the flooded river. As Darl, Cash, and Jewel are looking for the old ford to get over the high water, the older two brothers share thoughts about the fact that Vernon Tull, their neighbor, has been logging down by the river: "cut a sight of timber outen here" to pay off his mortgage, one says. Indeed, because Tull "cut them two big whiteoaks" by which folks had in "the old days … line[d] up the ford," the brothers cannot locate a path across the water (142). Another feature of the deforested riverscape is that, because an "old road" had been "cleaned out" of vegetation by Tull to transport his lumber, the road seems to Darl to be "soaked free of earth and floated upward, to leave in its spectral tracing a monument to a still more profound desolation than this above which we now sit" (143).

Tull, a name associated with the modernization of husbandry, represents a New South agriculturalist.[38] Unlike the younger Bundrens, who hire themselves out as wage laborers (transporting timber and clearing fields) even though Pa owns his small farm, Tull uses his property's surplus resources (trees) to operate in wider mercantile and credit markets. As such, Tull also represents the post-bellum practice of southern states that handled their straightened economies by selling off the region's forests, and other resources, to external financiers. Tull distinguishes himself from Darl, who he says "thinks by himself too much" (71), by averring that a brain should be "like a piece of machinery … best when it all runs along the same, doing the day's work and not no one part used no more than needful" (71). Like Darl, he too sees through "one of these here spy-glasses" (139), but, instead of the "beast with two backs" inside Darl's French optical apparatus, he sees his own prosaic mule, and in him "all the broad land and my house sweated outen it like it was the more the sweat, the broader the land" (139). In other words, Tull sees the surplus value created by his animal laborer and the various forms this surplus value will assume. Though Tull's mechanistic brain processes this input from his "spy-glasses" with assurance, Darl and Cash look out at the logged riverscape and, instead of seeing surplus, feel perilously disoriented. And while a human corpse lies in their cart ("above which we now sit"), it is especially how that body indicates the overall "specter" of earthly things being "soaked free of earth" that betokens for Darl "a still more profound desolation."

In the Water

What lies before and under the three brothers is not just a swollen river; it is a "flood" (157). As Tull explained, "a fellow" looking at it "couldn't tell where was the river and where the land. It was just a tangle of yellow and the levee not less wider than a knife back" (124). Armstid reported a tremendously long crevasse where "the levee through Haley bottom had gone down for two miles" (185). At Samson's, they "hadn't never see the river so high" and the old men there "hadn't never see nor hear of it being so in the memory of man" (111). Tuning into the novel's full epic, or apocryphal, dimension, this river operates in the text as a liminal zone of crossing from one world into another – from the land of the living into that of the dead, or from a place of exile into an ancestral home.[39] If we, instead, tune into the text as modernist regional historiography, we understand that Faulkner is giving an account of the Flood of 1927, that unprecedented catastrophe in the life of the South. Reminded of the "current" Darl had described running "all the time" through the center of the Bundrens's house, "tilting a little down the hill" (19–20), we recognize that, when we read the scale of the household as regional rather than familial, the gently tilted current running right through the deep South is none other than the Mississippi.[40] Faulkner, having provided, through Peabody, Darl, and Cash, the information about the deforestation of this watershed, as well as descriptions of the monoculture planting of cotton and corn – effectively providing much of the contemporaneous environmentalist explanation for flooding – it is no surprise that mid-river what upends Addie's coffin – or a reified, wasted territory – is a log, surging *"for an instant upright ... like Christ"* or like "an old man or a goat" (148). It is as if "something huge and alive" that lives "just beneath the surface" of the water, coming into "alertness" (141) only an instant at a time, has jetted out this log as its satyr-like agent of revenge.[41] Unlike all the journalistic commentators who, during the spring of 1927, personified the flooding river as something monstrous – a "giant, bloated snake," a "mighty old dragon"[42] – Faulkner's choice of an animated agent of destruction incorporates an environmental critique as he links the commodification and destruction of forests with flooding through the figure of the crucified tree.

Original Motion

Even before the flood, Darl has been made apparently "queer" in the head by his exposure to war, modernization, and modernist art in France (125). It is a mark of the traumatic psychological and epistemological force of the flood that, comparatively speaking, it is this event that causes the "majority" to see Darl as "crazy" (233). Indeed, Faulkner seems to give some substance to this diagnosis as he puts Darl through a transformation: while passing through the flood, Darl comes in contact with an intense vitalism. Below the water's surface is "something huge and alive" (141). Underneath the "false blandness the true force of it leans lazily against us" (158). This force is radically creative, working "like hands molding and prodding at the very bones"

(158) and turning the ford's "flat surface" into "troughs and hillocks" (147). While underwater, Darl seems to have been "dissolved into" this "myriad original motion," such that "seeing and hearing" become "blind and deaf" (163–4). Two key organs of the human perceptual sensoria, those channels for data through which the Lockean mind is filled and energized toward higher activities, have been terminated. Moreover, the Cartesian distinction between subject and object has been obviated. Before the flood, Darl had been a prodigy of super-sensory knowing, functioning much like the latest modern visual technologies as he saw at great distances and through solid matter. After the flood, though, his senses no longer provide a pathway to information. He now responds to his family's expectation of his seer-like perception with the phrase "I don't know" (162).

Cora thinks that "it was the hand of God" (153) that caused the flood, and that Darl, in particular, was "touched by God Himself" (167–8). Though the log avenger, really a composite of log-goat-Christ-old man, suggests that a much more syncretic divinity than Cora has in mind is at work here; Darl is in fact "touched" – indeed, molded, prodded, as well as blinded and deafened by its force.[43] Running through the river's "myriad original motion" are other, stranger, more latter-day velocities and forces. Darl feels in the river the "motion of the wasted world accelerat[ing] just before the final precipice" (146). With the words "accelerating" and "precipice," Faulkner makes this "wasted world" seem more apocalyptic engine than cyclical *bios*. This is the motion of an engine that has worn itself out in a kind of suicidal love of hyper-celerity. Elsewhere, Darl feels the river's altered motion to be like that of "machinery" capable of "sever[ing] ... at a single blow, the two torsos" of Jewel and Tull (163). These two dismembered torsos then appear to "mov[e] with infinitesimal and ludicrous care upon the surface" of the river (163). Blind Darl, unclotted and dissolved into water, watches two other half-men glide atop its surface.

Though there has, up until this scene, been an ambient doom in the sulfurous, world's-end kind of landscape atop the Bundrens' "mountain," it is only now, as the adulterated river shows its machine-like destructive capacity, that the trauma of Europe's Machine Age war comes back to Darl. Looking at the flood, he recalls, and superimposes, the trenches. In Mississippi mud is the doubled presence of the muddy battlefield. Thus all the abstract pictures Darl has been making with his mind since he returned from France, have, in the flooding river, at last found a fully stimulating, or radicalizing, objective correlative.[44] Which is to say that if the war made him see "queer" but not quite as "queer" as a Dadaist, the flood at his doorstep afflicted "Darl" with the most profound kind of un-homing and un-selfing possible.[45]

Figure 5.3. Untitled, 1920, photomontage, collage, and pencil on photographic reproduction mounted on board, 6 x 14.6 (2 3/8 x 5 ¾), The Menil Collection, Houston.

Consider the similarity in tone, then, between Darl's riverscape, in which a strange bearded satyr creature has left behind him the wreckage of gliding torsos and an earless, eyeless, unclotted man, with this untitled 1920 photomontage produced by German Dadaist Max Ernst (Figure 5.3). Playing with the reality-effects of photojournalism, Ernst turns this World War I bomber, which should be a mere prosthesis of the male will, into a silken, almost self-caressing, dominatrix who brings about male disintegration. Faulkner likewise turns the river from a mechanized canal of human wishes into a mockingly-alive, weird goat-tree-man montage who cuts men in half and drowns their tools. The river has become as uncanny a contrivance as Max Ernst's silken-armed bomber.

In the river, Darl's vision for the destination of Addie's wasted body – his vision for how the South will be reincorporated into the nation – is radicalized. Rather than belonging to the nation as a kind of dependent but vulnerable periphery, with its poverty, backwardness, and radical racism – in short, its degeneracy from apparently foundational national ideals – flouted in a time of disaster, Darl comes to doubt the very legitimacy of the concept of "property" itself (233).[46] If the transformation of land throughout the Mississippi watershed into highly capitalized zones where deforestation, industrial farming, and immured water have made the earth "spectral," then both property and the social underpinnings of its distribution need radical rethinking. Note that a politician as conservative as Herbert Hoover publicized, in the midst of the 1927 flood, his thoughts on a major redistribution of property in the Delta to small farmers, a plan he only seems to have abandoned because of his run for the presidency.[47] Darl's vision is bigger, it seems, because he does not see the problems to be only southern. His vision is bolder too than that of the anti-industrial age southern artists and writers known as the Nashville Agrarians, who, in their protests against northern factory encroachment, wanted to maintain their region's agrarian traditions, along with its race-based labor system.[48] Darl, "insane" as "the majority" saw him, wanted to burn the whole structure down, and the old South along with it. Having been unable to help the river divinity finish its work in the flood, Darl takes up what he perceives to be a new call, to "lay down [the] life" (215) of the South, that is, as Tzara put it, in the "the great spectacle of ... fire" he has staged in Gillespie's barn. Like a Dadaist, "he cultivates the curiosity of one who experiences delight even in the most questionable forms of insubordination," for he "knows that this world of systems has gone to pieces."[49] That he sees his incendiary act as an aesthetic performance is emphasized again when Darl relates that "we watch through the dissolving proscenium of the doorway" (221). If the barn door is a "proscenium," the barn is Darl's stage, his incendiary cabaret, and his words to the actors over the course of this scene have essentially been stage directions.

Interestingly, what he hears in Gillespie's barn, in the midst of the performance, is a "quite peaceful" sound, "like the sound of the river" (221). This comment indicates that Darl, having been dissolved into those strange currents, is trying, through his art, to reproduce the destructive vitalism he found to be at the core of modernized matter and to turn it against itself. Darl may have succeeded in recreating, through a work of art, the trauma of anthropogenic flood, but he ultimately fails to produce a political act of transformation. For in the barn, Jewel upstages Darl as, "enclosed in a thin nimbus of fire" (222), he achieves his own apotheosis, rescuing "the South" for its return to Jefferson, to a seemingly Jeffersonian agrarian ideal. At the novel's end, the law of property, and the use of others' labor to produce surplus value for accumulation and trade, are upheld. The view of "the majority," that anyone threatening these foundational southern, and indeed broadly capitalist, tenets must be incarcerated, is likewise sustained. Darl's absorption into the apparatus of the state as an insane criminal not only terminates his anarchic activities and cuts off his access to those creative/destructive forces of modern turbulence, but also reifies him *to himself* as an absurdist character. Any opportunity that the trauma of flood may have provided for reassessing environmental practices, as well as labor and race relations, has been lost. Fierce race hatred presents itself in Jewel as the family approaches Jefferson, even as it becomes increasingly evident – as blackness creeps up the Bundrens' bodies – that the position of the poor white farmer in the southern plantation zone has much in common with the darker races of the global South. Participation in distant networks of capitalism only provides the family with darkened bodies, double-dealing, consumer trinkets, and a kind of false belonging in this bigger world.[50] Indeed, as they sit in their wagon eating bananas, consuming a staple from some "Banana Republic"[51] in the nation's tropical imperium not very different from Mississippi in its economic and political weakness, Darl watches from the train, convulsing in laughter, because what the family thinks of as marks of their cosmopolitan arrival are to Darl actually marks of their peripheral subordination.[52] The final scene, of the Bundrens freshly accoutered with their new commodity blandishments, seems to fulfill Wilbur J. Cash's 1929 prophecy, namely, that after a great "upheaval," "the South will merely repeat the dismal history of Yankeedom, [so] that we shall have the hog apotheosized – and nothing else."[53] In his invention of Darl, Faulkner speculated about what happens when an aesthetics that responds to modernization's destructiveness tries to reproduce that violence.[54] Faulkner seemed to be querying what kinds of aesthetic acts of force, in his post-flood South (and in his post-crash nation), were possible. As I Lay Dying was the materialization of that question.

NOTES

1 Faulkner quoted in Joseph Blotner, *Faulkner: A Biography*, Volume 1 (New York: Random House, 1974), p. 634; Blotner describes the manuscript on 633.

2 See, for example, John Limon, "Addie in No Man's Land," *Faulkner and War: Faulkner and Yoknapatawpha*, Noel Polk and Ann J. Abadie (eds.) (Oxford: University Press of Mississippi, 2001) and Ted Atkinson, *Faulkner and the Great Depression: Aesthetics, Ideology, and Cultural Politics* (Athens: University of Georgia Press, 2006); Atkinson writes that "*As I Lay Dying* reads as arguably the first quintessential Depression novel" (194).

3 John Dewey, *The Public and its Problems* (New York: Henry Holt, 1927), p. 131.

4 *The Memphis Commercial Appeal* (April 24, 1927).

5 For the most thorough account, see John M. Barry, *Rising Tide: The Great Mississippi Flood of 1927 and How It Changed America* (New York: Simon and Schuster, 1997).

6 *New York Times* (May 4, 1927).

7 Hoover quoted in *Memphis Commercial Appeal* (May 29, 1927), p. 1 and in "Hoover Speeds Up Flood Restoration," *New York Times* (June 20, 1927). The phrase "bind their wounds" echoes Abraham Lincoln's 1865 "Second Inaugural Address."

8 According to Jesse O. Thomas in "The Path of the Flood," *Opportunity* (August 1927), approximately 555,000 were people of color (236); Thomas was part of the Hoover-appointed Colored Advisory Commission during the flood.

9 *The Gulf Coast Guide*, quoted in "Wasted Irony," *Wall Street Journal* (June 7, 1927).

10 Frederick Simpich, "The Great Mississippi Flood of 1927," *National Geographic Magazine* Vol. 52.3 (September 1, 1927). Walter Parker summarized, "Thus the

process which enriched the Northern landowner has resulted in the destruction of many valuable Southern plantations" ("Curbing the Mississippi," *The Nation* 124 (May 11, 1927), pp. 521–2).

11 See Mikko Saikku, *This Delta, This Land: An Environmental History of the Yazoo-Mississippi Floodplain* (Athens: University of Georgia Press, 2005).

12 See my "Faulkner and the Outer Weather of 1927," *American Literary History* 24.1 (Spring 2012), 34–58.

13 Limon, "Addie in No Man's Land," p. 39.

14 Harris Dickson, "Flood Changes Region Into Valley of Sorrow," *Los Angeles Times* (June 5, 1927), p. 1.

15 Ibid., p. 3.

16 L. C. Speers, "Louisiana Parishes Rotting in the Flood," *New York Times* (July 11, 1927), p. 21.

17 Saikku explains in *This Delta, This Land* that a "disturbance regime" is subject to external disturbances that nonetheless are "essential to the maintenance of the whole complex in longer perspective" (23).

18 These figures are from Lowell Juilliard Carr, "Disaster and the Sequence-Pattern Concept of Social Change," *American Journal of Sociology* 38 (1932), p. 209; Ted Steinberg roughly confirmed this claim, shifting the time span from 1880 to 1930, in *Acts of God: The Unnatural History of Natural Disaster in America* (New York: Oxford University Press, 2000) p. 69.

19 The Red Cross called these refugee camps "concentration camps." Giorgio Agamben has controversially described the concentration camp as "the hidden paradigm of the political space of modernity" because it combines the state's inherent totalitarian potential with its ostensible role in regulating the health and security of its population; *Homo Sacer: Sovereign Power and Bare Life*, Daniel Heller-Roazen (trans.) (Stanford, CA: Stanford University Press, 1998), 73; Henry A. Giroux echoes Agamben's claim in "Reading Hurricane Katrina: Race, Class, and the Biopolitics of Disposability," *College Literature*, 33.3 (Summer 2006), p. 180.

20 Faulkner told Harrison Smith in February 1934 that the theme he would explore in *Absalom, Absalom!* involved how "a man ... outraged the land, and the land then turned and destroyed the man's family," quoted in Charles Aiken, *William Faulkner and the Southern Landscape* (Athens: University of Georgia Press, 2009), p. 151.

21 Yrgo Haila and Richard Levins, *Humanity and Nature: Ecology, Science, and Society* (London: Pluto Press, 1992), p. 213.

22 For recent work on the importance not only of a symbolic or mythic "Nature" but of southern environmental history in Faulkner's work, see Donald M. Kartiganer and Ann J. Abadie (eds.), *Faulkner and the Natural World: Faulkner and Yoknapatawpha, 1996* (Jackson: University Press of Mississippi, 1999); Joseph R. Urgo and Ann J. Abadie (eds.) *Faulkner and the Ecology of the South: Faulkner and Yoknapatawpha, 2003* (Jackson: University Press of Mississippi, 2005); Bart H. Welling, "A Meeting with Old Ben: Seeing and Writing Nature in Faulkner's *Go Down, Moses*," *Mississippi Quarterly* 55.4 (2002), 461–96; and Matthew Wynn Sivils, "Faulkner's Ecological Disturbances," *The Mississippi Quarterly* 59.3/4 (Summer 2006), 489–502.

23 Limon, "Addie in No Man's Land," p. 45.

24 Cheryl Lester understands the novel to be an allegory of the "collective upheaval of traditional rural life" ("As They Lay Dying: Rural Depopulation and Social Dislocation as a Structure of Feeling," *The Faulkner Journal* 21. 1/2 (Fall 2005/ Spring 2006), 28). Susan Willis likewise argues that "The family's migration is a geographic metaphor describing [the] demographic change" of agriculturalism to urbanism ("Learning from the Banana," *American Quarterly* 39.4 [Winter 1987], 587). By contrast, John T. Matthews argues that the Bundrens' rural mode was not removed from modernity but rather had "already been *constituted* by the dialectical history of capitalist agriculture, commodified economic and social relations, and the homogenization of mass culture in the nineteenth-century South" ("*As I Lay Dying* in the Machine Age," *Boundary* 2 19.1 [1992], 74); and Jolene Hubbs argues that the novel is not so much about migration toward modernity/urbanization but about the ways in which modernity impinges on the rural world ("William Faulkner's Rural Modernism," *The Mississippi Quarterly* 61.3 [2008], 461–75). I read the river scenes not as a symbolic crossing into modernity but rather as a key symptom of modernity's decades-long presence in the rural world.

25 Watson G. Branch, "Darl Bundren's 'Cubistic' Vision," *William Faulkner's As I Lay Dying: A Critical Casebook*, Dianne L. Cox (ed.) (New York: Garland, 1985), p. 119.

26 See also Homer Pettey, "Perception and the Destruction of Being in *As I Lay Dying*," *Faulkner Journal* 19.1 (2003), who elaborates that Faulkner learned from Cézanne that art, more than representing the world, needed to materialize perception (27–8), and from the Futurists that art could mix memory and sight (28, ftn 1).

27 Quoted in Richard Cork, *Vorticism and Abstract Art in the First Machine Age: Volume One, Origins and Development* (London: Gordon Fraser, 1976), p 283.

28 See Leah Dickerman, "Introduction," *Dada: Zurich, Berlin, Hanover, Cologne, New York, Paris* (Washington, DC: National Gallery of Art/D.A.P., 2005), pp. 7, 9.

29 See Brigid Doherty, "'See: *We Are All Neurasthenics!*' or, the Trauma of Dada Montage," *Critical Inquiry* 24.1 (Autumn 1997), especially pp. 111–12.

30 Tristan Tzara, "Dada Manifesto," *Dada Painters and Poets: An Anthology*, Robert Motherwell (ed.) (Boston: G.K. Hall, 1981 [1951]), p. 78.

31 Tristan Tzara, "An Introduction to Dada," *Dada Painters and Poets: An Anthology*, Robert Motherwell (ed.) (Boston: G.K. Hall, 1981 [1951]), p. 405.

32 Dickerman, "Introduction," *Dada*, p. 7.

33 Richard Huelsenbeck, quoting his own German Dadaist manifesto in "En Avant Dada: A History of Dadaism" (1920) in *Dada Painters*, p. 24.

34 Aiken, *William Faulkner and the Southern Landscape*, pp. 145, 147; quote is from Eugene W. Hilgard, 1860.

35 Cora corroborates this impression as she sees Addie's body as "wasted," making "no more of a hump" under the quilt "than a rail would"; this over-industrialized iron rail body fittingly has eyes like "sockets of iron" (8).

36 See, for example, Willis, "Learning from the Banana," who sees Addie as representing "the unmediated connection with organic process," something that Faulkner treats in a "disparaging mode" (588); Mary Jane Dickerson

argues in "Some Sources of Faulkner's Myth in *As I Lay Dying,*" *Mississippi Quarterly* (Summer 1966) that specifically in Addie and Dewey Dell we see the Demeter-Persephone relationship (134) or really an inverted version of that myth, since both want to abjure their fertility.

37 I would argue that she is not then "a maternal Eve at one with the immemorial earth" (even if ironized) as André Bleikasten argued in *Faulkner's* As I Lay Dying, Roger Little (trans.) (Bloomington: Indiana University Press, 1973), pp. 76–7 but an index of the vulnerability and quasi-absurdity of cotton monoculture.

38 Jethro Tull was a well-known early eighteenth-century English innovator of the "New Husbandry" of mechanized farming, an implement designer, and writer of the treatise, *The horse-Hoeing husbandry*, in which he says such practical things as "fine Language will not fill a Farmer's Barn" (Jethro Tull, *The horse-Hoeing husbandry: or, an essay on the principles of tillage and vegetation. Wherein is shewn a method of introducing a sort of vineyard-culture into the corn-fields* [Dublin: Rhames, 1733], p. iv). See Ernest Clarke, 'Tull, Jethro (bap. 1674, d. 1741)', rev. G. E. Mingay, *Oxford Dictionary of National Biography* (New York: Oxford University Press, 2004).

39 See André Bleikasten, *Faulkner's* As I Lay Dying, p. 111. He appreciates the "liquid catastrophe" (112) at the novel's center, as well as the interpenetration of characters and environment, but interprets the water more symbolically and existentially than as a symptom of history.

40 Faulkner himself describes in his 1954 *Holiday* article "Mississippi" how the overflowing big river would push the little ones backward "as far upstream as Wylie's Crossing above Jefferson" (Leland H. Cox (ed.), *William Faulkner Critical Collection* [Detroit: Gale, 1982], p. 45), so even read as a small inland river, it could show the effects of a great Mississippi flood.

41 Christopher T. White, "The Modern Magnetic Animal: *As I Lay Dying* and the Uncanny Zoology of Modernism," *Journal of Modern Literature* 31.3 (Spring 2008), argues that animals in the novel "expose the limitations of *logos*" and the traditional philosophical privileging of "the (human) subject" (82); they "haunt the text" (84). Certainly, the animated, or animal, force that seems here to dispatch a part-goat emissary to foil the humans' plot seems to exemplify the "limitations" of human communication, epistemology, and sociality. Darl's attention to the language of this animal (its "clucks" and "murmurs" [141]) and his wanting to dissolve into its force pegs him as "insane" within human law.

42 Alfred P. Reck, "Utter Desolation Rules Flood Stricken Region," *The Atlanta Constitution* (May 2, 1927); Herschel Brickell, "Again the Old Dragon Mississippi Fumes," *New York Times* (May 1, 1927).

43 Erin E. Edwards, in "Extremities of the Body: The Anoptic Corporeality of *As I Lay Dying,*" *Modern Fiction Studies* 55.4 (Winter 2009), argues that there is "a blind, often grotesque familiarity with an ambient corporeality" (743), a familiarity which produces "epistemological aporia" (743); she also points out that "the natural world and one's sense of place are already Other, already an opaquely monitoring force that awakens self-reflection" (754). I very much agree with this reading but would argue that this is not a kind of ahistorical corporeality at work but Faulkner's representation of the disturbed corporeality of a modernized nature.

44 Interestingly, Calvin Bedient describes "Darl's mind" as "flowing everywhere like the flood waters of the river – but flowing because unformed, because it has no home in itself, no principle of containment" (Calvin Bedient, "Pride and Nakedness: *As I Lay Dying*," *William Faulkner: Critical Collection*, Leland H. Cox (ed.), [Detroit: Gale, 1982], p. 209). For Bedient, the river is a metaphor for epistemology; I would argue, by contrast, that, along with the war, it is the river's derangement by modernization that leaves his mind without a "home."

45 Cathy Caruth explains that "since the traumatic event is not experienced as it occurs, it is fully evident only in connection with another place, and in another time" (Cathy Caruth [ed.], *Trauma: Explorations in Memory* [Baltimore: Johns Hopkins University Press, 1995], p. 8).

46 Atkinson situates Darl's revolt against property in the context of rural unrest begun in the 1920s (186).

47 Hoover speaks of property redistribution in his interview with T. H. Alexander, "Herbert Hoover Wins Hearts of Folks in Flood District; 'He'd Make a Fine President,' Both White and Black Declare," *The Atlanta Constitution* (July 31, 1927)

48 See Louis D. Rubin (ed.), *I'll Take My Stand: The South and the Agrarian Tradition by Twelve Southerners* (New York: Harper and Brothers, 1930).

49 Hugo Ball, "Dada Fragments" (1916–17) reprinted in Robert Motherwell (ed.), *The Dada Painters and Poets: An Anthology* (Boston: G.K. Hall, 1981 [1951]), 51.

50 Lester argues in "As They Lay Dying" that the family's journey has shown how the forces of modernity "simultaneously solicit and reject them as middle class subjects, while neutralizing … the counter-hegemonic or alternative pressure they might otherwise exert as working-class subjects" (31).

51 A term coined by the short story writer O. Henry in *Cabbages and Kings* (New York: Doubleday, 1904), his fictional study of Honduras, its mixture of oligarchical rule and laborers' poverty, and its reliance on one export cultivar.

52 See Hosam Aboul-Ela, *Other South: Faulkner, Coloniality, and the Mariátegui Tradition* (Pittsburgh: University of Pittsburgh Press, 2007) for more elaboration on how post-bellum white southerners saw themselves as part of the United States' imperial periphery; see also Antonio Gramsci, "Some Aspects of the Southern Question," *Selections from Political Writings 1921–1926* (London: Electric Book Company, 1978).

53 Wilbur J. Cash, "The Mind of the South," *The American Mercury* 18.70 (October 1929), 192.

54 I am making a slightly different point here than does Matthews in "*As I Lay Dying* in the Machine Age" when he argues that Faulkner "needed to exorcise the strictly aestheticist impulse of his modernism" and forge instead a mode that was "critical, self-reflective" (91). I agree with Matthews that Faulkner achieved a "critical" relation to life in this novel, but I would say that – through his avant-garde artist character – he draws for himself a kind of limit-case of activist art.

6

GREG FORTER

Faulkner and Trauma: On *Sanctuary*'s Originality

Two central passages in *Absalom, Absalom!* (1936) concern the relations among trauma, history, and psychic experience. In the first of these, Quentin develops a striking extended metaphor:

> *Maybe nothing ever happens once and is finished. Maybe happen is never once but like ripples maybe on water after the pebble sinks, the ripples moving on, spreading, the pool attached by a narrow umbilical water-cord to the next pool which the first pool feeds, has fed, did feed, let this second pool contain a different temperature of water, a different molecularity of having seen, felt, remembered, reflect in a different tone the infinite unchanging sky, it doesn't matter: that pebble's watery echo whose fall it did not even see moves across its surface too at the original ripple-space, to the old ineradicable rhythm.*
> (*AA* 210)

Here, the organizing figure is of the historical event as brute materiality (the stone), which strikes and disturbs the waters of consciousness yet resists one's efforts to know or represent it: it is available only in the "watery echo" of its after-effects, in the recursive movement of the ripples it causes after sinking into the self's murky depths. The strong suggestion of such a figure is that the history with which *Absalom* contends is best understood as both *punctual* and *traumatic*. It is punctual in the sense that historical events are here imagined as discrete incidences of infraction upon a previously placid psyche. It is traumatic in that, according to this metaphor, such infractions are so overwhelming that they temporarily disable or absent consciousness from itself, making the event susceptible to knowledge only in its delayed repercussions (i.e., the ripples that spatially and temporally displace an initial break in the water's surface). The recursive effects of such an event are conceived as replicable across time and space. Not only will the person to whom the event happens be doomed to a kind of sustained reprisal in the form of those ripples' reverberations; even those who "*did not even see*" the pebble "*fall*" and who possess an entirely "*different molecularity of having*

92

seen, felt, remembered" will experience the initial event with undiminished force. This is, in short, an image of history as inescapable traumatic inheritance: no matter where or when one lives in relation to a traumatizing event, the fact of being connected to those who experienced that event – of being that second "pool" that the first one "*feeds, has fed, did feed*" – contaminates one with a "trauma" that cannot be distinguished from that of those who lived through it. This is what is implied by figuring the second pool as experiencing the disturbance at "*the original ripple-space, to the old ineradicable rhythm.*"

The second passage proposes a rather different vision of historical transmission, though one that still revolves around trauma. It concerns Thomas Sutpen, the self-made Southern planter whose dynastic ambitions lie at the novel's center. In chapter 7, Faulkner describes the genesis of those ambitions in the "affront" Sutpen suffers as an adolescent boy when he is turned away from the front door of a local planter by a black slave:

> before the monkey nigger who came to the door had finished saying what he did, he [Sutpen] seemed to kind of dissolve and a part of him turn and run back through the two years they had lived there like when you pass through a room fast and look at all the objects in it and you turn and go back through the room again and look at all the objects from the other side and you find out you had never seen them before, rushing back through those two years and seeing a dozen things that had happened and he hadn't even seen them before.... [He saw] his own father and sisters and brothers as the owner, the rich man (not the nigger) must have been seeing them all the time – as cattle, creatures heavy and without grace, brutely evacuated into a world without hope or purpose for them, who would in turn spawn with brutish and vicious prolixity ... a race whose future would be a succession of cut-down and patched and made-over garments bought on exorbitant credit because they were white people, from stores where niggers were given the garments free.
>
> (*AA* 186–90)

The passage resembles the previous one in a number of ways. Inasmuch as it seeks to answer the riddle of how Sutpen became Sutpen, it is about how history "happens" – more particularly, about how Southern planter masculinity is reproduced across generations. Inasmuch as it answers this question by describing a scene of psychic wounding, moreover – a moment of crippling, subjective violation in response to which Sutpen conceives a "design" to "beat" the planter by becoming him – the passage grounds the history it describes in an explicitly traumatic incursion.

And yet, the differences between the two passages are even more revealing. They pivot on how, in the current case, the historical event is not conceived as a brute, inassimilable materiality that intrudes punctually upon the psyche and cannot but induce trauma. The event is instead inscribed from the start in a dialectic of significance and meaning. It traumatizes not because it takes consciousness by surprise and so disables its functioning, but because it retrospectively gives meaning to a set of experiences that Sutpen's mind had "taken in" without being able to make sense of them. The pebble's punctual, non-significatory incursion is thus replaced by a sequence of events that are, from the start, potentially significant but whose meaning remains at first unrecognized. The experience is "like when you pass through a room fast and look at all the objects in it and you turn and go back through the room again and look at all the objects from the other side and you find out you had never seen them before." The temporal *delay* in the previous passage becomes now a temporal *resignification*: what had been opaque yet replete with significance is rendered meaningful and traumatic *for the first time* by an affront that crystallizes that traumatogenic significance. We are dealing, in short, with a model of trauma that hinges on the process Freud called *Nachträglichkeit*.[1] Within this model, trauma results from the interplay between two (or more) charged moments, the earlier of which arrives "too soon," before the self has the cognitive capacity to make sense of it, and the final of which retrospectively unleashes the traumatogenic significance of the previous.

It follows from this that trauma is not the Truth of a history that inflicts itself on each of us, whether or not we have experienced intensely destabilizing events. It is the result of specific historical forces that are capable of being named and represented and can in principle be resisted rather than passed on. Hence Sutpen *chooses* the oedipal reproduction of planter masculinity rather than, say, a course of political resistance. Following the affront, he retreats to a cave and debates with himself about how to respond to it, and even envisions his "design" as a kind of utopian effort to redeem the class wounds of all past and future (white) boys humiliated in similar fashion (see *AA* 210).

Two passages, then, two models of trauma. My argument is that these models uncannily predict or foreshadow a central tension in contemporary trauma theory. On one hand are theorists such as Cathy Caruth, Dori Laub, Shoshana Felman, and Bessel A. van der Kolk, who for all their differences adhere to something close to the first model.[2] The traumatic event is conceived in their work as the blow of a hard, overwhelming reality upon the psyche. The originary blow both produces trauma as its deferred effect and remains radically resistant to representation. For the dissociation of consciousness from itself means that the event *is not experienced* as it occurs; its basic mechanism consists in the paradox of a material intrusion whose disruption can never be "remembered" by the self, since the self was absent when it took place. The only way to "know" about trauma is thus through the flashbacks and crippling anxiety that disrupt psychic life with the specter of unprocessed memory-traces. This is, moreover, as true of those who have not been traumatized as of those who have: to seek to know the trauma of others "thematically," as it were – in propositional-representational form – is to betray the essence of trauma as anti-representational disturbance. Hence we are asked to cultivate an ethics in which we honor historical trauma through a "knowledge" that registers the impact of the event by reenacting its destabilizing power.

At the extreme, this view proposes to generalize trauma in much the same way as does Faulkner's first metaphor: to say (as does Caruth) that "history *is* the history of a trauma," or that "history is precisely the way we are implicated in each other's traumas," is to make it difficult to distinguish between traumatic and non-traumatic histories.[3] Indeed, in Caruth's influential arguments, and to a lesser extent in Laub's and Felman's, historical experience is itself assimilated to a model of language-as-trauma, in which to be human is to exist in language, and to be in language is to submit to a "traumatic" rupture with the Real whose exclusion founds representation but which forever returns to disrupt all efforts at symbolization.

On the other side are critics and theorists who either expressly critique such arguments or offer alternative, competing conceptions. Most prominent among them are Dominick LaCapra, Ruth Leys, Michael Rothberg, and Eric Santner. These thinkers rarely counter the view of trauma as dissociative incursion with one corresponding to the logic of Freud's *Nachträglichkeit* (as happens in Faulkner's text), but they each attempt to resist the generalizing assumptions that often underlie the former view. LaCapra draws on some of Santner's formulations, for example, to propose a distinction between *structural* and *historical* traumas – that is, between those intensely destabilizing events that all of us must undergo by virtue of our being-in-language (rupture with the Real, alienation from one's own body, the final unfulfillability of desire) and those that are the product of unique historical circumstances.[4] More recently, Rothberg has shown how arguments about the material-unrepresentable character of trauma often rest upon a tendentious reading of Lacan's conception of the Real, whereby what Lacan conceives of as a *modality* of that register – trauma as one way in which the Real can break into our lives – is generalized and metaphysicalized into the Truth of human experience – the Real defined as traumatic *tout court*.[5] Such critiques have the benefit of maintaining the ethically crucial distinctions between victims, perpetrators, bystanders, and latecomers: all of these would be subject to the originary decenterings so central to poststructuralist theory, but the question of whether and how each is traumatized by a given *historical* event is a matter for explication and analysis. This means that if perpetrators are "traumatized" by what they've done, that trauma can and must be ethically differentiated from the trauma of the victims. It also means that those who come to the event belatedly – those who did not experience the traumatic event directly – are not traumatized by *it* but (if they are indeed traumatized) by the stories transmitted to them about it. Finally, the implication of this line of argument is that it is possible to know about the trauma of others in a form other than its compulsive reprisal. Precisely because the trauma at issue is not the originary one that all of us share – because it is not the non-representable, decentering condition of consciousness itself – it can *in principle* be known and represented, even if its power is such as to short-circuit the protocols of memory and induce an acting out that seems to literalize and make the past present.

In *Absalom*, the two models I have been describing coexist side-by-side. It is as if Faulkner were struggling with the question of whether the history of racial dominion in the United States is best understood as a local instance of some transcendental principle of injury or as an irreducibly particular, *social* set of injurious institutions and practices. I have argued elsewhere that the novel in fact resolves this dispute in favor of its more historical impulse.[6] Here, I wish to move the analysis backward in time, to *Sanctuary* (1931). That novel occupies a curious place near the threshold of Faulkner's "major phase." Composed immediately after *The Sound and the Fury* in 1929, it retains evidentiary traces of the exhilarating, technical breakthrough in form that characterized Faulkner's first great book; and written (like *The Sound and the Fury*) after *Flags in the Dust* (1973),[7] it is marked by the new assurance about subject matter that Faulkner wrestled from that book's composition – the discovery that his "own little postage stamp of native soil was worth writing about" and that he "would never live long enough to exhaust it" (*LG* 255). Yet, formally speaking, *Sanctuary* is the *least* modernist book Faulkner published between 1929 and 1936 (the publication date of *Absalom, Absalom!*); the extensive revisions he made to the galleys eliminated the manuscript's subjectivist passages and transformed an associative narrative structure into one more conventionally linear.[8] The novel's interest in contemporary bootleggers signals, too, a break in what might otherwise seem a smooth progression from the familial concerns of *The Sound and the Fury* and *As I Lay Dying* (1930) to the historical excavations of *Light in August* (1932) and *Absalom, Absalom!*. *Sanctuary* might in this sense be read as a unique and uniquely liminal text, one which at once "knows" and resists the formal resources and historical insights developed in Faulkner's most productive years.

Nowhere is this clearer than in the way the novel registers and depicts trauma. On one hand, the book invites us to link the crime at its center to the traumas inflicted by slavery and its aftermath. Temple Drake is raped with a corncob at the decrepit remains of a once-functioning plantation; *Sanctuary* repeatedly calls her assailant, Popeye, "black" and metaphorically associates him with various kinds of "blackness"; the man eventually convicted of the crime (Lee Goodwin) is housed in a cell next to an African-American man and is himself lynched by an outraged mob before the state can hang him; and the novel exposes Goodwin's trial as a farcical vindication of Southern patriarchy, with the district attorney waving the bloodied corncob in the air and invoking the sanctity of white womanhood as he proclaims: "this is no longer a matter for the hangman, but for a bonfire of gasoline" (284).

On the other hand, and as this summary begins to suggest, attempts to clarify how these evocations "refer" to a history of racial trauma come up against insuperable difficulties. Popeye's blackness is more a literary or theological matter than an expressly racial one: until the final chapter humanizes him, he embodies what the novel suggests is the very principle of evil (his "black presence [lies] upon the house like the shadow of something no larger than a match falling monstrous and portentous upon something else otherwise familiar and everyday and twenty times its size" [121]), and he "smells [to Horace Benbow] like that black stuff that ran out of Bovary's mouth and down her bridal veil" (7). The falsely accused and lynched Goodwin resides in the cell *next* to a black man rather than himself "being" black. And Temple's resonant act of perjury – she testifies in court that Goodwin was her assailant – lacks the racist cast of such false testimony during Jim Crow and, in any case, dissembles an actual (rather than imaginary) rape.

The book's main plot thus asks to be read through the legacy of plantation slavery and the vigilante terror of Jim Crow, yet it representationally encodes that history in a way that scrambles its significance. Such a scrambling signals, I suggest, a double difference from the treatment of trauma we find in *Absalom, Absalom!* (and, in less developed form, in *Light in August*). *Sanctuary* offers a richer account than *Absalom* of the relations between the two models of trauma. It articulates (rather than opposes) the view of trauma as non-representational intrusion with that which links it to the processes of *Nachträglichkeit*, revealing how the first of these *need* not lead in the quasi-metaphysical direction taken by some theorists (and by Faulkner in what I've called *Absalom*'s first metaphor). This model is here largely adequate to a social understanding of such violence but must, Faulkner intimates, be supplemented with a model that stresses the resignification of prior meanings if we are to understand how trauma is historically "passed on." It will become clear that this notion of transmission or "passing on" is itself a misnaming of the processes at issue, at least as this novel conceives them. Finally, however, and despite these insights into the supplementary relation of the two models of trauma, *Sanctuary* moves to negate its most historically ambitious insights. It not only deforms historical reference "within" its representation (as described earlier with respect to slavery and Jim Crow) but also conceives its formal procedures in terms that allow us to "know" the characters' traumas only by having them repeat in us. Especially with this formal movement, *Sanctuary* mystifies the historical forces whose grip on the present it seeks to understand.

The book's exploration of trauma as disruption, dissociation, and delay emerges most clearly in the case of Temple's rape. Horace Benbow at one point observes that Temple seems unable to recount the horrors of the rape itself. In his capacity as Goodwin's lawyer, he visits her in the Memphis brothel where Popeye has taken her and tries to extract from her exculpatory evidence. She insists, however, on telling him not of her violation (which took place the morning after her night at the Old Frenchman place), but "of the night she had spent in the ruined house.... That was the only part of the whole experience which appeared to have left any impression on her at all: the night which she had spent in comparative inviolation" (215). This misplaced emphasis is just one way in which the novel links Temple's ordeal to a disordered sense of time. The sequence of chapters that chronicle her fate, for example, lead up to but do not culminate in the rape, ending instead with a temporal slippage through which the act slips away from her (and from us): "Something *is going to happen* to me," Temple thinks; "Something *is happening* to me.... I told you *it was*" (102; emphasis added). The slippage among tenses here underscores the elusiveness of the traumatizing event itself. It is a way of registering that dissociation of consciousness from itself by which some victims of violence respond to the unmanageable nature of the experience. This dissociation gives rise in turn to a kind of haunting compulsion. Not only does Temple come retrospectively to experience her "night of comparative inviolation" as already lacerated by the rape, but her subsequent sexual "depravity" (as the novel codes it) extends and reprises the brutal degradation of the event that initiates it.

Inasmuch as this depiction pertains to Temple and her violation by Popeye, it is amenable to a social analysis that emphasizes the violence of Southern patriarchy as mirrored in its transgressive "opposite" – Popeye as (in Temple's words) "Daddy" (231, 236), the underworld gangster as transgressor/enforcer of the violence that structures white-masculinist "civilization" but that such civilization also disavows. This is the reading developed by John T. Matthews in an essay that elaborates the logic I have described, though without calling it "trauma." It is compatible with Lisa Hinrichsen's analysis of the temporal "gaps" in *Sanctuary* as secreting the unrepresentable, traumatic genesis of Temple's plight. The rape exceeds Temple's conscious grasp, in Hinrichsen's view, because its horror absents her from it; and this very absence in turn explains her "dislocation in and confusion of time, her erratic physical movements, the grotesque glee with which she tells Horace Benbow ... what happened, [and] her final inability to bear witness to the event."[9] Even the fantasies through which Temple seeks to ward off her violation are legible in this context. She describes for Horace how, the night before her rape, she tried to eliminate her sexual vulnerability by sprouting a penis. The fantasy points to a radical dissociation of body (where she lacks a penis) from mind (where she "has" one), as if to suggest that the shock of impending violation gives rise to a gendered splitting of these domains. Similarly, Temple tells Horace how she fantasized being a middle-aged "teacher" who admonished Popeye with her "switch." This fantasy explicitly racializes an assailant she had earlier referred to as "that black man," figuring him now as "a little black thing like a nigger boy" (49, 219).[10] Such details suggest that Temple is so ensnared by the myth of the black rapist that she literalizes Popeye's "blackness" as a defense against the myth's shattering: she absents herself from her rape in part because to be present for it would mean confronting the horror of white women's violation by *white* men, thereby threatening a cultural narrative that underwrites her privilege in the Mississippi of the New South.

The emphasis on trauma as dissociative incursion diminishes when we turn to how this trauma gets "passed on": Temple's recounting of her ordeal devastates Horace, too, and here the model of trauma shifts to something approaching the logic of *Nachträglichkeit*. Upon returning to Jefferson after his interview with the raped girl, Horace remembers "the other morning when he had crossed" the town square on his way to visit her. "It was as though there had not been any elapsed time between: the same gesture of the lighted clock-face, the same vulture-like shadows in the doorways; it might be the same morning and he had merely crossed the square, about-faced and was returning; all between a dream filled with all the nightmare shapes it had taken him forty-three years to invent" (221–2). This dislocation in time uncannily reprises the one that befalls Temple. Just as her violation initiates a temporal-dissociative elision of consciousness, and just as she then finds herself marooned outside of ordinary time – the hours she spends in the brothel are measured by a one-handed clock that appears to have "nothing whatever to do with time" (148) – so one effect of her story on Horace is a negation of chronological sequence. His experience of crossing the square at once collapses the distinction between moments and enfolds those moments in an oneiric texture that exceeds them. The two moments reside, for him, "between a dream filled with all the nightmare shapes it had taken him forty-three years to invent." Such language points to a crucial condition for understanding traumatic transmission as an historical phenomenon. It indicates that Horace can be traumatized by listening to Temple not because *her* trauma becomes his but because it resonates with and resignifies his secret terrors and desires: her story brings into consciousness the unconscious fantasy around which his life has been organized as a defense (i.e., the "nightmare shapes" that he has "invented" but sought to confine to his "dream").

This dream is both a nightmare and one retrodetermined by Temple's story because it concerns Horace's transgressive longings toward his stepdaughter, Little Belle. Earlier, he had "looked ... with a quiet horror and despair" as some trick of the light transformed the step-daughter's photographed face into one "suddenly older in sin than he would ever be, a face more blurred than sweet, [with] eyes more secret than soft" (167). Now, immediately after hearing Temple's tale, he takes up the photo again: "the face appeared to breathe in his palms in a shallow bath of highlight, beneath the slow, smoke-like tongues of invisible honeysuckle.... The scent filled the room and the small face seemed to swoon in a voluptuous languor, blurring still more, fading, leaving upon his eye a soft and fading aftermath of invitation and voluptuous promise and secret affirmation like a scent itself" (223). The erotic dimension of this "invitation" is as unmistakable to Horace as it has been to critics.[11] It leads him moments later to *vomit*, in an effort to expel from himself the knowledge of female adolescent sexuality that Temple's story has activated. The vomit aims in fact to repudiate an "unassimilated" (221) set of desires that he has already internalized, a phantasmatic scenario in which he finds and loses himself equally in the pop-eyed violator of sexual girlhood and the violated Temple itself. Hence the fantasy that accompanies his vomit includes the phallic imagery of a train car "shot bodily" from a "black tunnel" "in a long upward slant," as well as a pronominal shift that marks the profundity of his identification with Temple: "he had not time to find [the bathroom light] and he gave over and plunged forward and struck the lavatory and leaned upon his braced arms while the shucks set up a terrific uproar beneath *her* thighs" (223; emphasis added). The shift from "his" to "her" here suggests that the fantasy traumatizes as much by its collapse of identitarian-gendered coordinates as by the desires in which it implicates the fantasist. At the same time, the "terrific uproar" of "shucks ... beneath her thighs" indicates that Horace's desire for the "daughter" is rendered both conscious and traumatogenic by Temple's tale of sleeping on corn shucks the night before being raped (with a corncob).

I'm suggesting that what traumatizes Horace is not some ineradicable ripple caused by Popeye's "unrepresentable" brutality and then relayed to him by Temple. The gangster's act is best understood as unrepresent*ed* rather than unrepresentable: it does not belong to the domain of the structurally excluded, pre-representational Real but to the realm of social reality; it fails to achieve memorial representation only because its horror overwhelms and thereby absents Temple from its blows. Horace is in his turn shattered not by the repercussions of an irrecoverable event that befell someone else but by the inner, latently significant fantasy of violating his own "daughter," which Temple's story renders conscious, retrospectively meaningful, and traumatic for the first time. This experience is traumatic because it reveals his implication in the violence that Southern patriarchy ordinarily masks. It confronts him with the ways in which the need to "protect our girls" is rooted in the fact that we "Might need them ourselves" (298) and, hence, with the precariousness of the borders between law and its transgression, chivalry and rape, incest and its legitimate, socially foundational displacements. It is the intertwining of Temple's and Horace's stories that thus gives the depiction of trauma such social and historical force in the novel. Through that intertwining, *Sanctuary* is able to honor both the power of social violence to short-circuit the perceptual-memorial apparatus *and* the way such violence may trigger trauma in others only when, in being narrated, it resignifies previously internalized social and psychic meanings.

The novel also blunts the force of its most instructive insights, however. It does so partly by exploiting an ambiguity in the "content" of Horace's traumatizing fantasy. If that content involves on one hand the lawyer's confrontation with his quasi-incestuous desire, it entails on the other a misogynist affirmation of women's "affinity for evil" (201) – that is to say, a judgment that Temple and Little Belle secretly want the violation Temple suffers. This is the meaning of the "invitation" Horace sees in the step-daughter's picture, as well as of his sense that her face is "older in sin than he would ever be." The view is equally evident when, in his drunken ramblings at the Old Frenchman place, he insists that "we know nature is a she ... because of [the] conspiracy between female flesh and female season" – a conspiracy by which the "female" profusion of grape blossoms in spring abets the step-daughter's "female" secrecy and, hence, her furtive acting upon her own sexual desires (13). Such associations between women, Nature, and dissimulation pose no interpretive difficulty so long as they remain rooted in Horace's perspective: they help flesh out his response to Temple's story as a traumatizing encounter with the desire for "evil" that he has sought to repudiate as "feminine." The trouble arises from the way the association exceeds the parameters of this character's mind. The misogynist links made by even some of *Sanctuary*'s best critics – Olga Vickery, for example[12] – derive from the novel's most authoritative pronouncements, rather than merely from Horace's rumina-tions. Faulkner describes Temple at the Old Frenchman place as "fac[ing] Popeye with a grimace of taut, toothed coquetry" (48); he amply bears out the suggestion made by Goodwin's lover, Ruby, that Temple could have prevented the rape "If she'd just stopped running around where they had to look at her. She wouldn't stay anywhere. She'd just dash out one door, and in a minute she'd come running in from the other direction" (162). Perhaps above all, the novel endorses this misogynist association through its treatment of the ease with which Temple transforms from spoiled yet undeflowered provoker of male desire to rapaciously sexual gangster's mol. The distance is both perceptible and slight between the Temple we meet, independent of Horace's consciousness, in chapter 4 – with her "squatting swirl of knickers" and her "fleet revelation of flank and thigh," "her bold painted mouth and soft chin, her eyes blankly right and left looking, cool, predatory and discreet" (28–30) – and the Temple whom Horace meets for the first time in bed in Miss Reba's whore-house: "Temple flung the covers back and sat up. Her head was tousled, her face puffed, two spots of rouge on her cheekbones and her mouth painted into a savage cupid's bow.... 'I want a drink,' she said, pulling up the shoulder of her gown" (214). This is a difference in degree, not kind. The girl whose lasciviousness leads her to plead with Red to ravish her rather than tell him to run from Popeye (who is about to kill him) merely actualizes and unleashes the depravity that *Sanctuary* makes latent in her from the start. In this sense, the depiction of Temple reproduces in the novel's own discourse that association between female sexuality, subter-fuge, and "evil" that characterizes Horace's view of women.

The result of this contamination of the novel's textures by Horace's vision is twofold. First, what gets "retrodetermined" by hearing Temple's story is now less the desires that implicate him in that story than a narratively con-firmed female "essence." Her story activates in him an awareness of the fictitiousness of prelapsarian origins, a "recognition" that the innocence of girls and young women is merely a dissimulation of woman as sexual incar-nation of "sin." Horace's encounter with Temple's story is thereby strangely departicularized; it ceases to be a resignification of fantasies irrevocably personal (if of course also social), becoming instead something akin to a reenactment of the Fall. It seems now an ontogenic recapitulation of Man's traumatic descent into Knowledge through the susceptibility to carnality of Woman. The leakage of Horace's views into the narrative thus has the effect of "structuralizing" the book's historical account of traumatic transmission. It renders such transmission no more than the ceaseless reenactment in the present of a mythically originary, traumatic initiation into femininity, carnality, and "the corruption [of] looking upon evil" (129).

The second result has to do with *Sanctuary*'s form.[13] That form is characterized by what I suggest is a traumatizing intentionality, an effort to induce in readers the dislocations and disruptions experienced by its characters, and, hence, by a stylistic extension of the inclination to structuralize trauma that I have described. This formal intention is closely bound up with Horace's own perceptions, as well as with the novel's peculiar form of "objectivity." For if, as intimated earlier, *Sanctuary*'s apparently conventional, objective technique distinguishes it from the other novels in Faulkner's major phase, this objectivity turns out to be deceptive. What seems at first like optical clarity is in fact a seductive obfuscation, as we can see by turning to the novel's opening paragraph: "From beyond the screen of bushes which surrounded the spring, Popeye watched the man drinking. A faint path led from the road to the spring. Popeye watched the man – a tall, thin mat, hatless, in worn gray flannel trousers and carrying a tweed coat over his arm – emerge from the path and kneel to drink from the spring" (3). This scene is staged as a visual transaction, in which Popeye peers unseen at Horace. The visual transaction is in its turn extended by a third-person style that invites the reader to engage in a kind of "meta-vision": we "watch" Popeye watching Horace, and do so from a position of apparently objective distance and clarity. This crisp, objective, ocular detachment is central to *Sanctuary*'s generic affiliation. It is a result of one aspect of the book's composition that Faulkner's mischievous comments about it give us no reason to doubt: that he set out to write a species of genre fiction – a pot-boiler – and that the genre most congenial to him was that of hard-boiled crime fiction.

But the opening scene is significantly more disturbing than this description implies. The reason for this lies not just in the ominous inequality the passage inscribes – one man watching another implies the vulnerability of the second – but also in the way the action is almost impossible to focus. The first sentence asks us to look at Horace already drinking from the spring; the third sentence then *moves back in time*, tracing his movement as he exits the path and begins to drink.[14] Such a procedure makes it hard to know where or when the novel begins. It would be wrong to choose one image and grant it chronological priority. For the main effect of this technique is to ask us to see both moments at once: to hold the past "within" the present, in the form of a palimpsestial image that wrecks the ordered heterogeneity of sequence. Horace emerges from the path to drink water *while he is already drinking* from the spring. Temporal sequence in this way dissolves in a present simultaneously captured and missed. This is, of course, another way of saying that the opening paragraph implicates readers in a traumatic temporality that echoes the one experienced (differently) by Horace and Temple.

Central to this ocular derangement is the way that *Sanctuary* links it both to Horace's style of looking and to a problematics of oral expulsion. Popeye is repeatedly shown to *spit into* the spring from which Horace drinks. And Horace's drinking is accompanied by an act of narcissistic gazing that fails to discover a coherent self-image: "In the spring the drinking man leaned his face to the broken and myriad reflection of his own drinking. When he rose up he saw among them the shattered reflection of Popeye's straw hat, though he had heard no sound" (4). This is the very first action that Horace performs in the novel. Its inaugural status encourages us to read it as an allegory for his subsequent efforts to "see" and master the world around him. The terms of that allegory are striking and disturbing. When Horace looks at the world before him, he discovers less an external object than a surface that seems to reflect his own image. The image of self is in its turn supplanted by an alien other (Popeye), as if to suggest that selfhood is grounded in visual identifications that alienate one from "oneself." But beyond both of these – and this is most crucial – the passage insists that this drama cannot even enable the self to find a coherence-in-alienation. For when the alien image "is" Horace, it is already torn into bits and pieces ("broken reflection"). And what comes then to take its place is less a human figure at all than an anti-reflective dispersion of matter ("straw hat") that fails to provide even a fleeting or illusory sense of coherence.

The encounter with Popeye thus enacts a traumatic disaggregation of self that *Sanctuary* metaphorizes by way of vision's encounter with oral expulsion. The scene marks the breakdown of vision's capacity to keep the objective world at bay, to distinguish between inner and outer when confronted with a substance that troubles that distinction. This ruin of ocular objectivity by the oral can be read back into the novel's first sentences. The second passage suggests, in other words, the retrospective *cause* of that opening's opacity. It is as if Faulkner were proposing that the novel frustrates our visual movements toward the world as a way of recalling us to a condition in which the self could not yet distinguish itself from what it abjected. *Sanctuary*'s narrative mode in this sense aims to induce in readers a version of the "structural" trauma out of which subjectivity is said to emerge. It solicits our ocular mastery through a kind of feigned, hardboiled "objectivity" but blurs our vision with the disruptive force of an abjected portion of self (spit), as a way of inducing in us a primordial dissociation and temporal disorder.

The visual encounter with oral abjection can also be read *forward* into the body of *Sanctuary*. The novel offers a sly analogue for Horace and the reader (as the book's opening construes them) in the blind old man, Pap, whom Faulkner describes more than once as having "phlegm-clots" for eyes (102). It also repeatedly confronts us with the blots to vision that result from this process, asking us to gaze upon matter clotted, whorled, gutted, stained, vomited, bled, and so forth.[15] Perhaps the most telling of these examples is one I mentioned earlier: "that black stuff that ran out of Bovary's mouth and down her bridal veil." This "stuff" condenses "evil" (blackness), oral expulsion, and the feminine (it is Emma Bovary who emits it) in ways that link it to the misogynist moment in Horace's regurgitative fantasy. The link is made explicit by the fact that the subject of that fantasy "watch[es] something black and furious go roaring out of her pale body ... the blackness streaming in rigid threads overhead" (223). Thus does the act of "looking upon evil" (i.e., hearing Temple's story) give rise to a visually devastated confrontation with the black expulsions of womanhood. Horace's traumatization by this process is relayed to readers by way of techniques that the novel's opening conceives as a visual confrontation with the oral. Or, to put the case slightly differently: *Sanctuary* conceives of its formal designs in terms of a (visually) traumatic induction into the eminently transmissible Truth of female carnality and sin.

André Bleikasten is surely right that Bovary's bile is also an evocation of the black "stuff" of writing; it is a way of giving material form to Faulkner's "ink of melancholy."[16] However, this is only another way of saying that the novel asks us to imbibe that bile. It seeks to induce in us through its forms the originary trauma that *Sanctuary* suggests, at the level of content, is the universal condition of Man since the Fall. Whatever truth there may be in that suggestion, it seems to me difficult to separate it in this book from a troubling misogyny on one hand, and an effacement of the more historically particular accounts of trauma on the other. Can we, then, in our approach to *Sanctuary*, keep ourselves open to its compelling designs without succumbing to the cosmic despair and misogyny that follow so easily from them?

NOTES

1 See, i.e., Sigmund Freud, *From the History of an Infantile Neurosis* (1918), *The Standard Edition of the Complete Psychological Works of Sigmund Freud*, James Strachey (ed.), vol. 17 (London: Hogarth, 1955). *Nachträglichkeit* is ordinarily translated "deferred action," but John Brenkman prefers "retrodetermination" for the way it stresses the determinative force of the later moment on the earlier (*Straight Male Modern: A Cultural Critique of Psychoanalysis* [New York and London: Routledge, 1996], pp. 21–2).

2 Cathy Caruth, *Unclaimed Experience: Trauma, Narrative, and History* (Baltimore: Johns Hopkins University Press, 1996); Caruth, ed., *Trauma: Explorations in Memory* (Baltimore: Johns Hopkins University Press, 1995);

Shoshana Felman and Dori Laub, *Testimony: Crises of Witnessing in Literature, Psychoanalysis, and History* (New York: Routledge, 1992); and Bessel A. van der Kolk, Alexander C. McFarlane, and Lars Weisaeth, *Traumatic Stress: The Effects of Overwhelming Experience on Mind, Body, and Society* (New York: Guilford Press, 1996).

3 Caruth, *Unclaimed Experience,* pp. 64, 24.

4 LaCapra, *Writing History, Writing Trauma,* pp. 76–86.

5 Michael Rothberg, *Traumatic Realism: The Demands of Holocaust Representation* (Minneapolis: University of Minnesota Press, 2000), pp. 135–40.

6 Greg Forter, *Gender, Race, and Mourning in American Modernism* (Cambridge: Cambridge University Press, 2011), chapter 3.

7 Faulkner completed the manuscript of *Flags* in 1927, but his publisher, Horace Liveright, rejected it. A version of that manuscript heavily edited by Ben Wasson was published as *Sartoris* in 1929.

8 Faulkner later claimed that he "paid for the privilege" of rewriting the book's galleys because the original was "terrible": basely conceived and rapidly composed in an effort to make money. His revisions (he wrote) aimed to make of the novel "something which would not shame *The Sound and the Fury* and *As I Lay Dying* too much." Many elements of this account have since been called into question. See Faulkner, Introduction to the Modern Library edition of *Sanctuary* (p. 324), and Noel Polk, Afterword to *Sanctuary: The Original Text.*

9 Lisa Hinrichsen, "A History That Has No Place: Trauma and Temple Drake in *Sanctuary,*" *Misrecognition, Race, and the Real in Faulkner's Fiction,* eds. Michael Zeitlin, André Bleikasten, and Nicole Moulinoux (Rennes, France: Presses Universitaires de Rennes, 2004), p. 129.

10 Dorothy Stringer has given these fantasies particularly detailed attention in *"Not Even Past": Race, Historical Trauma, and Subjectivity in Faulkner, Larsen, and Van Vechten* (New York: Fordham University Press, 2010), pp. 29–34.

11 See, i.e., John T. Matthews, "The Elliptical Nature of *Sanctuary,*" *NOVEL: A Forum on Fiction* 17.3 (1984), esp. pp. 247–51; Lawrence S. Kubie, "William Faulkner's *Sanctuary*: An Analysis," rpt. in *Twentieth Century Interpretations of Sanctuary,* J. Douglas Canfield (ed.) (Englewood Cliffs, NJ: Prentice-Hall), esp. p. 28; and David Williams, "The Profaned Temple," *Twentieth Century Interpretations of Sanctuary,* J. Douglas Canfield (ed.) (Englewood Cliffs, NJ: Prentice-Hall), esp. p. 96.

12 Olga Vickery, *The Novels of William Faulkner: A Critical Interpretation,* rev. ed. (Baton Rouge: Louisiana State University Press, 1964), esp. p. 111.

13 This discussion of *Sanctuary*'s form draws on while revising the more celebratory one I offered in *Murdering Masculinities: Fantasies of Gender and Violence in the American Crime Novel* (New York: New York University Press, 2000), chap. 3.

14 See George Toles, "*The Space Between: A Study of Faulkner's Sanctuary,*" *Twentieth Century Interpretations of Sanctuary: A Collection of Critical Essays,* J. Douglas Canfield (ed.) (Englewood Cliffs, NJ: Prentice-Hall, 1982), pp. 120–8.

15 André Bleikasten makes a version of this point in "Terror and Nausea: Bodies in *Sanctuary,*" *Faulkner Journal* 1.1 (1985), p. 29.

16 Ibid., p. 29.

7

JAIME HARKER

Queer Faulkner: Whores, Queers, and the Transgressive South

William Faulkner's writing portrays almost every kind of non-normative sexuality imaginable: rape, incest, homosexuality, sadomasochism, voyeurism, bestiality, prostitution, necrophilia, and garden-variety fornication and adultery. "Masculine" women and "feminine" men circulate in a cornucopia of gender identities that cut across racial and class lines. Faulkner's characters transgress gender and sexual norms liberally: Judith Sutpen, Charlotte Rittenmeyer, Laverne Schumann, Joanna Burden, Lena Grove, Emily Grierson, Addie Bundren, Temple Drake, Eula Snopes, and Linda Snopes violate conventions of femininity and sexual mores; V. K. Ratliff, Henry Sutpen, Charles Bon, Joe Christmas, Harry Wilbourne, Ab Snopes, and Quentin Compson flout masculine norms. Indeed, one can hardly find a major character in Faulkner who conforms to hetero-normative standards.

Faulkner criticism, however, has until recently imagined a very different Faulkner: a chronicler of virile Southern patriarchs obsessed with founding traditional families, a provincial novelist who perpetuated archetypal images of female fecundity as part of an idealized and unified Southern community. William Faulkner's ascent into the American literary canon after World War II was profoundly overdetermined by the cultural politics of the era; as Lawrence Schwartz so persuasively argued, Faulkner was elevated by New York intellectuals and the New Critics as an exemplar of American cultural superiority in the battle of Cold War aesthetics.[1] Malcolm Cowley's introduction to his edited anthology for Viking Press, *The Portable Faulkner* (1946), framed the master of Yoknapatawpha as the creator of a distinctively American mythology, a fearless innovator and craftsman whose writing embodied universal human truths.[2] Finally, Cold War intellectuals effused, we had an American writer to rival Tolstoy. Faulkner's Nobel Prize in 1949 provided international validation for Faulkner's American genius. This American/universal sleight of hand enmeshed Faulkner within Cold War geopolitics – a role he embraced dutifully through his numerous international trips for the State department.

Many historians and cultural critics have noted the gendered terms in which American Cold War geopolitics were articulated.[3] It is a strange irony that while American Cold Warriors were touting American individuality and innovation in contrast to the groupthink and cultural sterility of socialist realism, they were also enforcing rigid gender roles that bound the nuclear family to a culture of conformity. According to Schwartz, when Faulkner was canonized as an exemplar of American cultural superiority, Cold War critics embraced his writing for its complex experimentalism and deep moral purpose. Those same forces enlisted Faulkner as a heteronormative enforcer of traditional family values. Faulkner was read by Cold War critics as upholding the ideals of individualistic masculine virtues like honor, courage, truthfulness, and a willingness to fight for one's beliefs, while such readings tacitly approved the "universal" truths of female sexuality and subordination.[4]

But Faulkner as Southern patriarch obsessed with creating dynastic families and enforcing genteel sexual mores always required a breathtaking level of disavowal. After all, Faulkner first came to national prominence with the 1931 publication of *Sanctuary* – a novel that made New York sophisticates like Alexander Woolcott smirk and earned Faulkner the derisive moniker "the corncob man" in Oxford. If Faulkner dwells on the regime of "normal" heterosexuality, however extreme, that normality has nonetheless always been queerer than anyone ever imagined. It has taken Faulkner criticism a long time to catch up to the dystopian anarchy of Faulkner's genders and sexualities. John Duvall perceptively argues that the Cold War critical legacy makes us see things in novels that are not actually there and miss things that are there.[5] Cold War Faulkner critics saw a scion of Southern planters because that was a public role he had perfected by the end of his life. But Faulkner's relationship to gender and sexuality is much more interesting, diverse, and transgressive than those sonorous Cold War pronouncements ever imagined.

Minrose Gwin's *Faulkner and the Feminine* models a way to undo this critical blindness. "Faulkner's texts both explore and explode the boundaries of culture through creative probings of their limits and nuances," Gwin argues; "it is … this willingness to disallow the *idea* of center and to differ from itself in infinitely various ways that we find reverberating through Faulkner's narrative."[6] If Gwin is right about the deconstructive nature of Faulkner's narrative experimentations, then his sometimes monstrous genders and sexualities always produce an excess that refuses to be domesticated. Explicating Faulkner's genders and sexualities uncovers these disruptive textual moments and illustrates what I mean by the "queerness" of Faulkner's visionary fiction.

Biographical criticism has been crucial in complicating Faulkner's public persona and undoing many incorrect assumptions about him. An insider by birth, born to a prominent Oxford family, Faulkner was also, until his marriage at age thirty, an outsider in his Southern community. Joseph Blotner first noted that Faulkner's interest in books and his small stature provoked his classmates to call him "quair."[7] Faulkner's affectations on his return from World War I, when he pretended to be a decorated veteran for years, walking around town with a cape and a cane to assist him with a fictional war wound, earned him a moniker suggestive of the dandy: "Count No 'Count." Perhaps because of this, Faulkner had a special affinity for other outsiders in his community, especially sexual outsiders. He had a number of close friends who were gay, including Stark Young, Ben Wasson, who would become his first literary agent, and William Spratling, his New Orleans roommate with whom he travelled to Europe.[8] Faulkner exhibited no anxiety around these Southern gay men. Indeed, his time in New Orleans, in particular, was marked by thorough immersion in queer bohemian communities. Whatever Faulkner's personal sexual experiences, his artistic public persona in the Twenties circulated in explicitly gay communities.[9]

Though Faulkner was arguably less radical in his approach to gender, there, too, his experiences extend beyond the Cold War nuclear familial model. Judith Sensibar argues that his rearing by Maud Falkner and Mammy Callie Barr had a profound influence on his artistic development.[10] Outside the Southern patriarchal family structure, his associations with bohemian women and prostitutes prompted a sympathy and sensitivity that later blossomed in his writing. Even his marriage to Estelle, though it ostensibly legitimized him within a conservative Southern community, was unconventional; Estelle married someone else first, divorced, and came to the marriage with two children. Faulkner liked to represent their union as a product of his Southern gallantry, in saving a hysterical woman from suicide, but his daughter Jill maintained that both her parents enjoyed their dramatic, public altercations thoroughly,[11] both performing their respective "scripts" as hysterical lady and courtly gentleman with panache. The Faulkners' relish in the theatricality of their marital roles reaffirms Judith Butler's central insight that gender is fundamentally a performance: we are all drag queens. Add to that Faulkner's many extramarital affairs, which Estelle knew about and dismissed as a personality quirk, and Faulkner's marriage was anything but traditional. Despite his playacting as a Southern gentleman, Faulkner never escaped the "quair" boy he had been in the artist he became, and that "quairness" always fueled his art.

Faulkner's identification with sexual and gender otherness began early in his career. In *Mosquitoes*, he ascribes his own poetry to a lesbian character,

Eva Wiseman; Frann Michel uses *Mosquitoes* to claim Faulkner as a lesbian author.[12] But more broadly, Faulkner's explorations of sexual practices, including lesbian practices, mark the novel as a general critique of
gender norms. Young men, especially soldiers, also engage in homoerotics
in Faulkner's short stories, notably "Divorce in Naples," "Out of Nazareth,"
and "Moonlight." "Divorce in Naples" features a seaman "couple" and follows their estrangement and eventual reconciliation. "Out of Nazareth"
shows Faulkner and Bill Spratling surreptitiously cruising in Jackson Square
and meeting a beatific trick. "Moonlight" features a first sexual encounter in
which the adolescent protagonist is much more besotted with his male best
friend than his female paramour. All these early stories, in their emphasis on
male adolescent homoerotics, embrace sexual otherness as part of a larger
protest against repressive bourgeois sexual conventionality.

This embrace of sexual difference as modernist practice reaches its zenith
in *The Sound and the Fury*. The doomed Compson family is dominated
by the deviant: Benjy is a castrated sex offender, Quentin is consumed by
incestuous desires, and Caddy, Faulkner's "heart's darling," violates every
feminine code of sexual behavior. Faulkner's sympathy clearly lies with such
deviance, in all its dissident inscrutability. Jason Compson, in the most linear
and understandable section of the novel, is the contemptible voice of normative Southern sexuality, whose own hypocritical violation of the rules he justifies as the privilege of the ruling class. Readers cheer his comeuppance and
identify with the characters who defy prevailing sexual and linguistic rules.

Gender and sexuality become much more pointed tools of cultural critique
in Faulkner's next two novels through a pair of gender criminals: Temple
Drake and Joe Christmas. *Sanctuary* and *Light in August* are the textual
twins that bring gender and sexuality to the knife edge of his artistic vision.
In both, the cultural construction of "whore" and "nigger" highlight heteronormativity's disciplinary zeal. *Sanctuary*, of course, was the novel that
first gained Faulkner national notoriety. The story of Temple Drake is often
framed as a takedown of the liberated flapper, a deserved comeuppance
for women who forgot their proper place. The salacious details of Temple's
terror obscure Faulkner's pointed critique in the novel. Temple's descent
into nymphomania is orchestrated by men both respectable and unrespectable, from the Virginia undergraduate who abandons her at the bootleggers'
lair, to the "respectable" lawyer, Horace Benbow, who is more interested in
saving a violent criminal than in rescuing Temple from the whorehouse in
which she has been incarcerated. To the repressed romantic, Temple is now
damaged goods, unworthy of Horace's regard. That Benbow turns around
to support Lee Goodwin's woman, Ruby, suggests an ulterior sexual motive
that his sister, Narcissa, indicts as false gallantry. The sham of Southern

chivalry has never been so devastatingly exposed. Temple is educated into women's fate in patriarchy by the women she encounters – Ruby, the former prostitute, whose degraded status with the bootleggers leaves her no room for sympathy, and Miss Reba, the Memphis madam, for whom bloody sexual encounters are commonplace. Violence and sexuality are so intertwined within the Southern system that Popeye's violation of Temple is unrecognizable as rape to the prostitutes in Memphis. "'Now, now,' Miss Reba said. 'I bled for four days, myself. It aint nothing.... Us poor girls,' she said" (145). When Temple takes this lesson to heart and performs exaggerated sex acts with her "lover" Red to satisfy Popeye's voyeurism, she still finds no escape from a system both disgusted by and invested in the construction of women as "whores." Lee Goodwin has not actually raped Temple (although she accuses him of it to avoid Popeye's wrath), but the text makes it clear that he, like all the men at the house, would have raped her given the opportunity; Popeye simply got there first. The community outrage at Lee Goodwin is thus revealed to be a hypocritical show, not even bothering to conceal the voyeurism and violence at the heart of heterosexual masculinity. One of Lee Goodwin's lynchers offers a chilling benediction when he says of Temple, "I saw her. She was some baby. Jeez, I wouldn't have used no cob" (294). In this moment, Faulkner's larger critique becomes clear: for women, respectable and unrespectable alike, Southern patriarchy is one big whorehouse. Temple's terror, her dissociation from a traumatic event, her refrain in the barn – "something is going to happen to me" – reveals the helpless status of even the most privileged women, who can be transformed to "whore" in an instant (102).

That refrain – "something is going to happen to me" – also appears in *Light in August,* just before Joe Christmas kills Joanna Burden (118). That Faulkner uses precisely the same words to describe Temple's rape and Joe's killing of Joanna suggests that gender, race, and sexuality are mutually constitutive and disciplinary. Indeed, Siobhan Somerville argues, the "homosexual" was being invented as a species toward the end of the nineteenth century at the same time that eugenics was establishing elaborate racial hierarchies through an emerging racist science.[13] Black/white and homosexual/heterosexual binaries identified as essences what were really just differences, while racial and sexual definitions interlocked as a system of social discipline. *Light in August* is a devastating genealogy of this amalgam of racial and sexual misknowledge. The novel details the formation of that racial monster the "black rapist" through its flashbacks of Joe Christmas's childhood. No one knew what Christmas's racial heritage actually was, but that lack of knowledge was completely irrelevant to his grandfather, his fellow orphans, his teachers, and the police. He only had to be called a "nigger" to become one; framed as a racial and sexual deviant, Christmas was the invention of a pathological Jim Crow system that created its own bogeyman and then destroyed it.

Light in August exposes how sexual violence, both threatened and actual, is both a psychosis and a practical tool of racist intimidation in the Jim Crow South. Women who violate Southern racial codes, like Joanna Burden, a carpetbagger and "nigger lover," are seen to deserve a violent end (292). Joanna's death, and presumed rape, is celebrated by the town as her just deserts for rejecting social hierarchy, even as the men pretended to be outraged by the violation of a white woman they would not permit their wives to visit and used it as an excuse to terrorize the black community. The novel also shows us the fate of men who violate racial and sexual norms; they are framed as queer to dismiss protests to the Southern regime. Byron Bunch, a bachelor, and Gail Hightower, a preacher abandoned by his congregation when his wife's Memphis affair comes to light, are outcasts and friends and are taken to be queer by the larger community. Lucas Burch, living with Joe Christmas and selling bootleg liquor, is accused of Joanna Burden's murder and framed as a queer by the sheriff: "I aint interested in the wives he left in Alabama, or anywhere else. What I am interested in is the husband he seems to have had since he come to Jefferson" (321). It is only by denouncing Christmas as a "nigger" that Burch escapes his scapegoating as a queer and a traitor. "Whore," "nigger," and "queer" become the unholy trinity on which the Southern community is based. When Percy Grimm appears, the golem of American racism, with "a sublime and implicit faith in physical courage and blind obedience, and a belief that the white race is superior to any and all other races and that the American is superior to all other white races and that the American uniform is superior to all men" (451), it is the inevitable outcome of a psychotic disciplinary system. Hightower's ineffectual attempt to save Christmas makes the implicit misogyny and homophobia of the Southern system clear in Grimm's reply: "Jesus Christ!' ... Has every preacher and old maid in Jefferson taken their pants down to the yellowbellied son of a bitch?" (464). Repelled by Grimm's nausea-inducing castration of Christmas's corpse, readers are left to identify with rapists, murderers, cuckolds, and queers – Jefferson's despised outsiders.

The cultural critique in *Sanctuary* and *Light in August* laid the foundations for Faulkner's most thorough critique of the intersections of race, gender, and sexuality in *Absalom, Absalom!*. The novel tells the story of the South in microcosm through the queer familial drama of the Sutpen family. The South's "race problem" proves to be not outside but within the white southern family, materializing with the appearance of the purportedly mixed race Charles Bon, the disavowed first son who destroys Thomas

Sutpen's dreams of a planter dynasty requiring genealogical racial purity. But the seeds of Sutpen's demise are planted in his sexual dalliances at every stage of his career. From the mulatto mother of Charles Bon and the slave mother of Clytie to Ellen Coldfield, Rosa Coldfield, and the fifteen-year-old Milly Jones, Sutpen takes the privileges of his assumed upper class status to sexually humiliate and dominate women from all walks of life. But he is emphatically not in charge of what issues from those forced liaisons. Most of *Absalom, Absalom!* is narrated by white men, who are either of the planter class or aspire to be, and that narrative choice makes Sutpen a tragic figure, a loss to be lamented. Only in Rosa's eruptive middle section do those tragic narrative imperatives deconstruct and other disruptive queer energies become visible. In recent criticism, much attention has been paid to the male homoeroticism of the text.[14] The romantic entanglement of Charles Bon and Henry Sutpen, framed as a love affair and a marriage, destroys Sutpen's patrilineal pretensions, and Quentin and Shreve's erotic narrative reconstructions mirror that homoerotic pairing in its own attempt to construct a narrative of gay desire upon the past. That it took so long for critics to notice Bon's kimono is a testament to the power of Cold War heteronormativity, but *Absalom, Absalom!* is even more subversive than these readings allow.

Judith and Clytie represent another interracial, incestuous, homoerotic pairing,[15] one that does not end in homicide or suicide and that portends more radical consequences. The critical blindness regarding their union, queerly twinned with Henry and Bon's affinity, suggests that critics still prefer gay stories to be tragic and thus assimilable to a larger heteronormative narrative structure. Judith and Clytie become visible through Rosa's narrative, when Clytie, in an iconic scene from the novel, touches her arm to prevent her from going to Judith. Rosa's narrative immediately makes it clear that the touch, an intimacy between two women, incites in Rosa not just a racial revulsion but a lesbian panic:[16]

> We just stood there – I motionless in the attitude and action of running, she rigid in the furious immobility, the two of us joined by that hand and arm which held us, like a fierce rigid umbilical cord, twin sistered to the fell darkness which had produced her. As a child I had more than once watched her and Judith and even Henry scuffling in the rough games which they (possibly all children; I do not know) play, and (so I have heard) she and Judith even slept together, in the same room but with Judith in the bed and she on a pallet on the floor ostensibly. But I have heard how on more than one occasion Ellen has found them both on the pallet, and once in the bed together. But not I. Even as a child, I would not even play with the same objects which she and Judith played with, as though that warped and Spartan solitude which I called my

childhood, which had taught me (and little else) to listen before I could comprehend and to understand before I even heard, had also taught me not only to *instinctively fear her and what she was,* but to shun the very objects which she had touched. (112, italics added)

Rosa's thoughts here reveal a knowledge that she recognizes, even as she dissembles and then disavows her knowledge. Rosa "knew even then what I could not, would not, must not believe" and then cries out, in accusation, "And you too? And you too, sister, sister?" (112–13). As I argue elsewhere, this haunting refrain echoes the title of the novel; "like David, Rosa gladly would have died for Judith, but her place was usurped, and thwarted by love, she could only cry out against the two 'sisters' whose relationship excluded her."[17] Rosa's desire for and fear of this lesbian alliance culminates in a violent sundering of that too-intimate encounter with Clytie; Rosa's use of a racist epithet to break the encounter parallels the "queers" and "niggers" in *Light in August.*

The queer alliance between Clytie and Judith has disruptive, even transformative consequences. Judith seeks out Charles Bon's mulatto "wife" and places his son as the heir apparent to Sutpen's Hundred, creating a queer contact zone that, while not toppling the larger Southern system, seriously destabilizes one corner of it.[18] Judith destroys her father's designs and, after twenty years with Clytie, leaves the plantation to her and the mixed race grandson of Charles Bon, Jim Bond. Though the narrator insists on viewing this mixed race heir as an imbecile, he becomes the progenitor (however equivocal) of a new South that the implicitly lesbian couple, Judith and Clytie, midwife into the world. For Judith, "Jim Bond's triumph would simply extend the logic of the queer contact zone across the Southern landscape. She considered her dead fiancé's mixed race grandson as not only family but legitimate heir, the proper representative of the mulattas, queers, and maroons of her family tree."[19] *Absalom, Absalom!* is perhaps the most radical of Faulkner's queer visions, providing a blueprint for the dissolution of the Southern patriarchy, even if the novel's mostly male narrators simply mourn its passing.

Sexual and gender nonconformity thus figures prominently in what critics have come to call Faulkner's "major" novels. To understand more about the source and wider function of sexuality in Faulkner, however, one might look beyond Yoknapatawpha, to the "Signet" canon: *Sanctuary, Pylon, Wild Palms (If I Forget Thee, Jerusalem).* David Earle, in his book *Re-Covering Modernism,* maps the larger print culture of pulp magazines in the 1920s and pulp paperbacks in the 1940s and 1950s.[20] Contrary to Malcolm Cowley's claim, Faulkner was not out of print before the publication of

The Portable Faulkner; the New American Library had three of his books under its Signet imprint, and these not only sold well but were completely legible to pulp readers in their conformance to the genre's emphasis on deviant sexuality. *Sanctuary*'s rape and voyeurism, *Pylon*'s polyandry and sex mid-flight, and *The Wild Palms'* adultery and abortion were standard fare in the pulp tradition, where transgressive sexuality was a potent marketing tool. Both *Pylon* and *The Wild Palms*, outside the Yoknapatawpha mythology, feature some of Faulkner's most liberated women characters, who live in defiance of heteronormativity's strictures. Laverne Schumann, first seen in trousers, working as a mechanic, sleeps with two men and raises a son whose paternity cannot be established. Her rapacious sexuality binds both men to her and inspires the Reporter's devotion; in one memorable scene, after she straddles her lover as he pilots their biplane, Laverne parachutes from the wing, her underwear gone and her dress billowing in the air. The men of the town riot, and one police officer is driven insane, shouting "I'll pay you!" in one instant and "calling her whore and bitch and pervert in a tone wild with despair" the next (912); Laverne must escape from him in the dead of night. Liberated female sexuality like Laverne's, Faulkner suggests, risks breaking down the entire social order. In *Wild Palms*, Charlotte Rittenmeyer's embrace of sexual desire, regardless of consequence, is interspersed with the prisoner's engulfment by a flood, a symbol of feminine sexuality that culminates in his delivery of a baby and grateful escape back to the all-male refuge of prison. Faulkner punishes both women and the men who are drawn to them – Roger Schumann's death from a plane accident and Charlotte's from an abortion, performed by her lover Harry, who is convicted and sent to the penitentiary – but the danger, power, and allure of women's sexuality triumphs in both novels. Framing Faulkner's genders and sexualities within this larger pulp tradition might help us reassess the split between "major" and "minor" novels that still bedevils Faulkner criticism. A more thorough acknowledgement of how Faulkner absorbed and embraced the pulp tradition, even in novels that are seen as his most experimental and modernist, comes by taking the Signet canon seriously.

Faulkner's later writing loses some of the sharpness of its critique when he begins performing the country squire role more consistently; still, those later novels depend upon transgressive gender and sexuality for their most powerful moments. Unlike the consensual homoerotic incest of *Absalom, Absalom!*, *Go Down, Moses* exposes heterosexual rape and incest between father and daughter at the heart of Southern slavery. Ike McCaslin disavows his birthright and tries to make amends with Tomey Turl's descendants – the black McCaslins – but unlike Clytie, he cannot admit that the Southern family is already miscegenated and impure. His obsessive demand for purity leads him to destroy the things he claims to care about – his honor, his wife, the mythical bear Old Ben – and in the end, he, like his father and grandfather, disinherit the black members of the family. That final rejection of Roth Edmonds's black lover – "You're a nigger!" – exposes Ike's abdication as a hypocritical dodge (344). More recent scholarship, notably by Richard Godden and Noel Polk, focuses on the homoeroticism of Uncle Buck and Uncle Buddy, providing both a queer and a miscegenated genealogy.[21] In this later exploration of "deviant" sexual practices, Faulkner identifies their role in the most mainstream constructions of Southern culture – not only tolerated as long as they did not challenge the status quo (as John Howard argues in *Men Like That*) but even incorporated as a tool of sexual domination. Patriarchal heteronormativity privately embraced and publicly disavowed homoerotic practices; condemnations of "degeneracy" were used to neutralize threats to the status quo, even as those same practices were seen as a pleasurable indulgence by the privileged. Uncovering those hypocritical disavowals is one of the highlights of Faulkner's later work.

The Snopes trilogy is the repository for some of the most notorious stories of redneck sexuality – the sort of material with which Erskine Caldwell became most spectacularly associated. Framed by V. K. Ratliff, a closeted Russian and queer observer whose domestic "buggy" circulates across Yoknapatawpha,[22] the trilogy features American literature's most famous, and overwritten, seduction of a cow. But whatever Faulkner's interest in portraying bestiality as a metaphor of capitalist "diddling," it is Eula and her daughter Linda who dominate the male domain of the Snopes trilogy. Eula's unshameable sexuality is enabled, not contained, by Flem Snopes, but when he finally does shame Eula publicly on her gravestone, his daughter Linda systematically destroys the Snopes dynasty, just as Judith and Clytie undo Sutpen's Hundred. Linda's departure for Greenwich Village, her marriage to a Jew, her "race traitor" activism, and her revenge upon her father all mark her as an outsider and a formidable opponent.

Later queer coalitions – usually women, African-Americans, and children – against the oppressive white male establishment have more modest goals. In *Intruder in the Dust,* Chick Mallison joins with spinster Miss Eunice Habersham to save Lucas Beauchamp, acknowledged descendant but unacknowledged heir of the McCaslin estate, from a frame-up and lynching. That outsider coalition may not be able to undo the larger social order, represented by both the rabble of white lynchers and the highly educated Gowan Stevens, but it can intervene productively. *The Reivers* similarly traces the adventures of Lucius Priest, Boon Hogganeck, and Ned McCaslin on an unsanctioned trip to Memphis. Their alternative community includes "whores," whom Lucius insists deserve the gallant treatment afforded a lady. In the end, the social order reasserts itself; wealthy white men "save" them from their adventure but not before Ned McCaslin insists that the Southern patriarchy cannot understand the values of its outsider communities. Colonel Liscomb, mystified about the wild Saturday nights of African-Americans, asks "Why do you do it? I don't know" (960). Ned's reply is emphatic: "you cant know.... You're the wrong color. If you could just be a nigger one Saturday night, you wouldn't never want to be a white man again as long as you live" (960). These sudden eruptions of alternative knowledge and communities happen constantly in Faulkner, across gender, race, and sexual differences, and though the mainstream narrators quickly pass over such eruptions (or glamorize them in a patronizing way), they nevertheless threaten to undo the mainstream voice of Southern patriarchy.

Gender and sexuality are a bellwether of cultural fissures in Faulkner's fiction, exposing hypocrisies and cruelties and enabling disruptive alliances, however fragile. Sexual and gender outlaws are heroes in Faulkner's fiction, suffering at the hands of a disciplinary regime, even if the narrators and dominant voices do not always acknowledge them as heroes. Attention to these counter-narratives rescues Faulkner from his own planter class pretensions and outs the queer heart of his narrative genius.

NOTES

1 Lawrence Schwartz, *Creating Faulkner's Reputation: The Politics of Modern Literary Criticism* (Knoxville: University of Tennessee Press, 1990).
2 Malcolm Cowley (ed.), *The Portable Faulkner* (New York: Viking Press, 1946).
3 See Elaine Tyler May, *Homeward Bound: American Families in the Cold War Era* (New York: Basic Books, 1988); Suzanne Clark, *Cold Warriors: Manliness on Trial in the Rhetoric of the West* (Carbondale: Southern Illinois University, 2000); Alan Nadel, *Containment Culture: American Narratives, Postmodernism, and the Atomic Age* (Durham, NC: Duke University Press, 1995).
4 See Cleanth Brooks, *Toward Yoknapatawpha and Beyond* (Baton Rouge: Louisiana State University Press, 1990); Irving Howe, *William Faulkner, A Critical Study* (New York: Ivan R. Dee, 1991), Louis D. Rubin and Robert D. Jacobs (eds.), *South: Modern Southern Literature in its Cultural Setting* (New York: Doubleday, 1961).
5 John Duvall, "Faulkner's Critics and Women: the Voice of the Community," *Faulkner and Women*, Doreen Fowler and Ann Abadie (eds.) (Jackson: University Press of Mississippi, 1986).
6 Minrose Gwin, *The Feminine and Faulkner* (Knoxville: University of Tennessee Press, 1990), p. 32, emphasis in original.
7 Joseph Blotner, *Faulkner: A Biography* (New York: Random House, 1984), p. 38.
8 Gary Richards, "The Artful and Crafty Ones of the French Quarter: Male Homosexuality and Faulkner's Early Prose Writings," *Faulkner's Sexualities*, Annette Trefzer and Ann J. Abadie (eds.) (Jackson: University Press of Mississippi, 2010), pp. 21–37.

9 See Phillip Gordon, "Gay Faulkner: Uncovering a Homosexual Presence in Yoknapatawpha and Beyond," unpublished Ph.D. dissertation, University of Mississippi, 2013.

10 Judith Sensibar, *Faulkner and Love: the Women Who Shaped His Art, a Biography* (New Haven, CT: Yale University Press), 2010.

11 Ibid., p. 12.

12 Frann Michel, "Faulkner as a Lesbian Author," *The Faulkner Journal* 4.1–2 (Fall 1988–Spring 1989), 5–20.

13 Siobhan Somerville, *Queering the Color Line: Race and the Invention of Homosexuality in American Culture* (Durham, NC: Duke University Press, 2000).

14 See Norman W. Jones, "Coming Out Through History's Hidden Love Letters in *Absalom, Absalom!*" *American Literature: A Journal of Literary History, Criticism, and Bibliography* 76.2 (June 2004), 339–66 and Michael P. Bibler, *Cotton's Queer Relations: Same Sex Intimacy and the Literature of the Southern Plantation, 1939–1968* (Charlottesville: University of Virginia Press, 2009).

15 Jaime Harker, "'And You, Too, Sister, Sister?': Lesbian Sexuality, *Absalom, Absalom!*, and the Reconstruction of the Southern Family," *Faulkner's Sexualities*, pp. 38–53.

16 Ibid., p. 43.

17 Ibid., p. 43.

18 Ibid., pp. 49–50.

19 Ibid., p. 52.

20 David Earle, *Re-Covering Modernism: Pulps, Paperbacks, and the Prejudice of Form* (Burlington, VT: Ashgate, 2009).

21 Richard Godden and Noel Polk, "Reading the Ledgers," *Mississippi Quarterly: The Journal of Southern Cultures* 55.3 (Summer 2002), 301–59.

22 Noel Polk, "Around, Behind, Above, Below Men: Ratliff's Buggies and the Homosocial in Yoknapatawpha," *Haunted Bodies: Gender and Southern Texts*, Anne Goodwyn Jones and Susan V. Donaldson (eds.) (Charlottesville: University Press of Virginia, 1997), pp. 343–66.

8

MELANIE BENSON TAYLOR

Faulkner and Southern Studies

The great ruptures, the great oppositions, are always negotiable, but not the little crack, the imperceptible ruptures which come from the south.... Everyone has his south – it doesn't matter where it is – that is, his line of slope or flight.

– Gilles Deleuze[1]

The presence alone of Faulkner in our midst makes a great difference in what the writer can and cannot permit himself to do. Nobody wants his mule and wagon stalled on the same track the Dixie Limited is roaring down.

– Flannery O'Connor[2]

Faulkner is, of course, Faulkner, and not much more need be said.

– Michael Kreyling[3]

At a critical moment in the 2012 presidential campaign, Republican nominee Mitt Romney staged an elaborate play to court U.S. Southerners, whose support is deemed essential for a candidate to prevail in a national election. Importantly, Romney's Southern strategy teetered not on issues per se but on a zealous effort to embrace the region's characteristic cuisine and dialect. "I'm learning to say 'y'all' and I like grits. Strange things are happening to me," he told an amused crowd in Pascagoula that spring.[4] Romney credited his transformation to the tutelage of his bodyguard Garrett Jackson, a University of Mississippi graduate and licensed pilot who was scheduled to begin military flight school when he instead accepted a position on the campaign.[5] Leaving aside the irresistible echoes of Faulkner's own biography (a feature of which was his youthful misadventures as a trainee at the Royal Air Force flight school in Toronto during World War I), Jackson's stereotypical Southernness offered just the right air of authenticity to validate Romney's conversion. Ultimately, the tactic both succeeded and failed in revealing ways: while Romney did not win the election, he did manage to win over a substantial margin of conservative white voters – and not just in the South but nationwide. In the process, he issued a potent and complicated reminder that while the South remains a monolithic trope certain to signify in the cultural imagination, it is also a mobile phenomenon: at once "strange" and familiar, the South in the new millennium suggests a grits-loving cohort of conservatism that can be joined by seemingly anyone with a particular set of values, tastes, and speech patterns.

The field of Southern Studies has only recently begun to interrogate this paradoxical collision of permanence and plasticity, and especially its enduring impact on not just regional but national culture and politics. In their introduction to a 2001 special issue of *American Literature* devoted to "Violence, the Body, and 'The South,' " Houston Baker and Dana Nelson argue that "as a nation, we are always already in 'The South.' ... It is unequivocally and intricately lodged in us, a first principle of our being in the world." Baker and Nelson go on to call for a "new Southern studies ... [that] welcomes intellectual, multiparticipant, and revisionary complexity," that will disrupt "old borders and terrains" and "construct and survey a new scholarly map of 'The South.'"[6] Scholars in the new millennium have responded with the swift deconstruction of Southern Studies' old cartographies. Influenced by both postmodern and postcolonial thought, the "New" Southern Studies jettisoned narrow notions of region and its exceptional margins of race, gender, and sexuality, underlining construction over essence. Globalization studies have offered fruitful tools for placing the South within broader geographies of postplantation culture, where it mirrored and often influenced similar sites of colonial, racial, and economic trauma and extravagant cultural dissonance.[7] Symptomatic rather than exceptional, the South may now be seen as both an inveterate importer and exporter of global influences. These new conceptual frames have had broad applications for regionalist studies more generally: the South has been reconfigured as both an episteme for injustice elsewhere and itself a porous entity always already marked by global patterns of migration and influence. Most critics now concur with Richard Gray's assessment of the region as "an imagined community made up of a multiplicity of communities, similarly imagined,"[8] filtered through what scholars like Scott Romine and Michael Kreyling have deemed "the simulacra that crowd in upon the omnimediated experience of the present."[9] Yet, like any ideological construct, "the South" remains no less powerful and enduring for its artifice, and it seems that Faulkner – whose work both typifies and resists the tyranny of southern exceptionalism – remains its primary owner and proprietor.

From Postage Stamps to Federal Express: Faulkner and the South on a Global Stage

No longer dominated by attention to literary texts, the New Southern Studies' enlarged purview surveys cultural production more broadly, assuming that media, technology, foodways, and politics participate collectively in the heteroglot production of southern identity. More importantly, other fields – history, anthropology, cultural studies – have simultaneously undergone their own reconstitution in the wake of poststructural inquiry, paving the way for alliances among practitioners of various disciplines.[10] Notably, however, the turn to the global and the "new" is not simply a temporal shift seeking to document the contemporary evolution of the South or to signify the transcendent ethics of our current critical moment; rather, it reflexively interrogates regional ideology as a distinctively historical phenomenon, one nourished and maintained by active processes of invention, sublimation, and repression. Importantly, such gestures affirm that cultural discourse does not simply emanate a priori from a coherent environment, however lately deconstructed or reimagined, but is actively engaged in the manufacture of its own origins. Likewise, then, the rhetoric of newness suffusing the field often belies the dogged adherence of prior categories of analysis and inquiry, whether we realize it or not; and according to some critics, we may in fact exercise similar forms of repression and forgetting if we fail to look soberly "in the rearview mirror."[11]

Southern literary studies inaugurated not simply a cultural tradition but an ideological one. Compelled largely by the conservative Agrarian writers and scholars who collaborated on the 1930 manifesto *I'll Take My Stand* to decry the corrosive materialism of the modern age, the twentieth-century Southern literary "renaissance" was born into (and from) an epoch of dislocation and alienation. Southern literature was by definition a modern phenomenon, a collection of voices distinctly out of step with the world they were doomed to inhabit. As Allen Tate famously put it, they were men saddled with an acute awareness of "the past in the present."[12] Faulkner had his own version of this cliché: "The past is never dead," Gavin Stevens remarks in Act I of *Requiem for a Nun* (1951): "It's not even past" (535). The quip has flown as a kind of thematic banner over subsequent generations' efforts to interpret his demanding works and, in its habitual infiltration of recent pop-cultural texts, a testimony to Faulkner's persistent relevance. Indeed, as critics like Kreyling have demonstrated, the world that the Agrarians built continually exerts a powerful hold on the generations that came after. "Instead of forgetting the old," Sarah Ford suggests, "southern literary criticism seems indeed to be haunted by ghosts from the past."[13]

What the Agrarians gave voice to was a prevailing ideology of grief and resistance to change that could not be solved simply by admitting the region's more diverse and downtrodden members into the canon. To be sure, many of the major contributions to New Southern Studies have accomplished just that. Overlooked women writers finally received sustained attention in pioneering works by Anne Goodwyn Jones and Patricia Yaeger; simultaneously, African-American literature, often anxious to liberate itself from a poisonous southern context, began to be reintegrated into its conversations, perhaps most arrestingly in Houston Baker's autobiographical rereading of Booker T. Washington, *Turning South Again*.[14] Such measures were progressive mainly in their widened acknowledgement of suppressed voices and peripheries. Rediscovered black writers and emergent postcolonial methodologies rendered conversations about race far less insular and crude, though the tyranny of the black-white binarism has nonetheless proven exceptionally robust. Nor has the shift to global coordinates necessarily defused the stability of "regionalism"; in its place, "critical regionalism" strives to reconcile the durability of the local in the face of globalization. "To displace 'the American South,' " Katherine Henninger notes, "with all its canons and nationalist imaginings, entirely in favor of transnational, though no less valid, connections, would be, ironically enough, to risk re-performing the type of institutionalized forgetting that Benedict Anderson in *Imagined Communities* argued was essential to the process of nation-building."[15] Ultimately, most New Southern Studies critics acknowledge that for all their deconstructive potential, these new methodologies ironically do – and must – reaffirm the tenacity of "the South" as an ideological construction with discernible, tenacious influence.

In the crisis state witnessed by the Agrarians, John Grammer avers, "The personal virtue most useful ... was not imagination or energy or moral awareness but the one Faulkner praised most often, endurance."[16] Conveniently, Faulkner seems to satisfy a persistent urge to endure whatever crisis next rounds the bend, evincing what Ted Atkinson deems "a seemingly inexhaustible capacity for remaining relevant."[17] Primarily, these anxieties about social change hinge on economic fluctuations that destabilize perceptions of status, belonging, power, and humanism – a preoccupation that has persisted well beyond the South's most dire periods of depression and frustrated recovery. As Jon Smith notes,

> For at least the sixty-eight years between the Twelve Southerners' *I'll Take My Stand* and Michael Kreyling's *Inventing Southern Literature*, mainstream southern literary studies overwhelmingly and explicitly presented the region as precisely Douglas Holt's sort of populist world, and for nearly as long the

field of Faulkner studies – with some notable exceptions – has been about as guilty as anybody else, however paradoxically, of marketing the South, and the works of Faulkner in particular, as an antidote to the anxieties of Yankee capitalism.[18]

The trouble, Smith explains, is that "by their very nature, those fantasies [of Southern exceptionalism] don't necessarily go away, even should the scholars on the conscious, logical level no longer endorse them."[19] Indeed, Smith succumbs openly to the seductiveness of such fantasies – and Faulkner's role in sustaining them – by writing a book (*Finding Purple America*) about the power of those fictions. "But it is also," he avers, "I hope, a book about relative rationality and realism, about ways of living in modernity with Ruben Studdard, William Faulkner, and the older Neko Case instead of escaping into pre- or postmodern fantasy with the neo-agrarians, the religious Right, Johnny Cash, the L.A. school, or the editors of *American Quarterly*."[20]

Sandwiched between Studdard and Case, the veritable vanguard of the "new," Smith casually posits Faulkner – who is, he claims, "a good deal hipper than his critics have been."[21] By "hip," Smith refers to Faulkner's obvious impatience with the stultifying atmosphere of small-town rural enclaves and his attendant "need to negotiate between authentic southern yam-eating roots and a shifting cosmopolitan identity."[22] Faulkner biographers have vividly sketched "Count No 'Count'"'s efforts – and failures – to cultivate an urbane sophistication and bravado packaged in assorted uniforms of the military hero and the polished dandy. New Southern Studies methodologies quickly placed Faulkner's cosmopolitan yearnings into the more complex, ambivalent container of the South's demeaned and porous position within both the national and global imaginary. Smith knows this better than some: along with Deborah Cohn, he coedited the 2004 collection *Look Away!: The U.S. South in New World Studies*, which redirected the field's gaze toward a wider international world similarly wrought by colonialism and slavery, its ties to the South obscured by national mythologies and binarisms.[23] Despite its efforts to break new ground, the book devotes one of its four sections to exploring unseen relationships between "Faulkner and Latin America." Differently, and disturbingly, Robert Brinkmeyer's *The Fourth Ghost* suggested another, more modern kind of infiltration by arguing that southern writers of the 1930s and '40s, Faulkner included, were not nostalgically navel-gazing but turned "fearfully outward" toward "the ghostly presence of European Fascism lurking on the cultural horizon."[24]

Such works remind us that the South's inhabitants and artists have long registered these global refractions in ways that previous critics left unexplored. Complicated by such revelations, the South has reemerged in

American studies more broadly as an entity worth reconsideration after decades of being dismissed as, at best, quaint and provincial. Scholars such as Leigh Anne Duck and Jennifer Greeson have productively diagnosed the mechanics by which regions often function to facilitate national ideologies. Both offer sustained examinations of the ways that the South embodies what Duck calls the "nation's region": an easily bastardized foil to the ascendant values of the broader United States, at the same time that it functions, in Greeson's analysis, to nourish that very American distinctiveness – and not always in strict contradistinction.[25] At present, there exists a quiet equilibrium between those for whom the South endures, albeit as an imperfect, imagined community, and those who pursue more decentered, deconstructed paradigms in which the South is mere specimen or function. Remarkably, there is a version of Faulkner that satisfies each of these approaches, because his work so inimitably captures the ambivalent collisions of a region poised uncannily within and outside national culture. The Haiti episode in *Absalom, Absalom!*, for instance, functioned for many scholars as the connective tissue to a broader plantation organism felt palpably, by reverberation, throughout Faulkner's career. With his 1996 work *Faulkner, Mississippi,* the Caribbean writer Édouard Glissant demonstrated powerfully that Faulkner's function is simultaneously mimetic and migratory: for readers in America and elsewhere, the bard of Oxford represents "the South" in all its uncanny mystification at the same time that his world overlaps unnervingly with global sites of injustice.[26]

As Michael Kreyling has noted, mostly critically, "the perennial 'canonical figure' of the twentieth century, William Faulkner, still has the stage more or less to himself."[27] His enduring dominance occasionally troubles critics of the New Southern Studies, yet his work nonetheless manages to remain uncannily pertinent to – and uniquely illustrative of – its enlarged stage. In a recent essay, Richard King issues yet another bid for the suggestive significance of Haiti in *Absalom, Absalom!* but, in doing so, measures Faulkner's inimitable authority alongside eruptions of creativity in "Afro-modernity" rather than domestic contexts or the subjective (yet obstinate) standards of quality.[28] Efforts like King's evince that Faulkner's continued centrality actually marks something of a revision: previously one of few southern writers to transcend regional status – to be known as an "American" writer first and only secondarily as "southern" – his solid position within the New Southern Studies amounts to a reterritorialization, one that claims Faulkner as an ambassador to revamped territories of meaning and as a triumphant skeleton key to the myriad revelations that the South always already knew and that critics are only belatedly discovering.

Founding Yoknapatawpha: Faulkner's Imperial Fictions

By now, most Faulkner scholars are well-versed in the origins of Yoknapatawpha County, an imaginative domain that Faulkner christened with his interpretation of a Chickasaw word; "it means 'water runs slow through flat land'," he explained, to the apparent amusement of a class at the University of Virginia in 1957 (*FU* 74). As a founding father, Faulkner performs the by now prosaic act of eulogizing the indigenous predecessors in his discovered territory. This act of imperial imagination pairs strikingly with the story Faulkner tells about the founding of Jefferson, the fictional county seat of Yoknapatawpha. While it is an origin story of sorts, it appears in one of his later works, *Requiem for a Nun (1950)* – shortly before Gavin Stevens's pronouncement that "the past is never dead." As critics such as John T. Matthews and Spencer Morrison have demonstrated, Faulkner's late novels register distinct Cold War anxieties about the influence of a U.S. military-industrial complex yoked dangerously to unfettered market capitalism.[29] With *Requiem* in particular, Matthews sees Faulkner "diagnosing ... the unhealed trauma of the plantation South's violent origins in New World colonialism" as a direct response to the mid-century emergence of "imperial democracy – a paradoxical creature, for sure."[30]

In Act I of *Requiem*'s narrative drama, we learn that Jefferson was so named after a mail carrier named Thomas Jefferson Pettigrew. In a complicated and colorful series of events, the town founders need to compensate this mail rider for borrowing the lock from his mail pouch in order to secure the county jail – a building that importantly precedes the courthouse as the town's inaugural edifice. In exchange, the founders grudgingly agree to name the incipient town "Jefferson" after the crafty mail rider – not "Pettigrew," his actual surname, but the more patriotic and decorous "Jefferson." The superficial homage to Thomas Jefferson, an act of colonial reverence common in civic naming rituals, happens purely by accident here; moreover, it functions as a screen for an underlying narrative of theft, subterfuge, and bribery. That is, the original plan hatched by the founders was to pay for the lock by charging it to the Chickasaw account at the agency store (the town was originally settled as a trading post in 1800). They plan to thus obtain the necessary funds as reimbursement from the Bureau of Indian Affairs: "'You could call that lock "axle grease" on that Indian account,' Pettigrew himself suggests, 'To grease the wagons for Oklahoma'" (492–3). This was an idea Ratcliffe, the commissary agent, already had: "'Put it on the Book,' Ratcliffe said – the Book: not a ledger, but *the* ledger," confident that no Washington bookkeeper would ever notice (487). Pettigrew's sly

"moralizing" apparently dissuades them, though, ultimately, they are trou-
bled not by ethics but simply by the threat that they might get caught and
prosecuted, along with the baldness with which Pettigrew exposes the fraud-
ulent elision: the "grease" for Indian Removal is symbolically exchangeable
for a locked prison door, a sober commentary on what American liberal
democracy has purchased.

The founders appease Pettigrew by paying him honorary dividends worth
more than mere money in this act of naming. The shadow text continues
to haunt Ratcliffe, though, with the tragedy of missed opportunity: "That
lock," he laments, "That Indian axle grease." His companions "knew, understood.... It was neither the lock nor axle grease; it was the fifteen dollars
which could have been charged to the Indian Department on Ratcliffe's
books and nobody would ever have found it, noticed it, missed it" (496).
Ratcliffe is motivated neither by "greed" nor "corruption" but established
precedent: he has been inflating the accounts with impunity so long that it
seemed as if "it was the United States itself which had voluntarily offered to
show them how to transmute the inevictable lock into proofless and ephemeral axle grease" (497). The golden opportunity is squandered, "leaving in
fact the whole race of man, as long as it endured, forever and irrevocably
fifteen dollars deficit, fifteen dollars in the red" (497). Such a lament typifies
the peripheral manner by which Faulkner tends to create community among
those seduced, transformed, and ultimately shirked by the United States of
America. The "whole race of man" lives unalterably in arrears, very literally
paying for the crimes it was taught to commit and then foreclosed from
executing.

Such moments bear witness to Faulkner's dense entanglement in plural
modalities of dispossession that render his regional, national, racial, and
ethnic allegiances impossible – and perhaps irrelevant – to parse neatly.
What critics have lately acknowledged, though, is that his complex attitudes toward matters of economic and racial justice do, in important ways,
implicate "the whole race of man" polluted and deprived by American ideology and its perversions of market capitalism. Subsequently, Faulkner's
fictional town of Jefferson is itself instantiated over a composite loss – of
freedom, of prosperity, even of Indians, the lock hanging on the jailhouse
door an explicit collapse of freedom's travesties with the forcible exodus of
an entire people – a founding deficit compounded by the petty and monstrous thefts of removal, of slavery, of Reconstruction, of segregation, of
advanced capitalism. Faulkner's noted attraction to the particular tragedy of
Indian Removal as a genealogical episteme is on full view here, as the novel
presents his most extended meditation on the imperial machinations that
extirpated the South's tribes and thereby rendered man irrevocably "in the

red." The fateful exchange is never actually recorded "in the Book … not a ledger but *the* ledger" – suggesting that multiple versions of such accounting exist, but only one containing the real story of the South, the kind that might wait on the commissary shelves to be discovered by the Ike McCaslins or, for that matter, the Sam Fatherses of Faulkner's world.

New Southern Studies critics have been increasingly alert to the alternate ledgers of historical reckoning that lie dormant in Faulkner's fiction. Narratives about American Indian anteriority have been particularly difficult to access, mainly because Faulkner admitted that his Indians were products of pure imagination and that "no Chickasaw would recognize my Chickasaws" (*UVA 2 May 1958*). In his *Indians of Yoknapatawpha* (1974), Lewis Dabney endeavored to prove just how mistaken Faulkner was by measuring his romantic and often grotesque fictions against the historical reality of local tribes.[31] Poststructuralism and postcolonial theory provided critical tools for more complicated confrontations with Faulkner's creations – as the imaginative products he fully intended them to be, and not simply as misrepresented subjects in need of rescue.[32] Yet perhaps one of the trends slowest to develop in either the New Southern Studies or in Faulkner scholarship is a functional awareness of, in broad terms, the multiethnic disruptions to the region's black-white binary. Even Patricia Yaeger's otherwise visionary examination of women's writing fails to transcend its reductive racial contours; as she suggests, and her *Dirt and Desire* affirms, "southern literature, at its best, is … about the intersection of black and white cultures as they influence one another and collide."[33] Gradually, other scholars have since contributed nuanced work on the interactions of immigrant, Native, and other minorities long disturbing – and reinvigorating – the South's stark racial binarisms. Such inclusions are not just politically correct admonishments to the county seat of the culture wars; by exposing the pluralism obscured in a system deeply invested in its historical and ideological dualism, uncanny synergies emerge between the multiple "others" confronting coeval varieties of doom. In other words, unclassified specters on the margins of the traditional South function ambivalently not just as threats but often as allies to its black and white residents, uncomfortable mirrors for the widespread devolution suffered and repressed at various epochs of social, economic, and political upheaval.[34] Faulkner's characters repeatedly manage to align themselves, in uncanny and often outraged ways, with such presences.

Richer understandings of Faulkner's national and global consciousness help us to situate his Indian tropes even more pertinently. Captured in the dishonorable legacies of "Jefferson" at the heart of Yoknapatawpha County, for instance, we confront the paradox of Thomas Jefferson himself as accidental honoree: icon of democratic liberalism, and yet, the original author of the Indian Removal policies that Andrew Jackson enacted, Jefferson desired to eradicate Indians by absorbing them into the American marketplace, programming them for agricultural enterprise and participation in a capitalist economy. The town of Jefferson, then, is even more distinctly an expression of the labored subterfuge encoded in American memory: a heteroglot collision of colonial narratives screened by a valorous label and mythology. Thomas Jefferson Pettigrew's actual surname leaks the truth behind the fetish, as "Pettigrew" is a common name among the Eastern Band of Cherokee. If Faulkner is the self-appointed "sole owner and proprietor" of Yoknapatawpha County, the namesake of its county seat is naturally a proxy for the author himself. Thomas Jefferson Pettigrew is no Quentin Compson or Ike McCaslin, but, suggestively, he *is* described as a scrawny little windbag of a man who works for the post office.

It would be a gross overstatement to suggest that Faulkner harbors any sentient sympathy for Indians per se, save when they merge imperceptibly into the white and black races proper – which, for Faulkner, was simply what happened to the remnant Choctaws and Chickasaws in his home state. Sam Fathers, the part-negro, part-white descendant of tribal royalty functions explicitly as Faulkner's "Last of the Chickasaws" for the twentieth century, bequeathing to Isaac McCaslin the intimate knowledge of both wilderness and freedom imperiled by modernity's march into oblivion. *Requiem for a Nun* is anomalous, in that its Indians are not overtly ghostly or grotesque but tragic victims of the South's avarice. At this midcentury moment of disillusionment and fatigue, Faulkner mocks the American pageant of progress as "a furious beating of hollow drums toward nowhere" – a tune obviously set to the rhythm of indigenous extinction (476). It becomes a contemporary anthem, though, because he does not leave the poor Indians in the dust on the road to Oklahoma. In fact, by referencing Oklahoma at all in a scene set in 1833, he deploys an ideological anachronism, as the actual name for Oklahoma was not even suggested for three more decades and was made official only in 1890. In errors like this, Faulkner implies a knowledge that emerges only obliquely from his works: a notion that displacement is both geographical and psychological, that its iterations are frequent and foreordained, and that the aftermath haunts us and incites us in unnoticed ways.

According to Robert Kirk and Marvin Klotz's glossary of *Faulkner's People* (1965), there is only one other Mail Rider in all of Faulkner's work: in the 1931 story "Idyll in the Desert."[35] Anthologized in the *Uncollected Stories*, "Idyll" is a little-studied, early version of Harry and Charlotte's illicit love story in *The Wild Palms* (1939). The story is related to an unnamed narrator by the "Mail Rider" (named Lucas Crump[36]), effectively rendered the "author" of a narrative that Faulkner himself was busy developing. This tale is one of his rarer works set not in Yoknapatawpha but in the Southwest, at a tuberculosis camp that the mail rider serves. A man arrives there ill, and soon his lover – a married woman – arrives to nurse him. He recuperates and then promptly leaves her behind, now wasting away with the dreaded disease herself. Thinking that her lover will surely return, the woman waits there for eight subsequent years, slowly dying. Her cuckolded husband surfaces instead, sending money periodically; the mail carrier meets the man and engineers a plan to trick her into thinking the cash comes from her missing lover. Upon each delivery, she tosses away the money but savors the gesture of love; moreover, she is never seen eating. Palpably, she is sustained not by worldly goods or even food but solely by the memory and promise of love – and, importantly, by an "Injun" woman that the mail carrier commissions to help care for her.

It is fascinating, of course, that the Indian nurse is part of the intrepid woman's apparatus of survival beyond the bounds of civilization, propriety, and money. But the story ends badly anyway: the woman dies, and neither her remarried lover not her husband recognize her altered body in the end. The story is cryptic, to say the least, but it is the frame narrative that is finally more confounding – and revealing. Throughout the telling of this somber tale, the mail rider Crump habitually gets off track, forgetting where his story is going because he claims he "talks so seldom." When he finally finishes relating his story, the narrator asks in apparent exasperation,

> "Have you got any Indian blood?"
> "Indian blood?"
> "You talk so little. So seldom."
> "Oh, sure. I have some Indian blood. My name used to be Sitting Bull."
> "Used to be?"
> "Sure. I got killed one day a while back. Didn't you read it in the paper?"
>
> (411)

The story abruptly ends here. Both the absurdity and the levity of this exchange are striking in the aftermath of the sober narrative he tells, but when we consider the frame narrative as the real story here, the device that structures our understanding of the emotional turmoil and negotiations he oversees, the closing lines divulge more. Crump watches people arrive at the consumptive camp and drop out of the world and its codes, yet he observes that for most, "the hardest habit of all to break [is] owning things," even on their death beds: "They could live in a house on earth" with "something which, not having ever had any use for it at home, they had done forgot … for years without even knowing where it was, but just try to get them to start to heaven without taking it along" (403). It seems clear that the relationships he witnesses function in much the same way, structured as they are by cash, subterfuge, and dogged fixations on immaterial certainties that never bear fruit. The mail rider thus becomes a tempering influence, a long-silenced and ghostly emissary from another way, doling out cash only for necessaries like food and a buffalo robe to keep the man warm and engineering the pantomime of love that keeps the woman alive for eight long years. These habits of fiscal moderation and healing, we finally discover, are apparently tuned by his reincarnated indigeneity.

Reading the story through this odd frame, the specter of the Indian emerges as a nutritive antidote, as palliative care for those dying, literally, of *consumption* – that infectious disease of not just the lungs but the capitalist organism. The setting deepens the allegory: this "idyll" in the southwestern desert, away from commerce, away from the South, away even from marriage, peopled by Indians like the "Injun" nurse "who couldn't talk enough of any language" to give away the hoax or even to understand anything "better than a rich man sent her to wait there" (409). Neither the Indian woman nor Crump/Sitting Bull seems to speak the language of modern capitalism very well. In the end, though, they reveal and accomplish more than they seem to know or say. Crump "talks so seldom," reticent like most Indians dead or alive in the cultural imagination; and so, Faulkner seems to suggest, their voices and memory are channeled through the modern, conniving operatives of the federal government. It is Crump who is finally responsible for both the delivery of money and the deadly illusions that ultimately destroy. He may be the ghost of Sitting Bull, legendary enemy of the American government and martyr of colonial resistance, but he is also now the conniving spirit of *Requiem*'s Thomas Jefferson Pettigrew. Just before the closing revelation of his Indian blood, and presumably prompting it, the narrator asks: "'You must still have had some of the money the husband sent you to fool her with,' I said. The Mail Rider chewed.... He spat carefully. He wiped his sleeve across his mouth." The narrator follows immediately with the query – "Do you have any Indian blood?" Following his implied accusation, the narrator's question is actually a tacit suggestion that Crump's "Indian blood" is what makes him deceptive, greedy, doomed – and dangerous.

Elsewhere, Faulkner does seem to casually indict his Indian characters for aping the rapacity of the white men they lived among. The Indians sold what was not theirs to sell, setting in motion a multi-generational nightmare of land exchanges and exploitation that would ravage the countryside and its people; they epitomize the weakness of man before the temptations of capitalism, no more immune to its seductions than Pettigrew, or Ratliff, or Flem Snopes. Throughout his career, Faulkner both acknowledges and refuses this fate; his Indians, like his white and black creations, are never historically static or ethically transparent figures. Faulkner's own voice, like the mail carrier's, thus labors on "in the red," incessant but somehow "seldom" heard, wronged but not innocent, working steadily out of the deficit of human folly and exploitation. He absorbs the Indian voice not to absolve historical errors but to confront the more immediate anxieties, ambivalences, and infectious properties of a world in the death throes of consumption. Narratives like this one are about Faulkner himself peering into the "Book" of his nation's founding and, like Ike, repudiating what he sees there but knowing that the transgressions are emblazoned on his very nativity as *both* a Southerner and an American.

NOTES

1 Gilles Deleuze and Claire Parnet, *Dialogues II*, Hugh Tomlinson and Barbara Habberjam (trans.), rev. ed. (New York: Columbia University Press, 2007 [1987]), pp. 131–2.

2 Flannery O'Connor, "Some Aspects of the Grotesque in Southern Fiction," *Mystery and Manners: Occasional Prose* (London: Faber & Faber, 1972), p. 45.

3 Michael Kreyling, "Toward a 'New Southern Studies,'" *South Central Review* 22.1 (Spring 2005), p. 10.

4 Emily Wagster Pettus, "Mitt Romney Faces Skepticism in Republican South," *Huffington Post* (March 9, 2012).

5 Ashley Parker, "Starting the Day, and Ending It, at Romney's Side," *New York Times* (April 6, 2012).

6 Houston A. Baker and Dana Nelson, "Preface: Violence, the Body, and 'The South,'" *American Literature* 73.2 (2001), p. 243.

7 As James Peacock avers in *The American South in a Global World*, the seventeenth and eighteenth-century South "was a node in a network stretching from Europe through the Caribbean to the coast of what was still being colonized" (James Peacock, *The American South in a Global World*, James L. Peacock, Harry L. Watson, and Carrie R. Matthews (eds.), [Chapel Hill: University of North Carolina Press, 2005], p. 265).

8 Richard Gray, "Foreword: Inventing Communities, Imagining Places: Some Thoughts on Southern Self-fashioning," *South to a New Place: Region, Literature, and Culture*, Suzanne W. Jones and Sharon Monteith (eds.) (Baton Rouge: Louisiana State University Press, 2002), p. xxiii.

9 Michael Kreyling, *The South That Wasn't There: Postsouthern Memory and History* [CE: italics](Baton Rouge: Louisiana State University Press, 2010), p. 194. See also Scott Romine, *The Real South: Southern Narrative in the Age of Cultural Reproduction* (Baton Rouge: Louisiana State University Press, 2008).

10 Particularly influential for the New Southern Studies movement were vibrantly interdisciplinary, cross-cultural, and transnational works such as Paul Gilroy, *The Black Atlantic: Modernity and Double Consciousness* (Cambridge, MA: Harvard

University Press, 1995) and Joseph Roach, *Cities of the Dead: Circum-Atlantic Performance* (New York: Columbia University Press, 1996).

11 Michael Kreyling, "Toward 'A New Southern Studies,' " p. 9.

12 Allen Tate, "The New Provincialism," *Collected Essays* (Denver, CO: Alan Swallow, 1959), p. 292.

13 Sarah Gilbreath Ford, "Listening to the Ghosts: The New Southern Studies," *South Central Review*, 22.1 (Spring 2005), 23.

14 Houston A. Baker, *Turning South Again: Re-Thinking Modernism/Re-Reading Booker T.* (Durham, NC: Duke University Press, 2001).

15 Katherine Henninger, "How New? What Place?: Southern Studies and the Rest of the World," *Contemporary Literature*, 45.1 (Spring 2004), 179.

16 John M. Grammer, "Reconstructing Southern Literature," *American Literary History*, 13.1 (Spring 2001), 131.

17 Ted Atkinson, "Cultural Context: *Absalom, Absalom!*" In *Critical Insights: Absalom, Absalom!*, David Madden (ed.) (Baton Rouge: Louisiana State University Press, 2011), p. 64.

18 Jon Smith, *Finding Purple America: The South and the Future of American Cultural Studies* (Athens: University of Georgia Press, 2013), pp. 90–1.

19 Ibid., p. x.

20 Ibid., p. xii.

21 Ibid., p. 91.

22 Ibid., p. 92.

23 Jon Smith and Deborah Cohn (eds.), *Look Away!: The South in New World Studies* (Durham, NC: Duke University Press, 2004).

24 Robert H. Brinkmeyer, Jr., *The Fourth Ghost: White Southern Writers and European Fascism, 1930–1950* (Baton Rouge: Louisiana State University Press, 2009), p. 2. See also Jeanne A. Follansbee, " 'Sweet Fascism in the Piney Woods': *Absalom, Absalom!* as Fascist Fable," *Modernism/Modernity* 18.1 (Jan. 2011), 67–94 and Daniel Spoth's "Totalitarian Faulkner: The Nazi Interpretation of *Light in August* and *Absalom, Absalom!*," *English Literary History* 78.1 (Spring 2011), 239–57.

25 See Leigh Anne Duck, *The Nation's Region: Southern Modernism, Segregation, and U.S. Nationalism* (Athens: University of Georgia Press, 2006) and Jennifer Greeson, *Our South: Geographic Fantasy and the Rise of National Literature* (Cambridge, MA: Harvard University Press, 2010).

26 Édouard Glissant, *Faulkner, Mississippi*, Barbara B. Lewis and Thomas C. Spear (trans.) (Chicago: University of Chicago Press, 2000).

27 Kreyling, "New Southern Studies," p. 9.

28 Richard King, "From Haiti to Mississippi: Faulkner and the Making of the Southern Master-Class," *International Journal of Francophone Studies* 14.1–2 (May 2011), 94.

29 See John T. Matthews, "Many Mansions: Faulkner's Cold War Conflicts," *Global Faulkner: Faulkner and Yoknapatawpha 2006*, Annette Trefzer and Ann J. Abadie (eds.) (Jackson: University Press of Mississippi, 2009) and *William Faulkner: Seeing Through the South* (Malden, MA: Wiley-Blackwell, 2009) and Spencer Morrison, "*Requiem*'s Ruins: Unmaking and Making in Cold War Faulkner," *American Literature* 85.2 (2013), 303–31.

30 Matthews, *Seeing Through the South*, p. 226.

31 Dabney, *Indians of Yoknapatawpha: A Study in Literature and History* (Baton Rouge: LSU Press, 1974).

32 See, for instance, Annette Trefzer's *Disturbing Indians: The Archaeology of Southern Fiction* (Tuscaloosa: University of Alabama Press, 2009), which was the first to examine the use of Indian tropes in a specifically southern, modern, literary context.

33 Patricia Yaeger, *Dirt and Desire: Reconstructing Southern Women's Writing, 1930–1990* (Chicago: University of Chicago Press, 2000), p. 38.

34 As Michael O'Brien notes in his critique of Greeson's *Our South*, "[Greeson] may be too easily dismissive of alternate American 'others' (the West, women, Indians), who also helped to create what passed as American identity." Michael O'Brien, "Our South or Theirs?" *The Southern Literary Journal* 44.1 (Fall 2011), 147.

35 Robert W. Kirk and Marvin Klotz, *Faulkner's People: A Complete Guide and Index to Characters in the Fiction of William Faulkner* (Berkeley: University of California Press, 1965).

36 Suggestively, Lucas Crump's name phonetically echoes that of Lucas Beauchamp, one of Faulkner's most fully developed mixed-race characters (and one who goes digging for gold in an Indian mound); he appears prominently in *Go Down, Moses* (1942), *Intruder in the Dust* (1948), and *The Reivers* (1962).

9

MARTYN BONE

The Faulkner Factor: Influence and Intertextuality in Southern Fiction since 1965

In Barry Hannah's posthumously published short story "Fire Water" (2010), two Mississippi "literary women" ponder how "Both of them had worked in the shadow of this statue. Faulkner." They conclude ruefully that, "Compared, they were only mild grannies with a patient lightbulb inside."[1] Hannah's characters are merely the latest in a long line of U.S. southern writers who have confronted the daunting legacy of William Faulkner. What one might term the Faulkner factor in southern fiction was first identified by Flannery O'Connor fully fifty years before Hannah's story appeared: "The presence alone of Faulkner in our midst makes a great difference in what the writer can and cannot permit himself to do. Nobody wants his mule and wagon stalled on the same track the Dixie Limited is roaring down."[2] Faulkner himself was still alive in 1960, and critic Michael Kreyling has argued that, after winning the 1949 Nobel Prize for Literature, "William Faulkner lived with an additional burden[:] ... himself as institutionalized cultural force." Witnessing the retrospective valorization of his "great" period (from *The Sound and the Fury* in 1929 to, at the latest, *Go Down, Moses* in 1942), Faulkner was the first writer to come "under the influence of his own formidable example" – an "anxiety of influence" that, Kreyling suggests, Faulkner attempted to neuter through self-parody.[3]

The Faulkner factor in southern fiction – or perhaps more pointedly, in southern literary studies – has deep roots. Though Allen Tate declared in 1945 that "the Southern literary renascence ... is over," the hyper-canonization of Faulkner between publication of *The Portable Faulkner* in 1946 and the Nobel award in 1949 also renewed the cultural capital of southern literature.[4] Already in 1950, Tate's Agrarian fellow traveler Donald Davidson could answer his own rhetorical question, "Why does the modern South have a great literature?" by repeatedly referencing the singular achievement of Faulkner.[5] Even as the post-Nobel Faulkner was feted nationally and globally as "an emblem of the freedom of the individual under capitalism,"[6] he was elevated regionally as exhibit A for the burgeoning academic study of modern southern fiction. A sizeable side effect of such maneuvers was that emerging southern writers faced the dubious distinction of being compared to Faulkner by both book reviewers and scholars. William Styron's debut *Lie Down in Darkness* (1951) was the first novel to suffer critical comparison with the newly canonical Faulkner, though Styron's style and subject matter – the tribulations of a dysfunctional white southern family – practically invited comparison with *The Sound and the Fury*. Within a year of Faulkner's death, Louis D. Rubin, a critic who played a crucial role in the institutionalization of southern literary studies, identified Faulkner as the monumental figure that the "southern writer" had to work at "getting out from under."[7] The Faulkner factor became so familiar that, come 1977, a young Mississippi-born author named Richard Ford would offer the caustic yet considered opinion that "'southern writer' [is] an expression which limps from one 'critic' to the next but which almost always is pejorative, hazy in its essentials, and frequently born out of a simple poverty of wit, and which generally means simply *like Faulkner*."[8]

Given the repetitive, even reflexive nature of critics' references to Faulkner, it is perhaps not surprising that successive generations of southern writers have been inclined to regard the Dixie Limited less as a direct influence than an indirect inspiration to do something *different*. Furthermore, to each emerging generation, Faulkner has seemed less obviously the overwhelming individual talent that he appeared to O'Connor and her peers. For southern writers today, Faulkner's contemporaries and immediate successors – Eudora Welty, Richard Wright, Zora Neale Hurston, O'Connor herself, and Cormac McCarthy – have become alternative literary antecedents whose "shadow" must be negotiated. At scholarly conferences on southern literature, it is now commonplace to encounter more panels devoted to Welty than to Faulkner.[9] One recent southern novelist, Madison Smartt Bell, has remarked that another, the late Larry Brown from Faulkner's hometown of Oxford, Mississippi, saw Cormac McCarthy as "a more significant figure in the literary pantheon than Faulkner his own self."[10] For selected black southern writers since the Civil Rights era, Faulkner has remained significant but for somewhat different reasons: less a "statue" to get out from under, than still the most monumental white *male* southern author to write back against and beyond. As Alice Walker starkly remarked in 1975, "The fact that in Mississippi no one even remembers where Richard Wright lived, while Faulkner's house is maintained by a black caretaker, is painful.... For a long time I will feel Faulkner's house, O'Connor's house, crushing me."[11]

Among southern writers who began to publish after Faulkner's death in July 1962, the Faulkner factor became most immediately and perniciously apparent in the first decade of Cormac McCarthy's career. When McCarthy published his debut novel *The Orchard Keeper* (1965), a tragic family tale set in rural Tennessee, *The New York Times* review was headlined "Still Another Disciple of William Faulkner" and opined that McCarthy employed "so many of Faulkner's literary devices and mannerisms that he half submerges his own talents beneath a flood of imitation."[12] That McCarthy was published by Random House and worked with Faulkner's editor, Albert Erskine, no doubt fueled such comparisons, which culminated with the publication of McCarthy's third novel *Child of God* (1973). Less lyrical and pastoral than *The Orchard Keeper*, *Child of God* is a bleak, often brutal account of the protagonist Lester Ballard's displacement from his family home in the east Tennessee mountains, and descent into murder and necrophilia. Reviewing *Child of God* in the *Washington Post*, Jonathan Yardley enthused that "McCarthy is perhaps the closest we have to a genuine heir to the Faulkner tradition. Yet he is not merely a skilled imitator. His novels have a stark, mythic quality that is very much their own ... *Child of God* is an extraordinary book."[13] But in 1976, southern literary scholar Walter Sullivan lambasted *Child of God* as not merely a debasement of Faulkner's vision but "an affront to decency on every level." For Sullivan, though *The Hamlet* had charted "the victory of Snopesism," still "Faulkner retained hope about southern society" and emphasized "man's fidelity and his capacity to love"; even Ike Snopes's notorious sexual relationship with a cow derived from "selfless" love. Whereas, in *The Hamlet*, "enduring man is almost a match for original sin, and in this sense he will prevail," in *Child of God*, McCarthy had "declared war" on "myth" and "community."[14]

Matthew Guinn has noted that the "frantic level of vitriol" in Sullivan's assessment of McCarthy "represents in microcosm the unwillingness of the old guard of southern literati to accommodate younger writers of iconoclastic vision."[15] But if Sullivan's eschatological take on (the end of) southern literary history exaggerated the supposed moral decline from Faulkner to McCarthy – or from Ike Snopes to Lester Ballard – one might still recognize the contrasting visions of "community" in *Child of God* and another Faulkner novel, the one with which it shares some formal features. In *As I Lay Dying*, minor characters who narrate and participate in the Bundren family's journey to Jefferson express compassion and a sense of communal obligation or "Christian duty" during and despite the grotesque sequence of events: as Vernon Tull deadpans, "Like most folks around here, I done holp him [Anse Bundren] so much already I cant quit now" (69, 33). By contrast, while the character-narrators who comment on Lester's background provide some hints as to why he has become so unhinged – referring to the auction of the Ballard homestead, one community member observes early on that "Lester Ballard never could hold his head right after that" – it also becomes evident that they ostracize Lester from any potentially redemptive sense of participating in the "community."[16] Moreover, whereas *As I Lay Dying* features individualized participant-observers, in *Child of God*, the anonymity of each community member's voice, and the way in which those voices recede entirely as the novel proceeds, formally amplify Ballard's isolation.

Later critics and novelists have been rather more sanguine than Sullivan about the nature of McCarthy's relationship to Faulkner. In 2000, Madison Smartt Bell suggested that "McCarthy is one of the very few writers to walk through the shadow of Faulkner's high style and survive the experience." Bell appreciates in Faulkner and McCarthy's fiction a mutual mastery of vernacular dialogue combined with a denser omniscient form characterized by grand rhetorical flourishes. He does faintly echo Sullivan when qualifying that "despite a very strong current of fatalism in his work, Faulkner is a humanist, first and last.... McCarthy is not a humanist"; yet for Bell, it is precisely the "power and intensity of [McCarthy's] vision," in which man has no control over the order of the universe, that "sets McCarthy free of Faulkner's influence."[17] McCarthy further liberated his fiction from (critical comparisons to) Faulkner by relocating all five of his novels between *Blood Meridian* (1985) and *No Country for Old Men* (2005) from the Deep South to the Texas-Mexican borderlands.

When Richard Ford published *A Piece of My Heart* (1976), fellow novelist Larry McMurtry scored Ford's "neo-Faulknerism" in *The New York Times*: "The South–dadgummit–has struck again, marring what might have been an excellent first novel."[18] Here one can begin to fathom Ford's frustration circa 1977 that "southern writer" had come to mean "simply *like Faulkner*"; Ford's exasperation is all the more understandable if one reads *A Piece of My Heart* not as mere "neo-Faulknerism" but rather as an early (if not entirely successful) example of postsouthern parody. Drawing on Linda Hutcheon's notion of postmodern literary parody, Kreyling defines postsouthern parody as a metafictional mode of writing that "lightens the burden of southern literariness it must necessarily carry in the presence of 'Faulkner' triumphant."[19] Kreyling identifies postsouthern parody of Faulkner in the work of Reynolds Price, Harry Crews, and Barry Hannah, but Ford's early novels fit the bill too – especially, in *A Piece of My Heart*, with the character of Mississippian lawyer Sam Newel.

When we first meet Newel, he is living in Chicago but pondering a return trip to his home state to confront his family history. Newel's nocturnal conversations about that history with his cousin and lover Beebe Henley recall Quentin Compson in garrulous dialog with Shreve McCannon in their freezing Harvard dorm room. It becomes apparent, however, that Newel is merely acting out received ideas of southern identity as bound up with the inexorable burden of history and pull of place. Of boyhood trips with his father, a traveling salesman, Newel remembers "all those goddamned rooms, in Hammond, Louisiana, and Tuscaloosa.... Just come in late in the afternoon, have a drink of whiskey, go down and eat your dinner in some greasy fly-speck café ... go back to the *room*, and lie in bed listening to the plumbing fart, until it was late enough to go to sleep. And that was *all.*"[20] In contrast to Faulkner's fiction, where the phrase "And that was all" is interjected at moments of extreme tension, there really is nothing more to be said: for all that Newel wants to transmute the stuff of his family history into a fully Faulknerian tragic sensibility, his father's itinerant life signifies nothing. Later, disembarking the train in Memphis, Newel wades into the Mississippi river, self-consciously recasting a "Quentissential" scene: Quentin Compson's suicide in the Charles River.[21] But following this flirtation with a suitably southern literary suicide, the scene becomes comic rather than tragic as Newel realizes "that his shorts were now gone and he was floating with his privates adangle in the cold current, prey to any browsing fish"; humiliatingly, he has to be rescued by two unimpressed bargemen.[22] In these and similar scenes, it is not Ford but Newel who is acting out the "learned behavior" of "Quentin's 'experience' of the South"; eventually, Newel's entropic search for a burdensome southern family history runs down into a bathetic realization that his childhood in Mississippi "was boring as shit," and he slinks off back to Chicago.[23] Yet after the "heartbreaking" experience of being reviewed as still another disciple of Faulkner, Ford resolved "to get my work out of the South as much as I possibly could."[24] In the first two volumes of his award-winning Bascombe trilogy, *The Sportswriter* (1986) and *Independence Day* (1995), Ford followed McCarthy in moving his novels out of the South altogether – in his case, to New Jersey and Michigan. Furthermore, to the degree Ford maintained an intertextual dialogue with his southern literary precursors, the Bascombe books engaged with Walker Percy more than Faulkner.[25]

Kreyling singles out Barry Hannah's fiction as "aggressively postsouthern" in its use of parody to get out from under Faulkner.[26] Born in Mississippi in 1942, Hannah was shadowed by critical comparisons to Faulkner from the start of his career, when his ramblingly inventive bildungsroman *Geronimo Rex* (1972), like McCarthy's *The Orchard Keeper* before it, won the William Faulkner Prize. Hannah's fiction does occasionally acknowledge that Faulkner's legacy can seem daunting, perhaps especially for an author who moved to Faulkner's hometown in 1982 and lived in Oxford until his death in 2010. In Hannah's semi-autobiographical novel *Boomerang* (1991), the narrator remarks, "All the Confederate dead and the Union dead planted in the soil near us. All of Faulkner the great. Christ, there's barely room for the living down here."[27] However, Hannah frequently expressed chagrin at "lazy" interviewers "asking me what it's like to be an heir to Faulkner, or what it's like writing in the shadow of Faulkner," while his fiction disarms "Faulkner the great" with brazen humor and stylistic verve: in the midcareer novella *Hey Jack* (1987), cocaine-tooting, whiskey-swilling rock star Ronnie Foot simulates sex on Faulkner's grave, "never giving up the night until he came, with a shout."[28] Even when the two "literary women" in "Fire Water" ponder their inferiority to Faulkner, the narrative's free indirect discourse notes "the way he [Faulkner] wrote like an octopus with pencils" – the kind of surreal simile that Faulkner would never have employed and which established Hannah's own singular reputation for making language "juggle with its snout, standing on its tail."[29]

"Dragged Fighting from his Tomb," from Hannah's celebrated story collection *Airships* (1978), is especially noteworthy here for its intertextual recasting of the early scene from *Sartoris* (1929) in which Confederate soldiers "Carolina" Bayard Sartoris and J. E. B. Stuart gallivant through a Union camp. In *Sartoris*, it is initially Jenny du Pre who tells the tale of Bayard and Stuart's raid, allowing Faulkner's third-person narrator to offer a wry commentary on the way Jenny's verbose anecdote feeds into the wider white southern mythos of Confederate heroism: "as she grew older the tale itself grew richer and richer ... until what had been a harebrained prank of two heedless and reckless boys wild with their own youth had become a gallant and finely tragical focal point to which the history of the race had been raised from out the old miasmic swamps of spiritual sloth by two angels valiantly fallen and strayed" (9). Yet, as the story of Stuart and Bayard proceeds, the third-person narrator takes over the role of more and more richly telling the tale; only when the scene closes does the narrative return to Jenny's voice "proud and still as banners in the dust" (19). Furthermore, *Sartoris* renders Stuart as a cavalier figure operating in "a spirit of pure fun" (9): the narrator insists that "neither Jeb Stuart nor Bayard Sartoris, as their actions clearly showed, had any political convictions involved at all" (10). By contrast, Hannah's Stuart is repeatedly figured as a ruthless exponent of modern total war. In "Dragged Fighting from His Tomb," the narrator, a gay Confederate captain called Howard, sets aside his sexual attraction to Stuart to begin questioning both the role of slavery in the Confederate cause and the general's aggressive military strategy: "You shit! What are we doing killing people in Pennsylvania?"[30] Howard's disgust at Stuart's tactics becomes so deep that he deserts, joins the Union, and kills Stuart. As in the novella *Ray* (1980) and later stories like "That Was Close, Ma" (1995), here we see how Hannah not only parodies the southern literary legacy of

"Faulkner the great" but also interrogates his precursor's sometimes romantic representations of white southern masculinity.[31]

During the 1950s and until his death in July 1962, Faulkner struggled to reconcile his conflicted views on southern race relations with his post-Nobel status as a reluctant spokesman for the region and an elder statesman of both southern and American letters. Faulkner died only two months before the riot on the University of Mississippi campus that followed James Meredith's attempt to integrate the university; his nephew Murry was part of the local National Guard deployed to campus and suffered a broken arm after being struck by a brick.[32] In Hannah's story "Lastward, Deputy James" (2010), the narrator, who witnessed the riot as "captain of the state National Guard," remarks that "The Nobel Laureate William Faulkner died in the hot July preceding the September riots. It was good he didn't have to watch. He was a racial moderate, read *nigger lover* in these parts then, and left much of his estate to the United Negro College Fund.... not all of us were rot."[33] By Faulkner's death, however, many African-American writers had long since become disillusioned with the Nobel Laureate and what they saw as the "rot" he spoke about southern race relations. In 1956, Faulkner was widely criticized for the gradualist stance on integration expressed in his *Life* essay "A Letter to the North"; the attacks intensified following Faulkner's infamous remark to a journalist in London that he would "fight for Mississippi against the United States even if it meant going out into the street and shooting Negroes" (*LG* 261). James Baldwin ridiculed the "squire of Oxford" for being more concerned with transforming white southern recalcitrance into "high and noble tragedy" than supporting black southerners' civil rights.[34]

Though Baldwin was better known nationally and internationally, prominent black southern writers were, if anything, even more disillusioned with Faulkner. Alabamian Albert Murray seethed privately to Ralph Ellison that Faulkner was a "Son of a bitch [who] prefers a handful of anachronistic crackers to everything that really gives him reason not only for being but for writing." Georgia-born John Oliver Killens addressed his disappointment more directly to Faulkner, writing that "We deemed you much bigger than Mississippi" and "looked to you for intellectual leadership."[35] Over the next decade, Killens's disillusionment hardened. In the prologue to his third novel *'Sippi* (1967), Killens figured Faulkner as a "famous Mississippi plantation owner" who pals around with fictional planter Charlie Wakefield: "Oh yes, he and Willie Faulkner had emptied many a bottle of Scotch and bourbon together in their day, and laughed about the poor-ass peckerwoods and commiserated over the poor down-trodden colored people, especially those of the 'noble savage' genre."[36] Throughout *'Sippi*, Wakefield envisions himself in the Faulknerian vein as an enlightened figure: a progressive, even cosmopolitan alternative to both the local white power elite and "ignorant peckerwoods." Wakefield pays for the university education of Chuck Othello Chaney, the son of a black sharecropper on the Wakefield plantation, as part of a larger plan to groom Chuck as "a moderating influence" in the midst of the Civil Rights Movement. However, Chuck is radicalized by his time away at a black southern college, and his belated engagement with the grassroots activism of his fellow black Mississippians at home. When it becomes apparent to Wakefield that Chuck is less than receptive to his Faulknerian message of moderation – "I'm saying, go slow.... Willie Faulkner was a friend of mine.... All I'm saying is what he advocated" – the veneer of paternalistic benevolence vanishes. After exhorting Chuck to "slow up on this Black Power! This spreading racial hatred!," Wakefield himself recapitulates the violent racial antagonism of Faulkner's most notorious statement: "But can't you see, if it comes to that, I'll have to join up with the peckerwoods and shoot down Negroes on the streets of Wakefield City."[37] 'Sippi's searing critique of Faulkner's racial politics segued into Killens's scathing attack on Styron's controversial novel *The Confessions of Nat Turner* (1967), in which Killens dismissed "Willie Styron" as "inheritor of the mantle bequeathed to him by 'Sippian Willie Faulkner" and similarly unable "to transcend his southern-peckerwood background."[38] At such moments, the chasm between white and black southern writers sometimes seemed wider than ever before.

Yet, since the early 1970s, some black southern writers have developed deeper – if still often difficult – dialogues with Faulkner's fiction. Beginning with his first published story in 1958, Ernest Gaines produced a series of novels and stories set in the sugarcane country of southwestern Louisiana; this multi-volume, microcosmic literary geography almost inevitably generated critical comparison with Faulkner's Yoknapatawpha saga. Citing Gaines's "attention to place and community ... his awareness of the past in the present," and a sense that "none except perhaps Styron resembles Faulkner so much as Gaines," critic Fred Hobson identified Gaines's fiction with "the old power of southern fiction," at a time when Gaines's white southern contemporaries like Hannah and Bobbie Ann Mason seemed immersed in a "postmodern world."[39] Gaines himself has remarked that "Faulkner is one of my favorite writers, and what Southern writer has not been influenced by him in the past fifty years?"[40] However, Gaines has also stated that "I could no more agree with his [Faulkner's] philosophy no more than I could agree with [George] Wallace's"; indeed, it was not Faulkner's fiction or philosophy but Meredith's struggle to enroll at the University of Mississippi that "would change my [Gaines'] life forever" and inspire his writing.[41] For all that Gaines follows Faulkner in focusing on "*his* particular postage stamp of native soil," the defining locus in Gaines's fiction is the black quarters that originated in plantation slavery; if Gaines's characters practice a sense of place, community, and "Faulknerian fusion of the grave and the comic," they do so within and despite the South's oppressive historical and spatial structures.[42] *A Gathering of Old Men* (1983) is the Gaines novel that formally most resembles one of Faulkner's: like *As I Lay Dying*, it features fifteen different character narrators. Furthermore, as Hobson notes, it features a litany of characters "who would be at home in Faulkner's Yoknapatawpha," from the local sheriff to the alcoholic, Compson-like landowner.[43] However, whereas blacks remain at best marginal to *As I Lay Dying*, and critics have debated the lack of black characters and narrators in Faulkner's fiction generally, *A Gathering of Old Men* is formally and thematically focused on black southern males speaking and fighting back following decades of subjection to white supremacy.

Another, more recent novel by a black southern author that signifies powerfully on *As I Lay Dying* is Jesmyn Ward's National Book Award winner *Salvage the Bones* (2011). Completed while Ward was based in Oxford as visiting writer-in-residence at the University of Mississippi, *Salvage the Bones* details twelve days in the lives of a poor black family in Bois Sauvage, on the Mississippi Gulf Coast; on the eleventh day, Hurricane Katrina hits. Ward's second novel signals its intertextuality in the opening section, when the remarkable teenaged narrator, Esch Batiste, mentions that "After my ninth-grade year, we read *As I Lay Dying*, and I made an A because I answered the hardest question right: *Why does the young boy think his mother is a fish?*"[44] This early reference to Faulkner's fifth novel serves to alert readers to its numerous thematic echoes in *Salvage the Bones*. In both novels, the mother is deceased: Esch's Mama died giving birth to her younger brother, Claude Junior, who in turn recalls Vardaman Bundren's childish naivety about the complex realities swirling around the family. Esch herself, newly pregnant but largely ignored by Manny, a friend of her brother Randall, recalls Dewey Dell, abandoned by her lover Lafe; there are rhetorical resemblances too, as when Esch's vividly elemental description of how a gutted squirrel's "blood smells like wet hot earth after summer rain"[45] echoes Dewey Dell's figuration of herself as "like a wet seed wild in the hot blind earth" (64). Esch's middle brother Skeetah resembles Jewel Bundren in his obsessive relationship with a domesticated animal. Where Jewel works nights clearing Lon Quick's land to buy the "sweet son of a bitch" horse, which he curses "*in a whisper of obscene caress*" (13, 183), Skeet funds China's special diet by going "to the Catholic church and convinc[ing] them to pay him to cut the grass and pull weeds at the graveyard"; he addresses China as "my girl.... Always

my bitch."[46] Moreover, much as Darl is the only Bundren brother to perceive Dewey Dell's predicament, so Skeet alone among the three Batiste
boys intuits that Esch is pregnant. Such parallels surely inform novelist
Nicholas Delbanco's observation, in a blurb for the hardcover jacket of
Salvage the Bones, that Ward's "memorable clan deals with the threat and
then the actuality of Hurricane Katrina in much the way that Faulkner's
folk dealt with fire and flood." The *tour de force* eleventh section, in which
Esch describes the impact of Hurricane Katrina and the flooding of the
Batiste homeplace, resembles the sequence in *As I Lay Dying* when the
Bundrens attempt to ford the swollen river at Samson's bridge.

But for all that *Salvage the Bones* riffs on *As I Lay Dying*, it would be
much too simple to say that – in the words of John Frow's widely publicized plagiarism charge against Graham Swift's *Last Orders* (1996) – "its
plot and formal structure, is almost identical to that novel."[47] In contrast
to *As I Lay Dying*'s multiple character narrators, *Salvage the Bones* is
told entirely by Esch. And Esch does not make any further references to
Faulker's novel; instead, she repeatedly references the Greek myth of Medea
and Jason, through which Esch transfigures her own inauspicious love for
Manny. What is more, in interviews, Ward echoes Gaines by acknowledging
Faulkner's example as a fellow southern writer, even while emphasizing the
distance between Faulkner's worldview and her own. In 2011, *The Paris
Review* put to Ward a familiar question: "As a writer from the South, you
are fated to be compared with Faulkner. How do you contend with his legacy?" Ward responded that "The first time I read *As I Lay Dying*, I was so
awed I wanted to give up. I thought, 'He's done it, perfectly. Why the hell am
I trying?'" However, she then stressed that "the failures of some of his black
characters – the lack of imaginative vision regarding them, the way they don't
display the full range of human emotion, how they fail to live fully on the
page – work against that awe and goad me to write." One might argue that,
in social and economic terms, the black southern working-class Batistes are
(like the English working class family and friends who mourn butcher Jack
Dodds in Swift's *Last Orders*) not so far removed from the white southern
working class Bundrens. Nevertheless, the racialized "failures" of Faulkner's
fiction were for Ward not merely troubling but a negative example to write
back against. She insists that "The stories I write are particular to my community and my people," and, as with Gaines, Ward's literary geography
resonates powerfully with the author's home locale: Delisle, Mississippi,
is vividly rendered in Ward's 2013 memoir *Men We Reaped*, while Bois
Sauvage is also the setting of her 2008 debut novel *Where the Line Bleeds*.[48]
Hence, like Gaines's *Gathering* – or *Getting Mother's Body* (2003), the
debut novel of another black southern writer, Suzan-Lori Parks – *Salvage*

the Bones can be seen as a necessary *re*-vision, across the color line and at the local scale, of Faulkner's limited Dixie "vision" in *As I Lay Dying*.

Yet, in the same *Paris Review* interview, Ward also states: "It infuriates me that the work of white American writers can be universal and lay claim to classic texts, while black and female authors are ghetto-ized as 'other.' " Ward's desire to square (to adapt Kenneth Warren's phrase) black *southern* particularity with something more "universal" also helps to explain why she "wanted to align Esch with ... the universal figure of Medea, the antihero, to claim that tradition as part of my Western literary heritage."[49] But by the same token, and despite Ward's reservations about Faulkner's racialized "failures," *Salvage the Bones*' intertextual and cross-racial signifying on a major modern novel by a Nobel Prize-winning author can be seen as another way to locate herself within a larger "literary heritage" – both U.S. southern and "Western," regional and "universal." To Frow's charge that *Last Orders* plagiarized *As I Lay Dying*, Swift responded that it "is a story of how the living deal with the recently dead. It has been told by countless writers."[50] Ward's *Paris Review* interview includes a similar observation that *Salvage the Bones*' "larger story of the survivor, the *savage*, is essentially a universal, human one."[51] In this move from the local to the universal scale, then, both *As I Lay Dying* and *Salvage the Bones* become takes on archetypal tales "told by countless writers." This may illuminate not only the protean adaptability of *As I Lay Dying* (in theater, dance, and film as well as other novels) but also Faulkner's opinion that "there is nothing new to be said" in literature – that ultimately "Shakespeare, Balzac, Homer have all written about the same things" (*LG* 238).

Much more could be said here about how other post-1965 writing from and about the U.S. South compares with, adapts, parodies, or interrogates Faulkner. For example, though recent scholarship within Faulkner studies and "new southern studies" has engaged with Faulkner's impact on Latin American fiction, foundational texts in the field of Chicano literary studies, such as Tomás Rivera's *This Migrant Earth* (in Spanish, 1971; English translation, 1987) and Rolando Hinojosa's *Klail City* (in Spanish, 1976; English translation, 1987), remain largely off the radar of Faulkner and southern literature scholars alike – even though both writers were born in Texas and have been tentatively compared to Faulkner for their experimental form (Rivera) and multivolume literary geography (Hinojosa). As for those hoary accusations of neo-Faulknerism leveled at southern writers since the 1960s, they endure without prevailing. The publication in 2013 of *Southern Cross the Dog*, a novel set in 1920s Mississippi and written by Bill Cheng, a Chinese-American author from Queens, prompted the *New York Times* to observe that "Mr. Cheng might have dedicated his novel not to bluesmen but to Southern gothic writers like William Faulkner, Flannery O'Connor and Cormac McCarthy."[52] If the vein and venue of the review is familiar, it does at least demonstrate that the burden of bearing and defining southern literary history is no longer solely assigned to Faulkner, and that younger writers are as likely to be read by reviewers as needing to get (in Alice Walker's phrase) "beyond the peacock" as out from under the Dixie Limited. Finally, one suspects that Faulkner himself would have had little patience with narratives of (southern) literary history and influence that foreground decline, anxiety, inferiority, imitation, plagiarism, or the fear of being (like Gavin Blount in "A Return") "born too late" (*US* 567). For, as Faulkner remarked in 1956, any writer at any time should and "will rob, borrow, beg, or steal from anybody and everybody to get the work done" (*LG* 239).

NOTES

1 Barry Hannah, "Fire Water," *Long, Last, Happy: New and Selected Stories* (New York: Grove Press, 2010), pp. 388–9.
2 Flannery O'Connor, "Some Aspects of the Grotesque in Southern Fiction," *Mystery and Manners: Occasional Prose* (London: Faber & Faber, 1972), p. 45.
3 Michael Kreyling, *Inventing Southern Literature* (Jackson: University Press of Mississippi, 1998), pp. 130, 137.
4 Allen Tate, "The New Provincialism," in *Essays of Four Decades* (Chicago: Swallow Press, 1969), p. 535.
5 Donald Davidson, "Why the Modern South has a Great Literature," *Still Rebels, Still Yankees and Other Essays* (Baton Rouge: Louisiana State University Press, 1972), p. 161.
6 Lawrence Schwartz, *Creating Faulkner's Reputation: The Politics of Modern Literary Criticism* (Knoxville: University of Tennessee Press, 1988), p. 4.
7 Louis D. Rubin, "The Difficulties of Being a Southern Writer Today, or, Getting Out from Under William Faulkner," *Journal of Southern History*, 29.4 (1963), 486–94.
8 Richard Ford, "Walker Percy: Not Just Whistling Dixie," *National Review* (May 13, 1977), 561.
9 At the last five conferences of the Society for the Study of Southern Literature, the tally of panels focusing on Faulkner and Welty was: 2012: Welty panels 4, Faulkner panels 0; 2010: Welty 2, Faulkner 3; 2008: Welty 3, Faulkner 1; 2006: Welty 2, Faulkner 1; 2004: Welty 2, Faulkner 2 (in 2004, there were two other panels entitled "Confronting Racial Trauma in Welty and Faulkner," and "Teaching Welty Instead of Faulkner").
10 Madison Smartt Bell, "A Writer's View of Cormac McCarthy," *Myth, Legend, Dust: Critical Responses to Cormac McCarthy*, Rich Wallach (ed.) (Manchester: Manchester University Press, 2000), p. 6.

11 Alice Walker, "Beyond the Peacock: The Reconstruction of Flannery O'Connor," *In Search of Our Mother's Gardens: Womanist Prose* (London: The Women's Press, 1984), p. 58.

12 Orville Prescott, "Still Another Disciple of William Faulkner," *New York Times* (May 12, 1965), www.nytimes.com/1965/05/12/books/mccarthy-orchard.html.

13 Jonathan Yardley, "Alone, Alone, All, All Alone," *Washington Post Book World* (January 13, 1974), p. 1.

14 Walter Sullivan, *A Requiem for the Renascence: The State of Fiction in the Modern South* (Athens: University of Georgia Press, 1976), 71, pp. xviii, 72.

15 Matthew Guinn, *After Southern Modernism: Fiction of the Contemporary South* (Jackson: University Press of Mississippi, 2000), p. 92.

16 Cormac McCarthy, *Child of God* (London: Picador, 1989), p. 9.

17 Bell, "A writer's view," pp. 4, 10.

18 Larry McMurtry, review of Richard Ford's *A Piece of My Heart, New York Times Book Review*, October 24, 1976, p. 16.

19 Kreyling, *Inventing Southern Literature*, p. 161.

20 Richard Ford, *A Piece of My Heart* (London: Harvill, 1996), p. 81.

21 For "Quentissential," see Kreyling, *Inventing Southern Literature*, p. 110.

22 Ford, *A Piece of My Heart*, p. 88.

23 Kreyling, *Inventing Southern Literature*, p. 106; Ford, *A Piece of My Heart*, p. 229.

24 Graham Thompson and R. J. Ellis, "Interview with Richard Ford," *Over Here: A European Journal of American Culture*, 16.2 (winter 1996), 114.

25 See my book *The Postsouthern Sense of Place in Contemporary Fiction* (Baton Rouge: Louisiana State University Press, 2005).

26 Kreyling, *Inventing Southern Literature*, p. 161.

27 Barry Hannah, *Boomerang/Never Die* (Jackson: Banner Books, 1994), pp. 137–8.

28 Daniel E. Williams, "Interview with Barry Hannah," *Perspectives on Barry Hannah*, Martyn Bone (ed.) (Jackson: University Press of Mississippi, 2007), p. 185; Barry Hannah, *Hey Jack!* (New York: Penguin, 1987), p. 122.

29 Hannah, "Fire Water," p. 389; Ivan Gold, "Yoknapatawpha County of the Mind," review of Barry Hannah, *The Tennis Handsome, New York Times Book Review* (May 1, 1983), p. 19.

30 Hannah, "Dragged Fighting from His Tomb," *Airships* (New York: Knopf, 1978), p. 58.

31 See my essay "Neo-Confederate Narrative and Postsouthern Parody: Hannah and Faulkner," *Perspectives on Barry Hannah*, Martyn Bone (ed.), pp. 85–101.

32 See Charles Eagles, *The Price of Defiance: James Meredith and the Integration of Ole Miss* (Chapel Hill: University of North Carolina Press, 2009), p. 367.

33 Hannah, "Fire Water," 426.

34 James Baldwin, "Faulkner and Desegregation," *Nobody Knows My Name* (New York: The Dial Press, 1961), pp. 118, 119.

35 Murray and Killens quoted in Lawrence Jackson, *The Indignant Generation: A Narrative History of African American Writers and Critics, 1934–1960* (Princeton, NJ: Princeton University Press, 2011), pp. 415–16. Killens's essay was never published.

36 John Oliver Killens, *'Sippi* (New York: Trident, 1967), p. viii.

37 Ibid., p. 396, pp. 398–9.
38 John Oliver Killens, "The Confessions of Willie Styron," *William Styron's Nat Turner: Ten Black Writers Respond*, John Henrik Clarke (ed.) (Boston: Beacon Press, 1968), pp. 35–6.
39 Fred Hobson, *The Southern Writer in the Postmodern World* (Athens: University of Georgia Press, 1991), pp. 92, 95, 93.
40 Ernest Gaines, "Mozart and Leadbelly," *Mozart and Leadbelly: Stories and Essays* (New York: Knopf, 2005), p. 28.
41 Fred Beauford, "A Conversation with Ernest Gaines," John Lowe (ed.), *Conversations with Ernest Gaines* (Jackson: University Press of Mississippi, 1995), p. 19; "Mozart and Leadbelly," p. 24.
42 Hobson, *Southern Writer*, p. 95, p. 96.
43 Ibid., p. 97.
44 Jesmyn Ward, *Salvage the Bones* (New York: Bloomsbury, 2011), p. 7.
45 Ibid., p. 47.
46 Ibid, pp. 28–9, 101.
47 Frow quoted in Chris Blackhurst, "A Swift rewrite, or a tribute?" *The Independent*, March 9, 1997, http://www.independent.co.uk/news/uk/home -news/a-swift-rewrite-or-a-tribute-1271831.html.
48 Elizabeth Hoover, "Jesmyn Ward on *Salvage the Bones*," *The Paris Review*, August 30, 2011, http://www.theparisreview.org/blog/2011/08/30/jesmyn-ward -on-salvage-the-bones/.
49 Hoover, "Jesmyn Ward"; on "black particularity," see Kenneth Warren, *What Was African American Literature?* (Cambridge, MA: Harvard University Press, 2011), p. 46 and chapter 2 passim.
50 Swift quoted in Blackhurst, "A Swift rewrite."
51 Hoover, "Jesmyn Ward."
52 Dwight Garner, "Imagining a Past That Isn't His Own," *New York Times*, May 21, 2013, http://www.nytimes.com/2013/05/22/books/southern-cross-the-dog-a -novel-by-bill-cheng.html?_r=0.

10

BENJAMIN WIDISS

They Endured: The Faulknerian Novel and Post-45 American Fiction

Speaking with Jean Stein in *The Paris Review* in 1956, Faulkner famously rated his work and that of his peers a "splendid failure to do the impossible" (*LG* 238). This resonant formulation condenses a somewhat more elaborate self-accounting in a letter to Malcolm Cowley, editor of *The Portable Faulkner*, a dozen years earlier. There, Faulkner attributed his "involved formless 'style' " and "endless sentences" to the desire to go one step beyond the attempt he saw in Thomas Wolfe's work "to say everything, the world plus 'I' or filtered through 'I' or the effort of 'I' to embrace the world in which he was born and walked a little while and then lay down again, in one volume." Faulkner's yet more ambitious goal was to distill experience even further, "to say it all in one sentence, between one Cap and one period ... to put it all, if possible, on one pinhead." He again admitted defeat: "I don't know how to do it. All I know to do is to keep on trying in a new way."[1] But if the effort to condense the whole of world and self into the space of a novel, and then the novel onto the head of a pin, is where "the impossible" irrefutably rears its head, where Faulkner views the modernist project as foundering on the grandeur of its own ambitions, it has also in the decades since Faulkner's writing – and on the strength thereof – become a primary site of the literary possible, and of the possible conceived in uniquely literary terms.

Faulkner turns his adjectives of privation – "formless," "endless" – against themselves to convey the plenitude that accords his style to his aspirations: the caveats and corollaries forever linking one object or idea or event to the next, to the previous, and to the myriad others before and beyond. The world cannot be reduced to the head of a pin, but it can at least be reproduced in such a fashion that the pinpoint of any location within the text not only can but must open onto all the rest through ligatures that are primarily temporal and conceptual rather than spatial. Such a model, in which the referentiality of traditional realist representation is complemented and at length superseded by the cross-referential integument of the literary text, points to the core of Faulkner's endeavor. The impossibility of an infinite reduction of space is requited by the infinite elasticity and manipulability of novelistic time, layered again and again upon itself to create within the novel itself a space, an experience, and a mode of comprehension productively at odds with any to be had outside the text.

Faulkner's perennial concerns of inheritance, guilt, and other determinations bequeathed by the past are enabled by this style even as they undergird it, as are the tangles of consanguinity and the abiding domestic curses that express these themes through character, setting, and incident. In the pages that follow I will trace this representational nexus as itself an inheritance in a handful of novels marking out the literary generations succeeding Faulkner. The legacies of blood and the portentous but crumbling edifices that house them carry down through these generations, bringing with them the Faulknerian expedients of temporal skating and pleating (and those of neologism, syntactical daring, and perspectival multiplication) in pursuit of the continuing project of bringing literature to bear on the haunting burden of historical violence and dispossession. But Faulkner's notion of insufficiency eventually evolves into a far more sanguine estimation of the adequacy and value of a literary response, still reproducing failure within the text but at the same time proposing the accomplishments of the text in an increasingly positive light. Crucial to that development is the interpolation of the Latin American reception of Faulkner into the North American narrative, and emblematic for this discussion will be the utility of reading Gabriel García Márquez's *One Hundred Years of Solitude* as a relay point between Faulkner's *Absalom, Absalom!* and Toni Morrison's *Beloved*.[2] From the consideration of these three masterpieces, born of their authors' full artistic maturity, I will turn to *The Virgin Suicides* and *Everything is Illuminated*, Jeffrey Eugenides's and Jonathan Safran Foer's first novels.[3] Here we can see the Faulknerian inheritance, as transmuted by Morrison and García Márquez, being brought to bear as a means of inaugurating a novelistic praxis – one predicated, in part, on the enduring success of Faulkner's "failures."[4]

Failure of all sorts is of course endemic to Faulkner's corpus, and characters like Quentin Compson and Darl Bundren – who seem to share their author's sensitivity to the "all" that surrounds them and something of his ability to articulate it – come to particularly unattractive ends. *Absalom, Absalom!* is especially relentless, refracting Faulkner's personal sense of authorial failure in Quentin and his roommate Shreve's inability to arrive at any firm conclusions about the Sutpen family's tragedy two generations previous, in Quentin's anguished crisis of self-knowledge that closes the narrative, and in the repeated adumbration of historical documents – Rosa Coldfield's note to Quentin, Charles Bon's letter to Judith Sutpen, Mr.

Compson's to Quentin, Thomas and Judith Sutpen's headstones, and so on – that, as Quentin's father says, "just [do] not explain" (80). David M. Ball's elaboration of this "leitmotif of the text *as* ruin"[5] reflects Faulkner's sense of historical belatedness and loss, which Philip Weinstein accords with a broader modernist "obsess[ion] over the quandary" of its "slippage" away from the realist "project of *coming to know*," and thus over "the impossibility of getting the object right."[6] Because Faulkner works so hard in *Absalom* to align the reader's interpretive energies and desires with the characters' attempts to discern the truth of Bon's story, it is natural to find oneself at the conclusion sharing in Quentin's despair. If, as Weinstein argues, "Faulkner's Civil War resists coherent narration" so resolutely,[7] then so too might his novel be assumed to suffer from a fundamental incoherence of its own.[8]

The Latin Americans of the Boom generation – among them Carlos Fuentes, Mario Vargas Llosa, José Donoso, and most importantly García Márquez – thought otherwise, finding the evocation of failure in itself magisterial, Faulkner's articulation of a shared experience of defeat or depredation at the hands of Northern forces singularly successful and of unique value to their own fictional endeavors.[9] García Márquez (only "half facetiously," according to novelist William Kennedy, his interlocutor) declared *The Hamlet* "the best South American novel ever written" and elsewhere maintained that "the great difference between us and our grandparents ... is Faulkner. He was the only thing that happened between those two generations."[10] Deborah Cohn describes the grandparents' generation as still caught up in the "novel of the land," quoting Donoso's characterization of the genre as writing "for [the] parish ... cataloguing the flora and fauna ... which were unmistakably ours ... all that which specifically makes us different [from] other countries on the continent."[11] Faulkner makes it possible to move beyond this older fictional model through his own metaphorical and narrative transposition from land to house, announced in clarion terms already in *Absalom*'s second paragraph, as Quentin "watch[es]" in Rosa Coldfield's monologue while Sutpen and his men "overrun suddenly the hundred square miles of tranquil and astonished earth and drag house and formal gardens violently out of the soundless Nothing and clap them down like cards upon a table beneath the up-palm immobile and pontific, creating the Sutpen's Hundred, the *Be Sutpen's Hundred* like the oldentime *Be Light*" (4).

It is relatively well known that Faulkner's working title for both *Light in August* and *Absalom, Absalom!* was "Dark House"; Florence Delay and Jacqueline de Labriolle report that García Márquez's for *One Hundred Years of Solitude* was, similarly, "La Casa."[12] Sutpen's fiat of course emblematizes Faulkner's own, distilling regional history and national destiny in his "own little postage stamp of native soil" (*LG* 255), claimed as a private fiefdom by that imperious authorial "I" on the map of Jefferson that closes *Absalom* and concentrated in the vexed figure of the "Big House." García Márquez duplicates this move with the construction of the village of Macondo and the Buendía domicile in particular, but his own titular revision points to his recognition that equally as important as the spatial condensation in the house is the temporal distension of the house: the novel's ability to layer a century's worth of events in and around the house atop one another for the benefit of our scrutiny. His even more audacious chronological impasto in *The Autumn of the Patriarch* – a novel of six chapter-length paragraphs (the last out-Faulknering Faulkner himself in a single fifty-page sentence), each continuously careening across hundreds of years of Latin American history – yields what Jacques Pothier calls "the novel as suspended instant," in which "meaning is not born from succession as causality, but from the telescoping of events in the hybridization of plural scales of duration."[13] Pothier finds here a temporal recasting of Borges's Aleph ("the only place on earth where all the places are – seen from every angle, each standing clear, without any confusion or blending") and thus proposes the latter as "the paradigm of the design and of the poetic object of the South," both Faulkner's and the Latin American Boom's.[14] These formulations echo Fuentes's description of time in Faulkner (in contradistinction to Balzac's obsession with the future and Proust's with the past) as "always present, an obsession of the carnal incandescent memory," such that the novels become "works of sheer weight, sheer presence."[15]

García Márquez has already made resoundingly clear in the conclusion to *One Hundred Years of Solitude* that the novel is a singular technology, offering readers a means of temporal synthesis unavailable to those within its diegesis. The gypsy Melquíades, who stuns Macondo with the wonders of refrigeration and magnetism in the book's opening paragraph and who, on the next page, presents the magnifying glass and the telescope as a realization of the Aleph's promise of spatial contraction – " 'Science has eliminated distance,' Melquíades proclaimed. 'In a short time, man will be able to see what is happening in any place in the world without leaving his own house' " – leaves the Buendías with a lasting mystery in the form of a collection of indecipherable parchments.[16] Generations puzzle over what turns out to be a prophetic chronicle of the family's fortunes, but only the last Aureliano manages to decode them, in the book's final paragraphs, when he suddenly understands that the text "concentrated a century of daily episodes in such a way that they coexisted in one instant."[17] But while Macondo has by this point caught up with the industrial revolution and a range of twentieth-century scientific advances,

the knowledge contained in the parchments can arrive only apocalypti-
cally, projecting Quentin's closing despair and the catastrophic demise
of Sutpen's Hundred into the "wrath of the biblical hurricane" that will
leave not only the Buendía house but the whole of Macondo "wiped out
by the wind and exiled from the memory of men at the precise moment
when Aureliano Babilonia would finish deciphering the parchments ...
everything written on them ... unrepeatable since time immemorial and
forever more."[18] Just as Shreve's damning summation of Southern history, the Sutpen line, and Quentin's tortured psychology leaves Quentin
wracked by denial and effectively forces *Absalom*'s abrupt end, so in *One
Hundred Years of Solitude* is the synthesis of family history impossible
to both read and hold within the space of the novel. Roberto González
Echevarría argues that the book leaves us likewise desolated: "we, like
Aureliano, read the instant we live, cognizant that it may very well be our
last," "when the novel concludes ... we close the book to cease being as
readers, to be, as it were, slain in that role."[19] One can grant the symbolic
force of this conclusion, as one can Faulkner's, but still push back to note
that the aftermath of our reading is likely to be relatively prosaic in comparison with Quentin's or Aureliano's. In fact, a reader's strong emotional
response more often spurs a return to the text just completed for further
perusal – for the opportunity to suture together its various parts into new
patterns and coherences, to take advantage of Pothier's "telescoping" and
"hybridizing" optic to arrive at syntheses unavailable to those within. The
omnipresence of the past, unsupportable weight for Quentin and fatal revelation for Aureliano, is for the reader the boon that constitutes a novel as
something other than a fundamentally unrecoverable string of unspooling
events – that differentiates the novel, that is, from life.

Toni Morrison takes this demonstration a step further, gathering the
threads of lost history and incarnating them in Beloved in *Beloved*. The
nomenclatural confusion is exactly the point, asking as it does that we
compare our grasp of the novel with the tenuous hold those within it
have on its title character. At different moments, Beloved appears to be
Sethe's baby girl returned from the dead eighteen years after having been
killed by her mother in an attempt to spare her the experience of slavery,
or a figurative embodiment of the common hell of the Middle Passage,
or a young woman whose protracted sexual bondage to a white man in
a nearby community recapitulates one of the most intimate of slavery's
horrors. Effectively, she is all of these, giving bodily form to Faulkner's
oft-quoted assertion that the past is "never dead," that it is "not even
past" (*RN* 535). However, like Melquíades's parchments, and unlike
the typical ghost produced by and moored to a single personal trauma,

she synthesizes multiple historical registers. But if Morrison fleshes out Quentin and Shreve's vaporous imaginings, rendering history momentarily apprehensible in Beloved's human form and fitfully intelligible in her oblique and simple-minded speech, she also renders that history increasingly toxic. Beloved seduces and then drives away Sethe's lover, Paul D; she pulls the remainder of the household into a downward spiral of discord and destruction; and finally she brings Sethe to the threshold of repeating her own past in another spontaneous homicide, when she misconstrues the arrival of a friendly abolitionist as the return of her sadistic former owner. To hold history's hand, as Sethe does at the moment before the second attempted murder, is to find oneself held fast by it and held to its dictates, to lose the perspective that can discern differences within the patterns it weaves.

A group of neighbor women simultaneously averts the killing and exorcises Beloved, such that she flees the scene and "erupts into her separate parts,"[20] "subjected," Phillip Novak writes, "to a form of systematic dispersal."[21] He goes on to differentiate between Beloved's fate and Charles Bon's, arguing that the "loss of history [in *Absalom*] ... is itself a figure for the loss of meaning as such" – that the past in Faulkner is "an empty placeholder for the sheer desire for coherence" that "has always already been lost" – and contrasting that "universalized" claim with the "multiform, variegated" presentations of history, some of which "*can* be recounted," in *Beloved*. "Whereas in Faulkner, *all* the stories the novel tells eventually unravel," Novak concludes, "many of Morrison's stories do hang together."[22] Novak's insistence on the plural – "stories" – characterizes the way certain set pieces are indeed upheld more tenaciously in the latter novel than in the former, but that orientation leaves unconsidered the aggregated, unitary "story" that each novel proffers, qua novel. "Disremembered and unaccounted for," willfully repressed by even "those who had spoken to her, lived with her, fallen in love with her," Beloved is at the book's conclusion conferred upon readers alone.[23] Like the water from which she emerges and to which she returns, the diegesis closes about her, leaving only the reader with the wherewithal or the impetus to reassemble her component parts or the history for which they stand. For Morrison makes clear that any such project of reassembly within the narrative must be forward-looking. Paul D returns to Sethe, in the novel's penultimate scene, heeding their fellow slave Sixo's description of his own lover as a woman who can "gather ... the pieces [he is] ... and give them back ... in all the right order."[24] Paul D glosses such reassembly as a project of jointly embracing the future rather than continuing to worry the past, and rightly so, in that no other stance seems likely to bring Sethe even so far as the present. But this posture bequeaths to the reader the task of recovering Beloved, together with all the other pieces of the past in the novel, in "the right order."

To this end, Morrison lends *Beloved* a hint of Beloved's seductive power. She describes Beloved's final absence with a lyrical insistence – "a latch latched and lichen attached," "Certainly no clamor for a kiss"[25] – that undermines its own claims, commanding attention and asking to be unlocked, and at the same time recalling the eerie force with which Beloved compels Paul D to reopen the "little tobacco tin ... rusted shut" that he believes has replaced his heart.[26] This highly physical metaphor, like that of the body in pieces, anticipates the third generation's further transmutation of Faulkner's model. Eugenides and Foer go beyond García Márquez's and Morrison's imputations that the novel in sum offers a register of knowledge unavailable to the characters within, a means of amassing and organizing history that has no non-novelistic equivalent. They grant this epistemological advantage a shimmering ontological presence at the edges of their narratives, such that while the absent individuals around which Faulkner's and Morrison's novels circle do find new (and still absent) avatars here, they are countered by the material presence of the books themselves. The simple physical endurance and the ultimate canonization of Faulkner's corpus ramifies into the sense that a fictional text's existence in the world makes a positive difference even if it cannot in fact recuperate the lost or make restitution for history's damages. Against the continued spectacular immolation of the houses at the cores of these tales, and in spite of the continuing inability of the texts to explain history in full, the books come to stand as a means not only of staving off ruin but finally of carving out sustainable, inhabitable spaces of their own.

Jeffrey Eugenides adopts Morrison's puzzle metaphor in the conclusion to *The Virgin Suicides*: the final lament of the neighborhood men still attempting to process the mass suicide of the five Lisbon sisters back when they and the men were all teenagers, twenty years earlier, is that they will "never find the pieces to put [the girls] back together."[27] But in Eugenides's case a literalizing version of the metaphor has been in play throughout the novel. The men have amassed a collection of ninety-seven articles – personal effects and documentary ephemera – pertaining to the girls, in a doomed attempt to account for their behavior or even to preserve their memory adequately. These memorabilia (none of which is reproduced or represented in any fashion but verbally) are proffered by the first-person-plural narrators to the reader intermittently, sometimes airily, sometimes with an intense solicitousness for the objects' well-being – "Please don't touch. We're going to put the picture back in its envelope now"[28] – that is a teasing reminder of their absolute inaccessibility. But at the close, the men admit that the entire archive is "perishing" for want of having been kept "sufficiently airtight," the "Polaroid of the house, scummed by a greenish patina that looks like moss.... Mary's old cosmetics drying out and turning to beige dust.... Cecilia's canvas high-tops yellowing beyond remedy of toothbrush and dish soap," and so on.[29] In this moment, the novel flips the ontological priority, and with it the sense of an epistemological edge, that the men have heretofore enjoyed over the reader. The envy one may have felt at the solidity of these objects within the diegetic sphere dissipates with the recognition that the archive's decay will leave the narrative itself a more enduring and scrutable testament to the girls, that piecing together the logic of their actions must be a project of literary interpretation.

And, indeed, literary history appears to offer a series of determinants of the girls' actions and their fates that is finally more compelling than any the men can amass. Suicide remains a mystery within the novel, but the girls' actions are at the same time glossed to some degree of satisfaction by the novel. The men push their analysis as far as recognizing the force of a certain implacable authoritarian presence, observing for example that "as fall turned to winter, the trees in the [Lisbon] yard drooped and thickened, concealing the house, even though their leaflessness should have revealed it. A cloud always seemed to hover over the Lisbons' roof. There was no explanation except the psychic one ... that Mrs. Lisbon willed it to."[30] But what the boys gloss as the baleful force of parental malignance is more fully legible as the weight of the Faulknerian canon. "The house recede[s] behind its mists" and "miasmic vapors," becoming a "rain forest" of "rotten wood and soggy carpet," due to the family's neglect, to be sure, but also in deference to the fantastic decline of the Buendía estate and Sutpen's Hundred, and before them Poe's House of Usher, into nearby swamp or tarn.[31] Those within the novel are likewise mystified as to why the four older sisters time their massed exit to the anniversary of young Cecilia's first suicide attempt rather than to the date of her actual death, three weeks later; no one registers that her initial effort coincides with Bloomsday, but Eugenides – who reports that in high school he celebrated the date every year with his best friend – obviously does.[32] When Cecilia does manage to do herself in, it's by jumping from an upstairs window and impaling herself on the fencepost below, echoing Septimus Smith's demise in *Mrs. Dalloway*. Thus, when the hospital staff psychiatrist who ends up obsessed with the girls' case ultimately likens their actions to Russian Roulette with a fully loaded revolver – "A bullet for family abuse. A bullet for genetic predisposition. A bullet for historical malaise. A bullet for inevitable momentum" – and insists that even if the "other two bullets are impossible to name ... that doesn't mean the chambers were empty," he may be pointing as best someone inside the novel can to the magical realist inheritance, and that of the twentieth-century canon more broadly, as signing the girls' fate.[33]

Eugenides is fond of recounting the novel's origin in a chance conversation with his nephew's babysitter, who revealed that she and her sisters had once tried to commit suicide together. When Eugenides asked why, she responded only, "I don't know. We've had a lot of pressure."[34] The obvious insufficiency of this answer, and its extreme laconicism, produces the baroque efflorescence of the novel as an alternative explanatory system. Jonathan Safran Foer likewise routinely describes the origin of *Everything is Illuminated* by way of his woefully under-planned trip to Ukraine, armed only with a photograph and a first name, in search of the woman who saved his grandfather from the Nazis. Having found "nothing but nothing ... a landscape of completely realized absence," he stumbles instead upon the compulsion and the liberty to write his own version of the quest and of the Holocaust itself, predicated on what he calls "imaginative accuracy" rather than historical fidelity.[35] Both younger authors embrace, then, the kinds of historical gaps that dog Faulkner.

Neither Eugenides nor Foer turns his back on history, however; Eugenides offers his reader a rich and detailed evocation of 1970s malaise, centered on but not limited to Detroit's failing auto industry, and Foer's exuberantly counterfactual depiction of Trachimbrod, his grandfather's shtetl, collapses under the weight of the Nazis' inevitable ascent, concomitantly dragging the book from comedy to tragedy. But Foer nevertheless suggests yet more forcefully than does Eugenides – with a much more aggressive magical realism looping back to a more energetic engagement with Faulkner's imaginary – that indeterminacy and loss might be redressed through textual materiality. Foer riffs on Quentin and Shreve's joint storytelling in the interplay between the Jonathan Safran Foer character, who at first seems to be the book's protagonist (and who contributes chapters imagining the shtetl's past), and his Ukrainian translator, Alexander Perchov, who over time emerges as its soul (and who narrates the expedition itself and its aftermath). Quentin and Shreve's confabulation in *Absalom* is wavering and ethereal, "the two of them creating between them, out of the rag-tag and bob-ends of old tales and talking, people who perhaps had never existed at all anywhere, who, shadows, were shadows not of flesh and blood which had lived and died but shadows in turn of what were (to one of them at least, to Shreve) shades too," at length no more substantial than "the visible murmur of their vaporizing breath" (243). But by the midpoint of Foer's novel, Jonathan's protracted magical-realist fantasizing about his ancestors achieves a productive synergy with Alex's increasingly pertinacious sleuthing on his behalf, ultimately producing a lone, extremely aged survivor out of thin air (if propped up by the steps of yet another moribund house). In response to Alex's explanation that they are "searching for Trachimbrod," and in the wake of many denials, she at last affirms: "You are here. I am it."[36] She then introduces herself as Lista, a name common neither in Slavic languages nor in Yiddish, and one likewise not glossed directly by the kinds of consonances that undergird many of the text's other appellations. Rather, the name seems to derive from the Slavic root "*list*" – meaning "leaf, note, document, paper, sheet" – and constructs her as a body born out of the young men's literary reveries, keeping watch over a mass of communal relics heading in the opposite direction. For she presents Alex and Jonathan with a box labeled "REMAINS," "brimmed with many photographs, and many pieces of paper, and many ribbons, and cloths, and queer things like combs, rings, and flowers that had become more paper."[37]

Indeed, as the corporeal overtone of the box's label suggests, not just bodily adornments but bodies themselves are repeatedly supplanted in the novel by paper, eventually by that paper making up the book itself. In the first historical set piece, the imagined progenitor of Jonathan's line drowns in the shtetl's river (perhaps a suicide, perhaps an allusion to Quentin's demise), inspiring the community to take his name. His body never surfaces but "the bleeding red-ink script of a resolution: *I will … I will …*" singles itself out within the flotsam of his possessions.[38] This substitution is immediately echoed by the "several pages of death certificates … picked up by [a] breeze and sent into the trees" when the local doctor opens his bag – some certificates destined to "fall with the leaves that September," others lodging themselves to "fall with the trees generations later,"[39] effectively memorializing the "hundreds of bodies pour[ing] into the … river" in a failed attempt to escape the Nazi onslaught.[40] That early resolution then weaves through the novel's final paragraph, underscoring in one fell synthesis the medium's intertwined capacities for formal patterning, temporal conjunction, and material self-consciousness. The novel closes: "it is what I must do, and I will do it. Do you understand me? I will walk without noise, and I will open the door in the darkness, and I will"[41] This is, unequivocally, a suicide note – Alex's grandfather's, in the wake of confronting his role in the genocide – and it bookends the opening's irreverent plot device, Foer's means to countermand the inaccessibility of his own personal history, with an infinitely pained and loving (but doomed) endeavor to banish personal history, to "cut all of the strings" connecting Alex and his younger brother to the Holocaust.[42] The suicides track as well, then, the novel's development from Jonathan's puerile fantasizing to Alex's fraught achievement of self-knowledge and maturity – from a particularly hollow magical realism to the full weight of the past.

But at the same time, the repeated iterations of will, and Grandfather's final bitter accomplishment, still point to the novel's insouciance. Two-thirds of the way through, it presents a series of semi-playful definitions: of "art" and "artifice" and "artifact," and of "ifice," "ifact," and "ifactifice" as well. Foer defends the last as a nonsense word but also aligns it with "art," the signal difference being that a work of pure art (which he maintains does not exist) would be a "thing having to do only with itself," while "ifactifice" adds up to something like the "past-tensed fact" of a "thing with purpose, created for function's sake" – that is, something that has been willed to a specific end.[43] Foer's novel is such a thing, its willfulness in the face of the somber legacy of the Holocaust a provocation and also a response to Theodor Adorno's own famously provocative declaration that the writing of lyric poetry after Auschwitz was barbaric. Foer's humor and overwrought prose go well beyond the possibility, "however remote," that some kind of "enjoyment" might arise from the "artistic representation of … sheer physical pain" that concerns Adorno, but at the same time this means too that Foer steers well clear of the kind of "harsh and uncompromising," "committed" art that Adorno lambastes.[44] Instead, Foer proposes that writing with a full tonal range might indeed be an appropriate, constructive, emotionally palliative, and even moral response to the individual and societal losses of the Holocaust – as it might be in the wake of slavery, war, economic conquest, or suicide – that, in Faulkner's most infamous binary, "*Between grief and nothing*," there might be another choice (*JER* 273, emphasis Faulkner's). A novel may present an indelible record of grief and betoken the insuperable nothingness of that which has been forever lost and yet offer itself as that *something* – both physical and metaphysical – that endures and at length exceeds the inescapably negative sum of the conditions of its own possibility.

NOTES

1 Malcolm Cowley, *The Faulkner-Cowley File: Letters and Memories 1944–1962* (New York: Viking Press, 1966), p. 14.
2 By far the most expansive and energetic discussion of Faulkner's possible literary influence surrounds the work of Toni Morrison. Morrison's comments on the relationship are, as she herself observes, "typical … of all writers who are convinced that they are wholly original" – who, "recogniz[ing] an influence … abandon it as quickly as possible" ("Faulkner and Women," *Faulkner and Women: Faulkner and Yoknapatawpha, 1985*, Doreen Fowler and Ann Abadie [eds.] [Jackson: University Press of Mississippi, 1986], p. 296). While Morrison wrote her master's thesis at Cornell on Faulkner and Woolf and has allowed that "in a very, very personal way … William Faulkner had an enormous effect" on her, that she "spent a great deal of time thinking about" him, she has also maintained that she does not "really find strong connections between [her]

work and Faulkner's" (295–7), that she is "not *like* Faulkner ... in that sense" (*Unflinching Gaze: Morrison and Faulkner Re-Envisioned*, Carol A. Kolmerten, Stephen M. Ross, and Judith Bryant Wittenberg [eds.] [Jackson: University Press of Mississippi, 1997], p. xi).Critics have tempered the latter claims, and John N. Duvall has noted their echo of Faulkner's own insistence that he had not read Joyce – a statement belied by those who heard him "recite long passages of Joyce's work from memory" – but they have also recognized the danger that, in Duvall's words, an imputation of influence risks "calling up memories of racial and sexual abuse in the American past" by implying that "without a white Southern man's seminal texts, those of the African-American woman would never have come to fruition" ("Toni Morrison and the Anxiety of Faulknerian Influence," *Unflinching Gaze,* pp. 7, 3). A strong case has by now been made for replacing the implicitly hierarchical language of influence with the more evenhanded notion of dialogue. As Carol A. Kolmerten, Steven M. Ross, and Judith Bryant Wittenberg write in their introduction to a volume of essays on the two authors, "Not only does Morrison respond to Faulkner ... but no reader of Faulkner will ever read him in the same way after encountering the works of Morrison" ("Introduction: Refusing to Look Away," *Unflinching Gaze,* p. xi). My claim in the pages that follow is less resounding, more expansive, but fundamentally consonant with theirs.

3 Eugenides's second novel – the Pulitzer-winning *Middlesex* – is, in its bid for "Great American Novel" status, transparently indebted to the multi-generational splay of *Absalom, Absalom!*, but the subtler resonances in *The Virgin Suicides* are equally illuminating.

4 It is this looping itinerary of a thoroughly delineated indebtedness to Faulkner combined with energetic self-assertion equally enabled by his example that leads me to single out these novels. Obviously, one can identify many more inheritors. A still very partial catalogue might begin with those whose careers and concerns overlapped Faulkner's own and who had to wrestle through the fear that his style and subject might be indissolubly linked, the former not simply ideally suited to the latter but perhaps even enjoined by it in his wake ... or studiously to be avoided if one were to preserve an individual artistic identity. Flannery O'Connor likened the position of those "employing the same idiom" and "looking out on more or less the same social scene" to that of a "mule and wagon stalled on the same track the Dixie Limited is roaring down" ("Some Aspects of the Grotesque in Southern Fiction," *Mystery and Manners: Occasional Prose,* Sally and Robert Fitzgerald [eds.] [New York: Farrar, Straus and Giroux, 1969], p. 45), and William Styron averred that "whereas almost any fool could detect an influence of Faulkner in *Lie Down in Darkness,* I shook the more obvious qualities of Faulkner, and was left with a book which had its own distinctive and original stance" (*Conversations with William Styron,* James L. W. West III [ed.] [Jackson: University Press of Mississippi, 1985], pp. 54–5). Even as late an entrant as Cormac McCarthy, whose first novel appeared three years after Faulkner's death, has been characterized by Jay Watson as devoting *Suttree* (published another fourteen years on) to a book-length working through of "'the Quentin Compson problem,' a constellation of thematic motifs concerning time, change, the moral bankruptcy and irrelevance of an aristocratic southern legacy, suicide, death by drowning, and an overbearing father figure" as a means to "put some

distance between himself" and Faulkner's long shadow ("Lighting out of Civil Rights Territory: *Suttree*, the Quentin Problem, and the Historical Unconscious," *The Cormac McCarthy Journal* 4.1 [2005], p. 72).Further afield, Faulkner received an ambivalent embrace from African-American writers such as Ralph Ellison, Chester Himes, and Ernest Gaines, each of whom found stylistic resources in his example and credited as singular his effort to explore black experience, but each of whom also found reason for pause in Faulkner's sometime employment of black stereotypes and in his public statements on race relations in the South (see Ralph Ellison, "Twentieth Century Fiction and the Mask of Humanity," *The Collected Essays of Ralph Ellison*, John F. Callahan [ed.] [New York: Modern Library, 1995]; William Inge, "The Dixie Limited: Writers on Faulkner and His Influence," *The Faulkner Journal of Japan* 1 [1999], to which I owe several of the references in this note; and Margaret Donovan Bauer, *William Faulkner's Legacy: "What Shadow, What Stain, What Mark"* [Gainesville: University Press of Florida, 2005]). Ellison, in particular, is highly legible in dialogue with the lineage I trace here. The Invisible Man – secure in his bunker, infinitely savvier than the reader about the novel's events in the prologue and still running rhetorical circles around us at the close – inverts point-for-point the characteristics common to all the novels I discuss.

By the heyday of high postmodernism – which Brian McHale sees as anticipated by the moment in which Quentin Compson and Shreve McCannon, "apparently unanxiously," abandon "the intractable problems of attaining to realizable knowledge of *our* world" and instead commence to "improvise a *possible world*; they *fictionalize*" (*Postmodernist Fiction* [New York: Methuen, 1987], p. 10, emphasis McHale's; see also O'Donnell, and Duvall and Abadie) – Faulkner's influence can be felt in the ontological daring and contrapuntal storytelling techniques of writers as different as Thomas Pynchon, Leslie Marmon Silko, Maxine Hong Kingston, Kathy Acker, and David Foster Wallace, as well as (I will later argue in passing) in the broad swathe of magical realist stylings characterizing much late twentieth-century fiction.

5 David Ball, *False Starts: The Rhetoric of Failure and the Making of American Modernism* (Evanston, IL: Northwestern University Press, 2014), p. 126, emphasis Ball's. The catalogue of failed communications is Ball's also, reading the novel as organized around the "topos of the document that refuses to signify" (125).

6 Philip Weinstein, *Unknowing: The Work of Modernist Fiction* (Ithaca, NY: Cornell University Press, 2005), p. 237, emphasis Weinstein's.

7 Ibid., p. 235.

8 And, indeed, the existence of such a fundamental representational and psychic crisis is the thrust of Weinstein's argument for the "unknowing" at the heart of the modernist project. Nevertheless, he allows that "fiction's way of not-saying the world is no less resonantly a saying, a *wording*. It proceeds as though through a primordial belief, however vestigial, in a magic of mimesis seeded in words themselves" (254, emphasis Weinstein's). And Ball likewise observes that "this failure of language is an extremely productive force ... providing a generative power for both the creative artist and the theorist of language" (*False Starts*, pp. 143–4). In what follows, I will nudge the emphasis away from artist and world and toward the art object itself. My argument has much in common with John T. Matthews's in *The Play of Faulkner's Language* (Ithaca, NY: Cornell University Press, 1982)

but emphasizes the integrity of the accomplished work over the unfolding of the language within it.

9 See Deborah Cohn, "Faulkner, Latin America, and the Caribbean: Influence, Politics, and Academic Disciplines," *A Companion to William Faulkner*, Richard Moreland (ed.) (Oxford: Blackwell, 2006), pp. 499–518; Theo D'haen, "Magical Realism and Postmodernism: Decentering Privileged Centers," *Magical Realism: Theory, History, Community*, Lois Parkinson Zamora and Wendy B. Faris (eds.) (Durham, NC: Duke University Press, 1995) pp. 191–208; Mark Frisch, "Latin America," *A William Faulkner Encyclopedia*, Robert W. Hamblin and Charles A. Peek (eds.) (Westport, CT: Greenwood Press, 1999); Tanya T. Fayen, *In Search of the Latin American Faulkner* (Lanham, MD: University Press of America, 1995); Lois Parkinson Zamora, "Magical Romance/Magical Realism: Ghosts in U.S. and Latin American Fiction," *Magical Realism: Theory, History, Community*, Lois Parkinson Zamora and Wendy B. Faris (eds.) (Durham, NC: Duke University Press, 1995), pp. 497–550; and the dedicated issue of *The Faulkner Journal*: *A Latin American Faulkner*: XI.1–2 (Fall 1995 and Spring 1996).

10 Hamblin and Peek, *A William Faulkner Encyclopedia*, p. 222. As numerous critics have noted, and as García Márquez has sometimes allowed (see Bell-Villada), Faulkner's influence on *Leaf Storm*, García Márquez's first novel – at the level of plot, structure, narrative points of view, and overall scope – is pervasive. See Cohn for an eloquent discussion of the fashion in which multiple novelists of the Boom likewise combine *As I Lay Dying*'s "kaleidoscopic view" of the "life, family, and the social order" surrounding a deceased individual with *Absalom, Absalom!*'s "panoramic historical vision" to generate a "polyphonic novel of the dead in which the central figure's life recapitulates the history of an entire nation or region" ("Faulkner, Latin America, and the Caribbean," p. 503). Faulkner is not typically credited, however, with sparking the impassive commingling of the mundane and the fantastic that lends magical realism its name. García Márquez typically traces this narrative approach to his delighted shock at finding in the first sentences of Kafka's *The Metamorphosis* a high-culture literary praxis unexpectedly akin to his grandmother's mode of fabulation: "Holy shit! … Nobody had told me this could be done! … That's how my grandmother told stories … The wildest things, in the most natural way" (Gene H. Bell-Villada, "Journey Back to the Source: An Interview with Gabriel García Márquez," translated by Gene H. Bell-Villada, *Virginia Quarterly Review* 81.3 [Summer 2005]). But much of what we latterly come to recognize as magical realism is already nascent in Faulkner, as well, a tonal aspect of his ambition to "say it all in one sentence." García Márquez does draw this connection in the conversation with Kennedy, averring that "Faulkner was surprised at certain things that happened in life … but he writes of them not as surprises but as things that happen every day" (William Kennedy, "The Yellow Trolley Car in Barcelona, and Other Visions," *The Atlantic Monthly* 213 [January 1973]). Certainly, *The Hamlet*'s casual stylistic shifts, its almost obscenely plump metaphors, and its deadpan relation of narrative implausibilities anticipate García Márquez's mature style. But so, too, do the cyclical recursions and recombinations of name and personality in *The Sound and the Fury*, the French architect

who wears like a classical epithet the same "sombrely theatric" "frock coat ... flowered waistcoat and ... hat" through two years of swamp labor alongside his mud-caked but naked employer in *Absalom, Absalom!* (26), and the improbably bemused mixture of incredulity and acceptance with which *Light in August*'s Joe Christmas attends punishment and reward alike. It should be noted that even as he trumpets Faulkner's unique influence, García Márquez allows that he is "probably exaggerating" (Hamblin, Robert W. and Charles A. Peek [eds.], *A William Faulkner Encyclopedia* [Westport, CT: Greenwood Press, 1999], p. 222), and indeed in later years he attempts to walk back the significance of Faulkner's example for him (see, for example, Florence Delay and Jacqueline de Labriolle, "Is García Márquez the Colombian Faulkner?" *The Faulkner Journal* 11.1–2 [1995]). We have, of course, seen Toni Morrison make the same two moves and propose a convincing rationale for the latter. While I take it as axiomatic that no twentieth-century writer's testimony can always be read safely at face value, I lend more credence to statements of influence made in the heady rush of early success than I do to subsequent attempts to revise the record.

11 Deborah Cohn, "Faulkner, Latin America, and the Caribbean," p. 501.

12 Delay and de Labriolle, "Is García Márquez the Colombian Faulkner?" p. 122. Noel Polk points out the importance of houses, "ranging from shotgun sharecropper shacks, ephemeral and poisonous as mushrooms, to antebellum mansions" in the whole of the corpus, "inscribing on Faulkner's North Mississippi landscape the class structure of the plantation system" and at the same time playing "a particularly significant symbolic role" – which Polk reads in the most fraught Freudian terms – in the lives of his characters (*Children of the Dark House: Text and Context in Faulkner* [Jackson: University Press of Mississippi, 1996] pp. 25, 30). See also Jay Parini, "Afterword: In the House of Faulkner," *Faulkner's Inheritance*, Joseph R. Urgo and Ann J. Abadie (eds.) (Jackson: University Press of Mississippi), pp. 160–70 and James G. Watson, "Faulkner: The House of Fiction," *Fifty Years of Yoknapatawpha*, Doreen Fowler and Ann J. Abadie (eds.) (Jackson: University Press of Mississippi, 1980). One might likewise point to the centrality of a single house not just in García Márquez's masterwork but also in *Leaf Storm, Chronicle of a Death Foretold,* and *The Autumn of the Patriarch*.

13 Jacques Pothier, "Voices from the South, Voices of the Souths: Faulkner, García Márquez, Vargas Llosa, Borges," *The Faulkner Journal* 11.1–2 (1995), p. 114.

14 Ibid., p. 115.

15 Carlos Fuentes, "The Novel as Tragedy: William Faulkner," Trude Stern and Evelyn Taverelli (trans.), *The Faulkner Journal* 11.1–2 (1995), p. 25.

16 Gabriel García Márquez, *One Hundred Years of Solitude*, Gregory Rabassa (trans.) (New York: Harper and Row, 1970), p. 2.

17 Ibid., p. 415.

18 Ibid., p. 416–17.

19 Roberto González Echevarría, *Myth and Archive: A Theory of Latin American Narrative* (Cambridge: Cambridge University Press, 1990), pp. 26, 28.

20 Toni Morrison, *Beloved* (New York: Alfred A. Knopf, 1987), p. 274.

21 Philip Novak, "Signifying Silences: Morrison's Soundings in the Faulknerian Void," *Unflinching Gaze: Morrison and Faulkner Re-Envisioned*, Carol A. Kolmerten, Stephen M. Ross, and Judith Bryant Wittenberg (eds.) (Jackson: University Press of Mississippi, 1997), p. 212.

22 Ibid., pp. 213–14 (emphasis Novak's).
23 Morrison, *Beloved,* p. 274.
24 Ibid., pp. 272–3.
25 Ibid., p. 275.
26 Ibid., p. 116.
27 Jeffrey Eugenides, *The Virgin Suicides* (New York: Farrar, Straus and Giroux, 1993), p. 243.
28 Ibid., p. 114.
29 Ibid., pp. 240–1.
30 Ibid., p. 136.
31 Ibid., pp. 140, 154, 160.
32 Jeffrey Eugenides, "The Father of Modernism," Entry 2, *Slate* (16 June 2004)
33 Eugenides, *The Virgin Suicides,* p. 242.
34 James A. Schiff, "A Conversation with Jeffrey Eugenides," *The Missouri Review* 29.3 (2006), 104.
35 "A Reader's Guide: *Everything is Illuminated.*" *Houghton Mifflin Books.com,* n.d. Web. June 11, 2014, http://www.houghtonmifflinbooks.com/readers_guides/foer/.
36 Jonathan Safran Foer, *Everything is Illuminated* (New York: HarperCollins, 2002), p. 118.
37 Ibid., p. 151.
38 Ibid., p. 233 (ellipses in original).
39 Ibid., p. 12.
40 Ibid., p. 272.
41 Ibid., p. 276.
42 Ibid., p. 275.
43 Ibid., pp. 202–3.
44 Theodor Adorno, "Commitment," *Aesthetics and Politics* (London: Verso, 1977), p. 189.

II

HUGUES AZÉRAD

A New Region of the World: Faulkner, Glissant, and the Caribbean

"Yes, Faulkner is a moment, a beat in the world-thought"
— Édouard Glissant[1]

Glissant, Faulkner: An Infinite Encounter

The question "Do you really think there's something in common between Louisiana and the Caribbean?" that Édouard Glissant cites in his seminal essay *Faulkner, Mississippi* (1996) as one he occasionally had to face from a bemused white audience, seems merely rhetorical today.[2] By arguing that Faulkner had more in common with Caribbean culture than with North America or even with traditional conceptions of U.S. Southern states, Glissant radically changed the trajectory of American, New World, and comparative studies.[3] His positioning of Faulkner in a wider Caribbean context not only performed a postcolonial strategy of "détour" (diversion), it also displaced traditional Western taxonomies of literature, that is, the ways in which we classify and anchor authors or literary traditions within a national, imperial, or regional narrative, irrespective of disruptive features that actually form and motivate the very works being studied. This geographical displacement located Faulkner in a central line of questioning that Glissant had launched in the early 1950s from his own "little postage stamp of native soil," the island of Martinique (*LG* 255).

Glissant was acutely sensitive to the devastation that three centuries of French colonial rule and its subsequent assimilation within metropolitan France had caused the island and its people. In his early poem cycles *Un Champ d'îles* (1953) and *Les Indes* (1956) and in his first novel *La Lézarde* (1958), he realized that clear-sighted political diagnosis was difficult and necessary, but insufficient. At the same moment that Faulkner was stretching the boundaries of his *œuvre* along temporal and geographical axes in the 1950s (*Requiem for a Nun, A Fable, The Town, The Mansion, The Reivers*), Glissant was revolutionizing the western literary canon from the colonized periphery, upending literary tradition by exposing its obsession with the One, genealogy, filiation, the epic, root-identity, mimesis, chronology, and so on. This excavation of a poetic intention out of the wreckage of colonization and western imperialism took place not in world metropolitan centers but at the periphery, in the Caribbean. Crucially, this poetic intention is not rooted in the writer's self but is motivated by Caribbean geography as well as what Glissant calls the "non history" plaguing the region. Dispensing with hierarchies of knowledge, culture, or language, it ushers in a conception of space-time best summarized as "archipelagic thought."[4]

For Glissant, the Caribbean is an entanglement of landscape, culture, and language united by a common thread of negation: colonization, genocides, the Middle Passage, slavery, the plantation system. He eschews any imposition of a mechanical and unifying vision of the region, and this is where his analysis differs from the postmodern overview given by Antonio Benítez-Rojo in *The Repeating Island*. Even though both thinkers, taking their cue from Deleuze and Guattari, are perceptive to "the processes, dynamics and rhythms that show themselves within the marginal, the regional, the incoherent, the heterogeneous" and, more important, to the "meta- archipelagic,"[5] chaotic, and aquatic aspect of Caribbean culture, they profoundly diverge in the way they bring their theories to bear on the Caribbean. Benítez-Rojo defines Caribbean culture in terms of "poetic territory marked by an aesthetic of pleasure," of "light [that] keeps on being light." Such a view starkly contrasts with Glissant's conception of the region: "The Caribbean ... may be held up as one of the places in the world where Relation presents itself most visibly ... This has always been a place of encounter and connivance and, at the same time, a passageway toward the American continent.... The Caribbean is, in contrast [to the Mediterranean], a sea that explodes the scattered lands into an arc. A sea that diffracts. Without necessarily inferring any advantage whatsoever to their situation, the reality of archipelagos in the Caribbean or the Pacific provides a natural illustration of the thought of Relation."[6]

It is this geographical "commonplace" that brings forth what Glissant calls his poetics of Relation ("in which each and every identity is extended through a relationship with the Other").[7] Contrary, or, rather, as a corrective to Benítez-Rojo's thesis about *Mestizaje* (which he defines as "binary syncretism Europe-Africa" that "scatters its entrails"),[8] Glissant turns toward the only certainty that obtains in the Caribbean: erased traces of genocides (the Caribs, the Arawaks, the Tainos), what Jana Evans Braziel calls "genocidal legacies" that "haunt the entire Caribbean,"[9] and the hold of the slave ship, which he reads not simply as an annihilating void or abyss but *also* as a matrix, a womb[10] able to engender what will become the dynamics of creolization. Creolization is a continual process that originates in what Glissant calls a digenesis, the name he gives to the birth of composite societies, no longer founded on a sacred origin, the source of legitimacy and filiation for atavistic societies. Creolization is also the method of Glissant's works and, more contentiously and never explicitly, what was also perhaps always-already at work in Faulkner. Above all, it is a linguistic and communal dynamics: "What took place in the Caribbean, which could be summed up in the word *creolization*, approximates the idea of Relation.... It is not merely an encounter, a shock ... a *métissage*.... If we posit *métissage* as, generally speaking, the meeting and synthesis of two differences, *creolization* seems to be a limitless *métissage*, its elements and its consequences unforeseeable. Creolization diffracts, whereas certain forms of métissage can concentrate one more time."[11]

For Glissant, Faulkner's writing embodies crucial aspects of a poetics of relation not because the fictional world he had created depicted its effects openly (relation can never be fully described, even in Glissant's own novels and poetry) but because it progressively exposed the flawed foundations upon which western cultures asserted their domination, the U.S. South being one among many other avatars of European colonization (marked by white supremacy, economic exploitation, and nationhood increasingly defined in terms of imperialism). Faulkner, whom critics had categorized as one of the great modernists (alongside Proust, Joyce, Woolf, and Musil), but whose import in the then recent theoretical movements (postmodernism, postcolonialism) could not buck the loss of interest in most of his works (Faulkner risked at one point becoming once again "provincial"), was credited by Glissant as early as *Poetic Intention* (1969) with a poetics and a rhetoric that encapsulates Caribbean and "minority" literature concerns, and whose *œuvre* anticipates early twenty-first-century transnational and diaspora questionings. But what Glissant recognized in Faulkner was how he stuck to his provincial, peripheral, "defeated," and "colonized" county, and made it signify as a particular, pregnant with a non-generalizing universalism.[12]

"Yes, Faulkner is a writer of that 'Other America'," Glissant writes in his *Caribbean Discourse* (1981), meaning that the Southerner has more in common with the Caribbean than with the U.S. North (and writers such as Henry James). This designation is also a political gesture: for Glissant, the Antilles (and the Caribbean) is the "Other America" and the "Caribbean sea is not the preserve/pond of the United States. It is the estuary of the Americas."[13] This appropriation of Faulkner is found in Glissant's chapter on a new poetics of the novel of the Americas (South America, the Caribbean). With hindsight, such a gesture seems almost obvious and transparent, but that would be to forget their opacity and political import *then*. For Glissant – a key activist in the '50s and '60s in the struggles for Martiniquan independence and in opposition to U.S. and European economic exploitation of this region – politics is defined in terms of poetics. Glissant's interpretation of Faulkner's works reflects the prism of his own poetics, not Faulkner's.

What allowed Glissant to incorporate Faulkner's work within the Caribbean was their shared "quarrel with History" (a tragic "urge," "passion," obsession with the veiling/unveiling of the primordial "trace": the trauma caused by colonization and slavery and the lie that underwrites the myth of legitimacy).[14] Glissant's and Faulkner's poetics usher in the dynamics of creolization through an approach that rejects direct modes of representation (and therefore action) that could only reproduce the forces at stake in any form of domination, whether it be economic, social, or political. This complex aspect of poetics is essential to understanding Glissant's strategic reading of Faulkner. It opens up new ways to comprehend how Faulkner and the Caribbean form a constellation, a mode of seeing and of being that sheers away from our current cognitive and interpretative patterns.

What often seems unnecessarily rambling or repetitive in Glissant's text, his refusal to engage directly with current academic issues of race, identity politics, and postcolonialism, is an integral part of the politics of his poetics:[15] it is only by distancing itself from the "real" that poetics can signify it differently and therefore, never predictably, change it. Style, as Proust said, is a question of "vision," and what this vision sees is what Glissant calls indifferently the "insu" [unknown/unknowing] or the "invu" [unseen/invisible]. This is perhaps yet another aesthetic commonplace (Conrad, Dickinson, Proust, Joyce, Woolf, and many others have said it as well, all slightly differently), but commonplaces can paradoxically be diverted strategically and turned into something productive: in Glissant's words, commonplaces are "a place where a world-thought encounters another world-thought"[16]; they redeem the "given" of the real and evince the inextricability of language, ordinary life, and thought. This distancing effect and emphasis on "(poetic/technical) vision" crystallize the commonplace that unites Glissant and Faulkner:

> The principle of [Faulkner's] work is indisputable, and we must not forget it: what is founded on slavery and oppression cannot last.... It is through sounding this damnation, this denial, that the work draws, not a lesson, but a new vision ... the new experience of the Relation – can become deliberate. Faulkner's work struggles toward this change of direction, not through moral lessons, but by changing our poetics.[17]

For Glissant, it is this poetic "commonplace" that will reverberate through Caribbean writings. Faulkner's work taken as a whole is revolutionary and liberating not so much because of what the author says but *how* he says it. More important, Faulkner's style combines a writerly "modernist" dimension, described in terms of tragic "veiling/unveiling," "modified streams of consciousness," "strokes of consciousness," "deferral," paralipsis ("to say without saying while still saying"),[18] with traditional oral techniques found in storytelling, which Glissant includes at the end of his study: "the oral techniques of accumulation, repetition, and circularity combine to undo the vision of reality and truth as singular, introducing the multiple, the uncertain, and the relative instead."[19] If the written dimension conveys an obsession with filiation, genesis, myth, and History, the Creole oral tales oppose History by narrating an "anti-History,"[20] the trace of "Digenesis": "not ... the creation of a world" but the "birth of the Antillean or Caribbean people."[21]

Faulkner, Mississippi is testament to the infinite encounter between Faulkner and Glissant, an encounter that happened when both Faulkner and Glissant were at work simultaneously but geographically separated by the Atlantic Ocean. Glissant started reading Faulkner when he lived in Paris, during the early '50s, at a time when Faulkner's novels were on all the intellectuals' lips (notably Sartre, Malraux, and Camus) however much they differed historically, politically, and culturally. But it is probably this difference that makes their literary encounter all the more profound and effervescent. It is not a coincidence that Glissant declares Faulkner "the greatest writer of this century (despite Proust and despite Joyce, or because of them)."[22] The century had started with a notorious failed encounter between a recently decolonized writer (Joyce) and the epitome of "western" culture (Proust)[23]; here, now, another encounter occurred that would prove infinitely successful because of, and not despite, their inexhaustible differences, specificities, and historical traumas.

Faulkner, Mississippi, as many critics have noticed, is a composite text that enacts Glissant's now familiar technique of weaving many genres (ethnopoetic/graphic and literary essay, poetry, fiction), abstaining from any stable authorial control over the narrative (repetitions, spiral narratives, and digressions disrupt the order of chapters and themes) or the narration. The Glissantian text denies itself univocal interpretation of Faulkner, setting itself up as a continuous dialogue that bears witness to an infinite encounter. After his *Caribbean Discourse*, which had laid out the principles of an Antillean (and, more broadly, Caribbean) independence and non-exclusive archipelagic identity, *Faulkner, Mississippi* ushers in a Caribbean poetics that injects *equality* between previously hierarchized cultures and literatures. *Faulkner,*

Mississippi will remain as a landmark of Caribbean writing, not because it lays claim to any privileged insight into an iconic American writer, but because it shows how a poetics of relation regenerates literature by inaugurating a dialogue between equals and heralds a time when such encounters could forge a politics of friendship[24] across seemingly insuperable frontiers. Beyond the ideological limitations he perceives in Faulkner's work (vertiginously perched on the threshold of creolization but unable to accept or explore its potentialities), Glissant openly welcomes Faulkner's influence within his own writings. Crucially, the Martiniquan writer no longer considers literary influence a source of anxiety, based on a hierarchical and unilinear "sacred filiation," replacing it instead with a *reciprocal* influence, a confluence that remains respectful of each other's opacities: "the unbounded openness is such that anyone can find a suitable path ["trace"] among those Faulkner proposes without betraying or losing oneself."[25]

If we now return to the initial question about a commonality between Louisiana and the Caribbean, Glissant's reply, which has now percolated through Faulkner and New World studies at large, unravels another type of relation: "the plantation system, the thrilling persistence of Creole languages ... and, most blatantly in all of these slave societies, the insistent suffering of the blacks and the runaway slaves."[26] However, there is one "revolutionary" trace Glissant alludes to but leaves relatively unexplored: the presence of Haiti (and indeed of Martinique) in *Absalom*: "Haiti, the Caribbean, the elsewhere, in any event, is a place where, one suspects, the stain of miscegenation marks every corner of the Plantation ... actually, there is an intuition that what surrounds the county assails it, but the county does not know this. Faulkner points to this elsewhere that is menacing, misunderstood, and charged with everything problematic."[27] It is, however, through Glissant's earlier writings that Haiti suddenly heaved into sight among Faulkner studies, in the mid-'90s, and it is to this island that we will now turn.

The Politics of Influence: Haiti, Faulkner, and the Unthinkable

Haiti, the first black Republic (1804) in the world and the second independent state of the hemisphere, was the inverse mirror image of the antebellum South: a world that could only seem upside-down for a Southerner, where the color lines had not only been irreversibly broken but inverted, and not only inverted but vertiginously (to use a Glissantian term) reshuffled. Haiti, in the Southern imaginary, was a historical fact, like the process of creolization already at work in New Orleans (Louisiana had been sold to the United States a year earlier, in 1803). In his study of the impact of the

Haitian revolution, Nick Nesbitt, taking his cue from C. L. R. James's masterpiece *The Black Jacobins*, examines Michel Rolph Trouillot's thesis that the Haitian revolution (1791–1804) was "unthinkable," "that for which one has no adequate instruments to conceptualize."[28] This paradigmatic "unthinkable" richly resonates with *Absalom*, Faulkner's deepest foray into the liminal spaces, at once openly visible but blindingly suppressed, between the Caribbean and the antebellum South, and into the alleged "innocence" of the American imperial expansionism after the Civil War. Whether the insurrectional import of the Haitian revolution was "unthinkable" for Faulkner and/or for the protagonists of *Absalom* (let alone for Faulkner scholarship until the mid-'90s), or if, on the contrary, *Absalom* was Faulkner's attempt at exposing the corrupt ideology that held sway in the politics of colonial expansionism that took place during his lifetime, one thing is certain: this multiplicity of interpretations attests to the persistence and resistance of the "unthinkable" – call it gaps, a Glissantian "insu,"[29] an unsayable – that is woven within the intricate textual and aural looms of the novel.

The most notorious bone of contention concerns whether Faulkner meant a blatant anachronism when he depicted Sutpen's years spent in "the West Indies" (early 1820s to 1833). Sutpen becomes the overseer of a sugar-cane plantation. He subdues a rebellion of blacks besieging his employer, a "French" planter, and marries the planter's daughter Eulalia (whose mother was "Spanish"), then abruptly repudiates her and their son (Charles Bon) when he realizes that the planter has not stuck to his side of the bargain: "they deliberately withheld from me the one fact which I have reason to know they were aware would have caused me to decline the entire matter" (212). On the one hand, as Matthews reminds us, "Sutpen seems to experience events that could not have happened as he thinks they have if he is indeed in Haiti during the 1820s. By 1804, the western half of the whole island of Hispaniola had undergone a revolution led by mixed-race insurgents."[30] How could Sutpen's design be implemented in the land whose new black leaders had asserted the rights of enslaved men not only to freedom but to *universal equality*, where slavery had been abolished at least in principle in 1793, and where the military efficiency of the black and mixed-race leaders and armies had overthrown the most potent imperial army in the world?

That accurate historical knowledge of Haiti was scarce in the early 1930s, in spite of the American occupation and, as Leigh Anne Duck has shown, of the subsequent spate of books written on the island, would not explain such an anachronism on Faulkner's part.[31] As Ladd has pointed out, "there is little doubt that Faulkner wrote *Absalom* out of a deep familiarity with the political and cultural situation in New Orleans and in Haiti, especially as it was perceived by and important to nineteenth- and early twentieth-century southerners."[32] On the other hand, Sutpen's quelling of the black "insurrection" (a word that was excised in the final draft[33]) could well coincide with the period (1820–43), during which the government of the mulatto Jean Pierre Boyer united the island by incorporating the Spanish eastern side of the island in 1822, then still called Santo Domingo. White Spanish Creoles had to flee, mainly to New Orleans (as the French Creoles who had survived the revolutionary period of 1791 to 1804 had done), and it is likely that Sutpen found himself employed by the (mixed-raced) *jaunes*, who had taken over all the plantations previously owned by either French or Spanish nationals. This was a very unstable and often violent period, throughout the island (particularly in the eastern part), as "code rural" had been introduced and forcefully implemented in 1826, coercing the mainly black peasant freeholders (mostly ex-revolutionary soldiers) to work in conditions akin to forced labor. Sutpen's rise to fortune occurs in 1827 during one of the scuffles that shook plantations on many occasions, but he would have been unable to decode a culture that would have confounded anyone who did not live in Haiti or had close connections with it. Sutpen's "innocence" is not simply tantamount to ignorance or incomplete schooling (indeed, one wonders how much he could have learned about Haiti even had he paid attention to his geography lessons, given the limitations and interests of antebellum southern education). The sole knowledge Sutpen accepts and is willing to receive is that of stories he heard about the West Indies (and "innocently" trusted because they came from books he could not read). How he ended up in Haiti remains a mystery, an "unknown." Ladd, Matthews, Godden, and Bongie demonstrate that Haiti represents a screen upon which the narrators (Quentin, Grandfather, and Jason Compson, each with a different agenda) project their own fantasies and anxieties. But they also show, on a metanarrative level, that Sutpen allegorizes an imperialist trajectory or "design" which mimics that of the United States' relationship with its immediate Caribbean surroundings, leading to the colonial occupation of the island, very much in view of all Americans in the 1920s and early 1930s. Haiti and all the Caribbean references that pervade the novel point to a convenient politics of obliviousness, which Matthews identifies as "the colonial representation of *fetish*" whereby "Sutpen's 'innocent' 'mistakes' ... exemplify an extensive cultural apparatus dedicated to preserving masterly innocence in new-world colonial Souths, and U.S. imperial innocence in the postcolonial world."[34]

This "knowledge that can be held while being ignored, a kind of vision that looks but does not see"[35] should be viewed in turn within the kaleidoscopic structure of the novel, which eschews any form of definite "order of knowledge," never revealing anything as clear as facts or meaning, and, as Glissant reminds us, revealing nothing else but the process of its unveiling: the rawness of words hitting minds and of minds hitting words but, above all, of what could be called a chaotic silence. *Absalom* implicates whoever reads it, and whatever it touches is dragged within the abyss of unknowing, the only possible knowledge that could be said to exist in the novel: this knowledge is "vertiginous" but never abstract. Any mode of interpretation must accept the risk of finding itself undone on the next page. This principle holds for how the Caribbean is represented in the novel. As Jeff Karem puts it in *The Purloined Islands*, reprising Matthews's (and Bhabha's) heuristic template of disavowed knowledge but now emptied of its anti-imperialist critique: "in *Absalom, Absalom!* the Caribbean is both overdetermined and underrepresented at the same time," at once a "dangerous and fertile" source of wealth and a place that is "abstract and unvoiced."[36]

However, close examination of the Haitian passages reveals a striking lucidity regarding the island's "two hundred years of oppression and exploitation" (202), both in spite of and because of Grandfather Compson's subjectivity. As is usual with Faulkner, his style makes us "see" and "sense" what escapes meaning and historical control. The succession of alliterative sounds creates a phonemic landscape that is both withering and suspended in time and space, "halfway" between the representable and the unrepresentable: witness the alliterative plosives ("black blood"; "bones"; "oppression," "exploitation," "paradox," "peaceful," "expelled," "sprang," "pound"), liquids ("little lost island," "latitude," "smiling," "lurked"), and fricatives ("ravished," "violence," "vengeance") (202). Those few Haitian pages tucked within the novel constitute "intertextual fragments" lifted from *Heart of Darkness*, reaching out and calling on other regions of the world to address colonialism as a global plague. By keeping Haiti cloaked in opacity, a term Glissant has coined to describe how Faulkner refuses to impose his voice on his black characters (his two attempts at "voicing" two black characters in *New Orleans Sketches* left him vulnerable to ideological prejudices) and irrespective of his public pronouncements, Faulkner's style is always ethical in the way unmediated transparency (alongside any claims to historical veracity) is constantly deferred in favor of oppositional opacity, the *modus operandi* of his works.

Opacity does not negate the possibility of knowledge, but, by opening up gaps in its homogeneous flow and by holding it in abeyance, it creates moments of interruptions – possibly revolutionary – that allows the unthinkable to be, if not taken in, at least thinkable and brought to bear on consciousness. Sutpen's "innocence" constitutes such an "unthinkable" in *Absalom*, but so does the Caribbean (whether it be New Orleans,[37] "foreign and paradoxical" (86); Eulalia, Charles Bon, his unnamed wife under plaçage and child; the French architect from Martinique; Sutpen's "wild" slaves) and the Haitian revolution. Historically and ideologically determined, what is glaringly unthinkable for the narrators in *Absalom* is the possibility of *equality* – between races and between classes – a possibility that is not so much repressed as foreclosed, even though it was plainly in evidence in New Orleans and perceptible in the distant echoes of the Haitian revolution.[38] Creolization, as a possible interracial dynamic that could open up a future for a regenerated South, United States and beyond, is unthinkable within an ideology of radical racism. In Ladd's words, "the years between 1890 and 1930 had been, in the South, years of hysterical white reaction to any possibility of integration, which was seen as a dangerous infection of the white cultural body and a threat to the very foundations of Anglo-American civilization.... The figure [of the mulatto] ... embodied the threats and the promises of integration in a racist culture that had defined itself chiefly through tropes of mastery ... rather than through tropes of equality and difference."[39] Charles Bon, whose very surname is synonymous with "good," at once moral and material (cf. Godden), happens to mean in eighteenth- and nineteenth-century French a "gain" that "returns," a "revenant-bon," a "phantom-like" surplus that haunts the narrative with its insurrectional potentials in spite of having been destroyed, still holding out the promise of a "profitable" creolized future, not only a moral gain, but a moral "bond." The very existence of Charles Bon resonates with the declaration of "reciprocal" *equality* made by the black leaders of the Haitian revolution, best expressed in their famous letter to the French revolutionary government: "And you, gentlemen, who would enslave us, have you not ... forgotten that you have formally sworn the declaration of rights of man that say men are born free and equal under the law."[40]

If *Absalom* "seems repeatedly to introduce revolutionary energy only to dispel it" and is shot through with clear indictments of "economic privilege," it is not tied to a failure to act on or respond to this knowledge.[41] On the contrary, *Absalom* keeps the idea of equality alive in the grips of destructive forces by maintaining its opaque and silent resistance to annihilation. Silence or "background silence" (gaps, aposiopesis, paralipsis, ellipsis), which is key to Faulkner's aesthetic, is no "silencing" but what, for Pierre Macherey, "gives a meaning to the meaning."[42] In effect, *Absalom* sidesteps the "unthinkable" and the impossibility of change by raveling and unraveling a Caribbean critique, cloaked in opacity, that differentiates itself from existing ideologies, whether they be racialist, imperialist, or Jacobinic revolutionary. This also applies to the discreet insurrectional French presence in the novel. Rousseau (his *Social Contract* [1762] and his *Discourse on the Origin and Basis of Inequality Among Men* [1754]) and Montesquieu (the good and bad "troglodytes" fable in his *Persian Letters* [1721], a term used to describe Sutpen and Henry), are summoned in the description of Sutpen's Appalachian community, where property and social and racial inequality do not exist ("because where he lived the land belonged to anybody and everybody and so the man who would … say 'This is mine' is crazy" [179]). Of course, Faulkner does not indulge in a nostalgic portrait of Sutpen as a "good savage" who will fall from grace, Candide-like, after his descent into plantation hell: this French universalist discourse of equality will prove inefficient and easily corruptible in contact with the reality of inequity. Other visible references to the French Revolution, via the French Caribbean, the "swarthy man resembling a creature out of an old woodcut of the French Revolution erupts" (89) and the "French architect" (26) from Martinique, represent inadequate models for a truly creolized terrain, not because they are foreign but because they are "indifferent." The French architect – described as an "artist" (29) – is "sardonic" and fearless, and his knowledge of maroon escape techniques, blended with his "rationalist" use of nature (he "architects" himself on treetops), applies to himself only: his insurrectional knowledge is not shared or transmitted; his body, science and art do not touch "ground."

In the grips of ideologies and myths that are either destructive or ineffectual, *Absalom*'s "counternarratives" are frayed but for one exception: language itself, or rather, languages, in their *creolized* form.[43] Languages (aural, gestural, and written) are the most purloined of all "letters" in *Absalom*, to reprise Matthews's Poesque image about a form of looking that does not see, but also to point up the most irruptive moments in the novel: Bon's letter, the vulnerable and fragile "scratch" "mark," "trace." A potent definition of language (as written and spoken) is given by Grandfather and Jason Compson, in a textual fragment framed by Sutpen's Haitian venture: "riding peacefully about on his horse while he learned the language (that meager and fragile thread, Grandfather said, by which the little surface corners and edges of men's secret and solitary lives may be joined for an instant now and then before sinking back into the darkness)" (202). This conception of language, defined as a linguistic umbilical cord that can unite individuals, is left vulnerable to silence and effacement. Faulkner's authorial comment on the very texture of his narrative and of his style is strangely coupled with Sutpen's capacity to learn languages: Haitian patois, French, and "bombastic" English. Sutpen's innate ability to learn by mimicry is closely linked to his entry into language – he is constantly groping for analogies, knowing that language can be used as the ultimate tool of control and power. It is at the very moment he understands this, in the darkness of the room in which he sleeps with all his family, that his brooding "revolution" metamorphoses into his "design": "it was like that, he said, an explosion" (192). Sutpen's choice between direct *action* (to kill using a rifle) and his "design" are shown to be equally sterile.

In *Absalom*, Sutpen's use of languages, however dexterous and potentially rich as a tool for *equality*, is perversely inverted: he subdues the insurrecting Haitian blacks, his own slaves, the French architect, *everyone*, through his control of language. However, Sutpen's polyglossia does intimate language's capacity for heralding equality, in spite of his misuse of it as a tool for exerting tyrannical power. Unwillingly, Sutpen's tyranny serves as a catalyst for future emancipation. The novel dwells on his chameleon-like capacity to become indistinguishable from his slaves, fighting on equal terms with them to assert his authority, looking like them. Sutpen's figure is doubly revolutionary. By espousing and replicating to excess an iniquitous system, he shatters its principles; by his capacity for "becoming-other" and addressing others (represented as Caribbean) on their own terms, he involuntarily sows the seeds of the main principle of equality: language as a shared "good," as a "bond." These revolutions are not willed by Sutpen, but they form another thread, another invisible motif, in the novel's tapestry. Language, that most "fragile" thread, offers an infinite oppositional force that does not use force. As Jean-Luc Nancy explains: "In order for language to exist, in order for us to speak, it's necessary that there should be mutual recognition. Language signifies our understanding of one another, and to make oneself understood, one must be equal."

The presence of Creole (in all its forms or patois) in *Absalom* irresistibly and paradoxically unites Sutpen and his son, his "slaves," and all the characters linked to the Caribbean; it would also intimate a linguistic exchange between the Caribbean, the South and the United States at large, bringing porosity where intransigence held sway. New Orleans, beyond its "decadent" exposure through the eyes of the southern speakers, is also the place where all languages meet and where a new language, which Glissant names but does not straitjacket into a single definition, opens up a sense of equality that trumps national, class, and color boundaries. Glissant calls it creolization, a multidimensional and multilingual process that betokens an "Imaginary of languages." Equality, a word most dreaded by the white supremacists and their cheerleaders in the 1930s, is a principle already at work in *Absalom* through the slow and difficult process of creolization and catalyzed by its most unlikely, indeed impossible, agents.

Other Caribbean writers were to give not only direction but structure to Jim Bond's howling, so akin to this "notlanguage" with which Faulkner wrote *Absalom*. It is not merely a language of negativity but a poetic intention, a call to be relayed ("howl(ing) the structure, structure the howl(ing)" as Glissant put it), rippling through the Caribbean landscapes and beyond, wherever "a new region of the world" – Glissant's phrase to locate the multiple traces of Relation at once historically anchored in a specific place and geographically dispersed through all places – is emerging, however unpre-*dict*ably and unfore*see*ably.

A New Region of the World: Kincaid, Condé, Glissant

In her seminal article "Border and Bodies: The United States, America, and the Caribbean," Vera Kutzinski cogently interprets the cross-cultural "ripples" that Quentin Compson imagines "moving on, spreading" from one "pool" to the next, as if linked by "a narrow umbilical water-cord" (210): "Most striking about the Sutpen saga in Faulkner's *Absalom, Absalom!* is its insistently trans-American reach.... It is the Americas, not just the southern parts of the United States, that constitute Faulkner's literary and cultural 'region,' and he, in turn, is reconstituted by the perspectives and claims of this larger territory."[44] Literary regions, no longer strictly defined by fixed cultural boundaries and monolithic identities, would form a semiotic and semantic "ripple-space" whose new geographies could be perceived in the works of writers such as Harris, Glissant, Faulkner, Brodner, Condé, and so on.

Opening up this line of enquiry further, Jana Evans Braziel pays closer attention to the blurring of "genres" in *Faulkner, Mississippi*, its "weavings of physical world and literary texts" whereby "the relation between 'genre' and 'genealogy' also traces the contours of a deep connection between [Faulkner's] novel and the world it depicts."[45] Taking her cue from Mycéa's presence in *Faulkner, Mississippi*, and from Clytie's neglected role and "act of resistance" in *Absalom*, Braziel offers a rich reading of Jamaica Kincaid's *The Autobiography of My Mother*, seen as a "powerful narrative rejoinder to Faulkner's novel that allows us to shift from Faulkner's genealogical preoccupation with illegitimate sons to a consideration and revaluation of the genealogical role of dis-inherited black daughters in the Americas."[46] Kincaid's "autothanography"[47] engages in a profound dialogue with Clytie's apocalyptic narrative in *Absalom*, but, as Braziel shows, via Michael Dash and Glissant, *with* Kincaid, these "Antillean detours" weave together an "imaginary region" and usher in "an alternate way of thinking about regions from their traditional designation as a smaller, distinct, or clearly bound geographical space within a larger nation-state, as a transnational yet specific cultural zone."[48]

Like Glissant, Kincaid distrusts any universalist claims to narratives, creating instead a writing closely bound to landscapes, geology, and plants. She forges a style that is at once based on repetitive self-erasure and regenerative grafting of traces. Her latest novel, *See Now Then* (2013), embodies this organic counterpoetics, carefully re-grafting narrative techniques that are reminiscent not only of Faulkner's *As I Lay Dying, Absalom, Requiem for a Nun* and *The Sound and the Fury* but, more crucially, Woolf's modernist trilogy (*Mrs. Dalloway, To the Lighthouse*, and *The Waves*) as well as Gertrude Stein. Faulkner's "the past is not dead, it's not even past" (*RN* 535) is equally applicable to the intertextual memory that constitutes literature, in which language is as much a memory-trace (Chamoiseau) as a resilient seed that can fertilize all terrains.

See Now Then is a threnody for the voiceless dead and a secret and whispering song of and to life, reiterating the writing of death and replanting its own words into new landscapes. Traditional boundaries are not blurred but rendered senseless; as we have seen earlier with regard to Glissant, Caribbean literature has turned the notion of literary influence into an irrigating circuit that dispenses with hierarchical verticality, replacing it with an archipelagic transversality that now holds for *all* literatures and art forms. In Kincaid's novel, Mrs. Sweet, a vulnerable "arrivant" from Antigua, becomes the narrator of the incipit of another book, *The Autobiography of My Mother* ("My mother died at the moment I was born, and so for my whole life there was nothing standing between myself and eternity").[49] Mrs. Sweet, wholly taken by the beauty of her garden in Vermont and seeking refuge in the contemplation of serene North American landscapes, simultaneously sees and hears an inner "tormented landscape": "the Caribbean sea and the Atlantic Ocean … Mrs. Sweet's eyes were impenetrable … for behind her eyes lay scenes of turbulence, upheavals, murders, betrayals, on foot, on land, and the seas where horde upon horde of people were transported to places on the earth's surface that they had never heard of or even imagined, and murderer and murdered, betrayer and betrayed, the source of the turbulence, the instigator of the upheavals, were all mixed up, and the sorting out of the true, true truth."[50] Kincaid's writing pushes back the reaches of literature – past and present – pushing it past the Glissantian Abyss/matrix, still further back to where lie the traces of the Carib people who are now all but extinct. In *See Now Then*, time is an inward gaze that does not look but sees: "for even now I don't understand what Then was Now, even now I see then as translucent, as if it is all taking place on a pane of glass and sliding that way and just when it is about to disappear into nothing the pane of glass tilts this way, back into seeing Now and Then there as it all is just before it goes into another Then and Now, another Then and Now and seeing all of it only in a blink."[51] As with Faulkner's and Glissant's novels, *Malemort* in particular, literary experimentation turns into an invisible, subterranean and a-chronic form of literary solidarity. Kincaid inflects Glissant's poetics of relation, carrying it over into nature, into a language that incessantly repeats its caesura from a mankind irreparably guilty of genocide.

What Braziel aptly calls an "imaginary region" encompasses many other writers: from the Haitian novelists (Roumain, Alexis, Frankétienne, Danticat[52]) to the Martiniquan writer Patrick Chamoiseau[53] and the Guadeloupean writer Maryse Condé. Condé's *Crossing the Mangrove* (1989) offers particularly fertile ground for an openly intertextual dialogue with Faulkner's novels, not only with *As I Lay Dying*, as Michael Lucey pointed out, but also, as Celia Britton and O'Regan[54] have deftly noticed, with *Absalom* and *Light in August*. In an interview with Françoise Pfaff, Condé explicitly refers to Faulkner, whose books were on her desk as she was writing her novel: "Transgression and guilt constitute one of the profound and essential themes of any literature. If you consider Faulkner, whom I have read quite a bit, you notice that he depicts many characters affected by a fault that is not within, but rather outside them, in the community to which they belong."[55]

Through Condé's skillful and strategic diversion of Faulkerian "intertextual fragments," what Derek O'Regan calls "deliberate slippage from the intertext," Condé inscribes her own writerly design, allowing her to decompose and expose the harmful foundations of Guadeloupean community and suggest possible models of recomposition, at once removed from the inherited trauma of the past and from the post/colonial condition of the Guadeloupean present. Condé's use of Faulknerian techniques, the "modified stream of consciousness" that Glissant had identified in *Faulkner, Mississippi*, and which finds itself "modified" by Condé (as was the case with Kincaid) with a view to "foregrounding the multiple voices of her Rivière au Sel microcosm," enables her to compose a narrative "with a sense of the kaleidoscopic social atmosphere of present-day Guadeloupean reality so that she may eschew a past-determined and, above all, race-determined discursive point of view."[56] Contrary to Glissant, whose adoption of Faulknerian techniques and homonyms gives way to an entirely "other," Condé conducts a textual politics based on a creolization of Faulkner's writing, whereby textual borrowings resonate with unfamiliar closeness. By creolizing the hypertext – *Absalom* but also *Light in August* – Condé preempts any suggestion of hierarchical influence and "graft[s] the theme of inherited damnation relating to race and the crime of slavery, of which Burden and Joe Christmas are the avatars *par excellence*, onto the family curse that haunts Sancher himself ... underscoring the disabling obsession of Antilleans with their slave history [and proposing] its rewriting whereby the negativity of a race-determined past of arrant victimisation gives way to enabling stories of the collective memory."[57]

In his penultimate book, Glissant ushers in the idea of "a new region of the world." This concept, shot through with intuitions and ideas that had emerged from his earlier study of *Caribbean Discourse*, opens up the spatial and temporal boundaries that had still hampered his theory; it also tangibly alludes to a revolutionary way of looking and making sense of the emerging new art forms that cross known cognitive and geographic boundaries. This new region of the world *was once* the Caribbean space, and still is, but it is also now *one* among many others: "we are all now entering into a *new region of the world*, which marks its territories on all known and imaginable places, and of which only a few could have foreseen the wanderings and obscurities."[58] Glissant's region is already with us, *everywhere*. He sees it in terms of a threshold that has now been irreversibly crossed, opening new ways of traversing the Tout-monde (the "whole world") and new ways of interpreting – perhaps even changing – it.

Finally, to his unanswered question about the community – "always lacking"[59] – his work has constantly addressed, the trace of a reply emerges: "at the point at which *we all* enter together this *new region of the world* in which we are entering, the varieties or identities of peoples without exception and of their communities (in all) are neither lost nor distorted nor imprisoned by exaggeration, and finally differences come together, here resisting and there engendering more beauty."[60] The Tout-monde, in all its regions, in all its languages, is also accompanied by new art forms, which Glissant will soon stop calling literature, and whose categories we do not yet know. Glissant suggests that Faulkner was already there, one foot firmly in a new region he had apparently closed off in order to signify all the others. Glissant's concept of this new region of the world could open up new readings of Faulkner's late work, *A Fable* in particular, whose Creole character Tooleyman (everyone/*toutlemonde* in Creole) could well have prefigured the Glissantian Tout-monde (*Ti-moun, timoun* meaning "child" but also "person" and "world" in Creole). Glissant's "prophetic vision of the past," which has changed American and New World studies the world over, has so far been construed as a look backward, but it is also a prophetic vision, a gift *from* the past, *of* the past, to the future that is our present. Yes, the Caribbean is no longer an "estuary" of the Americas, it is its "préface"[61] and the foreword to new regions to come.

NOTES

1   Édouard Glissant, *Faulkner, Mississippi*, Barbara B. Lewis and Thomas C. Spear (trans.) (Chicago: University of Chicago Press, [1997] 1999), p. 102. We shall be referring to the English translations of Glissant's books when available, with

slight emendations when required; otherwise all other translations of Glissant's quotes are by Anthony Cummins.

2 Glissant, *Faulkner, Mississippi*, p. 29.

3 Ramón Saldívar introduced postcolonialism to Faulkner studies but before Glissant's theories, via Michael Dash's translation of *Caribbean Discourse*, had time to ripple through the United States: Ramón Saldívar, "Looking for a Master Plan: Faulkner, Paredes, and the Colonial and Postcolonial Subject," *The Cambridge Companion to William Faulkner*, Philip Weinstein (ed.) (Cambridge: Cambridge University Press, 1995), pp. 96–120. On how Glissant's writings have since then impacted on Faulkner, New World, U.S. South, and Caribbean studies, see Maritza Stanchich, "The Hidden Caribbean 'Other' in William Faulkner's *Absalom, Absalom!*: An Ideological Ancestry of U.S. Imperialism," *Mississippi Quarterly* 49 (1996), 603–17; Chris Bongie, *Islands and Exiles: The Creole Identities of Post/Colonial Literature* (Stanford, CA: Stanford University Press, 1998); Michael Dash, *The Other America: Caribbean Literature in a New World Context* (Charlottesville: University Press of Virginia, 1998); George Handley, *Postslavery Literatures in the Americas: Family Portraits in Black and White* (Charlottesville: University of Virginia Press, 2000); Barbara Ladd, "William Faulkner, Édouard Glissant, and a Creole Poetics of History and Body in *Absalom, Absalom!* and *A Fable*" in *Faulkner in the Twenty-First Century*, Robert Hamblin and Ann J. Abadie (eds.) (Jackson: University Press of Mississippi, 2003), pp. 31–49; *Resisting History: Gender, Modernity and Authorship in William Faulkner, Zora Neale Hurston, and Eudora Welty* (Baton Rouge: Louisiana State University Press, 2007); Vera Kutzinski, "Borders and Bodies: The United States, America, and the Caribbean," *New Centennial Review* 1.2 (2001), 55–88; Randy Boyagoda, "Just where and what is 'the (comparatively speaking) South'? Caribbean writers on Melville and Faulkner," *Mississippi Quarterly* 57.1 (2003), 65–73; John T. Matthews, "Recalling the West Indies: From Yoknapatawpha to Haiti and Back," *American Literary History* 16.2 (2004), 238–62; Jon Smith, "Postcolonial, Black, and Nobody's Margins: the US South and New World Studies," *American Literary History* 16.1 (2004), 144–61; *Look Away! The U.S. South in New World Studies*, Jon Smith and Deborah Cohn (eds.) (Durham, NC: Duke University Press, 2004); John Lowe, "'Calypso Magnolia': The Caribbean Side of the South," *South Central Review* 22.1 (2005), 54–80; Matthew Pratt Guterl, "'I Went to the West Indies': Race, Place and the Antebellum South," *American Literary History* 18.3 (2006), 446–67; Jessica Adams, Michael P. Bibler, and Cécile Accilien (eds.), *Just Below South: Intercultural Performance in the Caribbean and the U.S. South* (Charlottesville: University of Virginia Press, 2007); Richard C. Moreland (ed.), *A Companion to William Faulkner* (Oxford: Blackwell Publishing, 2007); Valérie Loichot, *Orphan Narratives: The Postplantation Literature of Faulkner, Glissant, Morrison, and Saint-John Perse* (Charlottesville: University of Virginia Press, 2007), "Faulkner's Caribbean Geographies" (forthcoming); Jana Evans Braziel, *Caribbean Genesis: Jamaica Kincaid and the Writing of New Worlds* (Albany: State University of New York, 2009); Annette Trefzer and Ann J. Abadie (eds.), *Global Faulkner: Faulkner and Yoknapatawpha* (Jackson: University Press of Mississippi, 2009); Elizabeth Christine Russ, *The Plantation in the*

Postslavery Imagination (Oxford: Oxford University Press, 2009); Kristin E. Pitt, *Body, Nation, and Narrative in the Americas* (London: Palgrave Macmillan, 2010); Jeff Karem, *The Purloined Islands: Caribbean-U.S. Crosscurrents in Literature and Culture (1880–1959)* (Charlottesville: University of Virginia Press, 2011); Seanna Sumalee Oakley, *Common Places: The Poetics of African Postromantics* (Amsterdam: Rodopi, 2011); Bethany Aery Clerico, "Haunting the Good Neighbor: Faulkner's Caribbean Imagination in *Go Down, Moses*," *The Faulkner Journal* 26.2 (2012), 5–26; Cynthia Dobbs, "Vernacular Kinship, The Creole City, and Faulkner's 'New Orleans,'" *The Faulkner Journal* 26.1 (2012), 57–74; Martin Munro and Celia Britton (eds.), *American Creoles: The Francophone Caribbean and the American South* (Liverpool: Liverpool University Press, 2012).

4 Glissant, *Philosophie de la Relation: Poésie en étendue* (Paris: Gallimard, 2009), p. 45.

5 Antonio Benítez-Rojo, *The Repeating Island: The Caribbean and the Postmodern Perspective*, James Maraniss (trans.) (Durham, NC: Duke University Press, 1992), pp. 3–4.

6 Benítez-Rojo, *The Repeating Island*, p. 21; Glissant, *Poetics of Relation*, Betsy Wing (trans.) (Ann Arbor: University of Michigan Press, [1990] 1997), pp. 33–4.

7 Glissant, *Poetics of Relation*, p. 11.

8 Benítez-Rojo, "The Repeating Island," *Do the Americas Have a Common Literature?* Gustavo Pérez-Firmat (ed.) (Durham, NC: Duke University Press, 1990), p. 105. For a probing comparison between these two thinkers' theorization of the plantation, see Elizabeth Christine Russ, *The Plantation in the Postslavery Imagination* (Oxford: Oxford University Press, 2009), pp. 95–115; see also Lorna Burns, *Contemporary Caribbean Writing and Deleuze: Literature between Postcolonialism and Post-Continental Philosophy* (London: Bloomsbury, 2012), pp. 23–6.

9 Jana Evans Braziel, "Antillean Detours through the American South: Édouard Glissant's and Jamaica Kincaid's Textual Returns to William Faulkner," *Just Below South*, p. 253. On the crucial notion of genealogy, see also Loichot, *Orphan Narratives*. Braziel's and Loichot's books and articles brilliantly bring forth the heretofore invisible and silenced female narratives that have been "orphaned" not only in Faulkner but also in Glissant's works, among other Caribbean artists.

10 See Loichot's interpretation of the Faulknerian "Dark House" (the aborted title of both *Light in August* and *Absalom, Absalom!*) as a possible echo of the Glissantian notion of the "belly" of the slave ship and of the plantation as a paradoxical "womb" of "memory" and as the site "of a birth-carrying-death-and-suffering," pp. 140–3.

11 Glissant, *Poetics of Relation*, p. 34.

12 Ibid., p. 34.

13 Glissant, *Le Discours antillais* (Paris: Gallimard, 1997 [1981]), p. 17, 427.

14 Ibid., pp. 254–60.

15 For a more elaborate exploration of this creative tension between politics and poetics, see *Les Entretiens de Baton Rouge* with Alexandre Leupin (Paris: Gallimard, 2008), pp. 55–64; see also Nick Nesbitt, *Caribbean Critique: Antillean Critical Theory from Toussaint to Glissant* (Liverpool: Liverpool University Press, 2013).

16 Glissant, *Traité du Tout-Monde* (Paris: Gallimard, 1997), p. 161; for a wide-ranging study of commonplaces in Caribbean poetics attentive to stylistic commonalities across African Atlantic writers, see Seanna Sumalee Oakley, *Common Places*.

17 Glissant, *Faulkner, Mississippi*, pp. 95–6.

18 Glissant, *Mémoires des esclavages* (Paris: Gallimard, 2007), pp. 61–3.

19 Glissant, *Faulkner, Mississippi*, p. 197.

20 Glissant, *Le Discours antillais*, p. 263.

21 Glissant, *Faulkner, Mississippi*, p. 195.

22 Ibid., p. 35.

23 On May 18, 1922, Joyce and Proust met at a supper party organized by Sydney Schiff. As Arthur Power commented: "Here are the two greatest literary figures of our time meeting and they ask each other if they like truffles," Richard Ellmann, *James Joyce* (Oxford: Oxford University Press, 1982), pp. 508–9.

24 See Patrick Ffrench, "Friendship, Asymmetry, Sacrifice: Bataille and Blanchot," *Parrhesia* 3 (2007), 32–42.

25 Glissant, *Faulkner, Mississippi*, p. 254.

26 Ibid., p. 29.

27 Ibid., pp. 87–8.

28 On the Haitian Revolution and its historical and philosophical impact, see Nesbitt, *Caribbean Critique*; Michel Rolph Trouillot, *Silencing the Past: Power and the Production of History* (Boston: Beacon, 1995); C. L. R. James, *The Black Jacobins: Toussaint L'Ouverture and the San Domingo Revolution* (New York: Vintage, 1989); Barbara Ladd, *Nationalism and the Color Line in G.W. Cable, Mark Twain, and William Faulkner* (Baton Rouge: Louisiana State University Press, 1996) and Ladd (2000); Richard Godden, *Fictions of Labor: William Faulkner and the South's Long Revolution* (Cambridge: Cambridge University Press, 1997); Michael Dash, *Haiti and the United States: National Stereotypes and the Literary Imagination* (New York: Palgrave, 1997); Bongie, *Islands and Exiles*; Susan Buck-Morss, *Hegel, Haiti, and Universal History* (Pittsburgh: University of Pittsburgh Press, 2009); *Haiti and the Americas*, Carla Calargé, Raphael Dalleo, Luis Duno-Gottberg, and Clevis Headley (eds.) (Jackson: University Press of Mississippi, 2013). See also Matthews (2004).

29 See Philip Weinstein, *Unknowing: The Work of Modernist Fiction* (Ithaca, NY: Cornell University Press, 2005).

30 John T. Matthews, *William Faulkner: Seeing Through the South* (Oxford: Wiley-Blackwell, 2009), p. 192.

31 See Leigh Anne Duck, "From Colony to Empire: Postmodern Faulkner," in *Global Faulkner*, pp. 24–42. Duck astutely points up the possible echo of William Seabrook's *The Magic Island* (recounting in particular the tale of Faustin Wirkus, a "Marine who had reportedly been crowned king") in *Absalom*, Sutpen's description as "this Faustus" (145) and as an "explorer" (24), let alone the few references to voodoo warnings found in the planter's house, may indicate a familiarity, if not with this book and its "innocent" protagonist, at least with other tales of Haiti that circulated during the American occupation of the island.

32 Ladd, *Nationalism*, 142.
33 See Jeff Karem, *The Purloined Islands*, p. 117. Bongie and Godden also noticed that Faulkner does not use the word "slave" within the context of Haiti.
34 Matthews, "Recalling the West Indies," p. 239.
35 Ibid., p. 239.
36 Karem, *The Purloined Islands*, p. 116.
37 On New Orleans as the liminal space between the U.S. South and the Caribbean, see Dobbs, Clerico, and Munro and Britton's *American Creoles*, pp. 19–76.
38 See Jaime Harker's essay in this volume on the question of imagining sexual equality in the plantation regime.
39 Ladd, *Nationalism*, pp. 139–40.
40 Letter of Jean-François, Belair and Biassou/Toussaint, July 1792, quoted in Nesbitt, *Caribbean Critique*, pp. 288–9.
41 Duck, "From Colony to Empire," p. 37.
42 Pierre Macherey, *Pour une théorie de la production littéraire* (Paris: François Maspero, 1966), p. 106. Translation Britton, "Ancestral Crime," p. 218.
43 Matthews, *Seeing Through the South*, p. 196.
44 Kutzinski, "Borders and Bodies," p. 59.
45 Braziel, "Antillean Detours," pp. 240–1.
46 Ibid., p. 241.
47 Ibid., p. 257.
48 Ibid., p. 259.
49 Jamaica Kincaid, *The Autobiography of My Mother* (New York: Macmillan, 1996), p. 3.
50 Jamaica Kincaid, *See Now Then* (New York: Farrar, Straus, and Giroux, 2013), pp. 18–19.
51 Ibid., p. 178.
52 See Michel Serres, "Roumain et Faulkner traduisent la littérature," *Hermès* III (Paris: Minuit, 1974). On Danticat and Faulkner, see Patrick Samway, "Homeward Journey: Edwidge Danticat's Fictional Landscapes, Mindscapes, Genescapes, and Signscapes in *Breath, Eyes, Memory*," *The Mississippi Quarterly* 57.1 (2003), 75–83.
53 Chamoiseau's admiration for Faulkner is explicitly stated in *Écrire en pays dominé* (Paris: Gallimard, 1997) and *Un dimanche au cachot* (Paris: Gallimard, 2007), and implicitly present in *L'Esclave vieil homme et le molosse* (Paris: Gallimard, 1997).
54 Michael Lucey, "Voices Accounting for the Past: Maryse Condé's *Traversée de la Mangrove*," *L'héritage de Caliban*, Maryse Condé (ed.) (Pointe-à-Pitre: Éditions Jasor, 1992), pp. 123–32; Celia Britton, "Ancestral Crime in the Novels of Faulkner, Glissant and Condé," *American Creoles*, pp. 216–29. For a magnificent analysis of Condé's novel in light of Faulkner's novels, see Derek O'Regan, *Postcolonial Echoes and Evocations* (Oxford: Lang, 2006).
55 Quoted in Britton, "Ancestral Crime," p. 224.
56 O'Regan, *Postcolonial Echoes*, p. 54.
57 Ibid., p. 57.
58 Glissant, *Une nouvelle région du monde: Esthétique I* (Paris: Gallimard, 2006), p. 21.

59 Deleuze, quoted in the epigraph to Édouard Glissant, *Sartorius* (Paris: Gallimard, 1999). For a detailed analysis of Caribbean community in light of Jean-Luc Nancy's philosophy, one that could fruitfully be brought to bear on studies about communities in Faulkner, see Celia Britton, *The Sense of Community*, pp. 37–8.

60 Glissant, *Une nouvelle région*, p. 98.

61 Glissant, *Philosophie de la Relation*, p. 49.

12

RAMÓN SALDÍVAR AND SYLVAN GOLDBERG

The Faulknerian Anthropocene: Scales of Time and History in *The Wild Palms* and *Go Down, Moses*

As part of what has become a robust body of criticism putting Faulkner's work into conversation with theories and literatures of the Global South, Hosam Aboul-Ela has recently argued for the need to attend to Faulkner's formal strategies for registering modes of historical knowledge that contest the linearity and progressive teleology of Western history. Aboul-Ela challenges a longstanding attention to Faulkner's stylistic repetition as mere modernist aesthetics by claiming that repetition marks a *formal* expression of Faulkner's understanding of the American South as a colonial economy, a post-Reconstruction dependent of the North. Like the postcolonial theorists and writers with whom Aboul-Ela compares him, Faulkner's temporally experimental narration "equates history with continuing processes of peripheralization and disruption, which are better expressed through a narrative that keeps ending up back at the beginning."[1] Thus, Aboul-Ela aligns Faulkner's narrative strategies not with the high modernist writers (Stein, Eliot, Joyce) who exhibited similar nonlinear formal features as an aesthetic escape from the teleology of history, and with whom Faulkner has never quite fit, but rather with the Latin American, Arab, and other third-world writers who have long claimed Faulkner as an influence.

Faulkner's aesthetic strategies are not an effacing of history but rather, like his thematic attention to race, class, gender, and sexuality, another mode of articulating otherness that brings history, and historical violence, into the frame with more precise mimetic accuracy. Because these stylistic features offer a formal expression of ideological confrontations within colonized societies, writers from the peripheries and semiperipheries find in Faulkner useful strategies for "connect[ing] literary form and material conditions," as Aboul-Ela writes of Gabriel García Márquez, who claimed Faulkner as a formative influence. García Márquez, like Faulkner, thus "argu[es] for a kind of experimental neorealism, for a literary phenomenon invested in verisimilitude, more than for a borrowing of modernism's fascination with the aesthetic realm."[2] Juan Carlos Onetti, José María Arguedas, and Mario

Vargas Llosa also have characterized their affection for Faulkner in similar formal terms. But even before García Márquez and other celebrated Latin American "Boom" novelists of the 1960s and '70s embraced Faulkner, Jorge Luis Borges, Faulkner's near-contemporary, had done so more fully than had readers and critics in the United States. In 1940, shortly after the original publication in 1939 of *The Wild Palms*, for example, Borges translated Faulkner's experimental neorealist novel under the title of *Las palmeras salvajes*.[3] Unlike Faulkner's earlier masterpieces such as *The Sound and the Fury* (1929), *As I Lay Dying* (1930), or *Absalom, Absalom!* (1936), which had immediately resonated with U.S. readers and critics, *The Wild Palms* had not been well received. That Borges turned to Faulkner's less well-known novel of interwoven temporalities, mixed literary modes, and primordial psychic and physical nature fresh from his own explorations of similar topics in two his most powerful stories, "Tlön, Uqbar, Orbis Tertius" and "El Sur" ("The South"), is a clue to the link between Faulkner's aesthetics and those of the Global South. Focusing on the fundamental structures of time, reality, and the imaginary, these and other of Borges's fictions animated the wholesale reconfiguration of Latin American literature under what would become the mode of magical realism. As another form of realism, magical realism can be seen as one unexpected avenue for the confluence of Faulkner, writers of the Latin American boom generation, and the new novelists emerging from South Asia, Africa, the Middle East, and other sites of dependency in the Global South during the era of decolonization.

Why vocabularies of the Global South and dependency theories arising from the social sciences and from mid-twentieth-century postcolonial critical traditions are of significance to students of literature is evident when one considers Borges's and other Latin American novelists' concern with the real in literature and with the continuing importance of nation-based literary history. Given that the ideas of the real and the nation are still the main ways we categorize literature, what happens when we think *across* nations and national categories to other conceptions of the real? In what follows, we wish to consider Faulkner in the context of the new critical terms that include globalization, concern with hemispheric environmental questions, and the world culture of the Global South.

The idea of the Global South first emerged in the postwar era from the fact that, with few exceptions, practically all of the world's industrially developed countries lay to the north of the so-called developing countries. According to sociologist Saskia Sassen, the term "Global South" refers to a new phase of global capital and designates primarily the territories that have been subjected to a post-Keynesian financial logic of land grabs, to the imposition of debt as a disciplining regime, to the massive extraction of mineral and human value, and to the massive expulsion of people from middle-class status into abject poverty.[4] The key words here are "expulsion" and "extraction." The underdevelopment of countries at a peripheral remove from the core of metropolitan economic power did not just happen; underdevelopment occurred as the result of active forces shaping regional societies. For this reason, it is fair to say that various southern economies and cultures share comparable experiences of marginalization and unequal access to the resources of globalization that differentiate them from fully developed and hegemonic cultures in their respective locations and the spaces they inhabit.

What does all this have to do with Faulkner and the history of the American novel that he helped so powerfully to shape? In the context of issues concerning the mid-twentieth-century era of decolonization and the emergence of a postcolonial Global South, Faulkner's southern reach is of great importance. Focusing attention on the modernizing processes of the U.S. South and of the southern portions of the Americas, Faulkner helped initiate the transnational and globalizing themes that are of such concern to humanities and social-science scholars today. He did so by focusing on the dependency of the South on the processes of modernization and by shaping his fiction as a formal response to and expression of those processes of dependency. As Susan Willis has accurately noted, "what makes dependency theory so useful for literary analysis is that it defines the historical contradictions of domination in terms which can then be related to the form and language of the literary text."[5] This is the crucial point of Willis's analysis: dependency theory as formalized by the idea of the Global South allows us to see how the economic and racial politics of our time are enmeshed with *the form and language* of the literary texts that describe the modern world.

To this mix, we add one other consequence of placing Faulkner in the context of the Global South. At the same time that we may see Faulkner as hemispheric regionalist, he continues to attend to the classic American theme of the wilderness versus settlement culture and the increasing eclipse of primordial nature by the encroachment of industrial modernization in the post-Reconstruction era. This attention locates Faulkner on another hemispheric plane, namely one offering a much more skeptical view of the romantic notion of a primordially pure natural world "immune from village and town institutions."[6] Faulkner's perspective on wilderness and the impact of modernization on the natural world is tinted by colonial and peripheral economic relations: in the U.S. South, the industries extracting resources and reshaping the Southern landscape were often dominated by Northern capital. The emphasis in literary studies on the trans-Atlantic aspects of modernism have typically prevented critics from seeing the connections between modernisms and modernists in the Americas, keeping northern and southern Americas oddly separated from each other, and from shared political and cultural events in the hemisphere. In particular, the Eurocentric focus in American literary studies has tended to obscure the numerous ways that Faulkner's connection with the issues of coloniality and postcoloniality also mark much Latin American literature of the pre- and post–World War II years and thus link Faulkner to that other South, the Global South – especially Latin America and its cultural history. By contrast, Latin American writers have often been very clear about their Faulknerian connection. Chief among the themes Faulkner addresses that make his fictions of such moment to Latin America are those having to do with subject formation in relation to racial and social ideologies and the frightening pressures emerging from the colonized world as it begins to throw off its colonial burden, including those pressures exerted on a natural world deeply tied to the identities of the colonized.

Place has always held a central position within Faulkner criticism, but the advent of ecocriticism has led to a reevaluation of Faulkner's representations of the natural world. The same year, in fact, that saw the publication of the field-inaugurating *The Ecocriticism Reader* (1996) also witnessed the annual Faulkner and Yoknapatawpha Conference elect as its theme "Faulkner and the Natural World." Though wilderness had long been considered an analog reflecting more deep-seated psychological concerns, ecocritical readings have encouraged critics to see Faulkner's real-world environment as subtending his fiction and to "rethink which are the manifest and which the hidden realms" of Faulkner's novels, as Susan Scott Parrish writes.[7] For Parrish, references to floods and rising waters in *The Sound and the Fury* allude to the 1927 Great Flood of the Mississippi River, in whose aftermath Faulkner wrote that novel, marking the centrality of environmental disaster within Faulkner's unconscious. The natural world, alongside issues like race, gender, and sexuality, comes to seem an equally compelling manifestation of Faulkner's interest in histories of violence, aligning human and natural histories as structuring traumas.

Critics who have attended to the natural world in Faulkner's work have been quick to note that wilderness often appears as ravaged landscape and thus as the locus of a sentimentalized nostalgia, and increasingly scholars have put these representations into conversation with the environmental history of the South and of the Mississippi Delta. "The Bear," in particular, with its lament for a disappearing wilderness sold off to logging interests, has been at the center of much of this critique. Lawrence Buell notes that this longest section of *Go Down, Moses* evokes "both a plot of wilderness destruction and an ethos of forest preservation" appropriate to the 1930s in which Faulkner wrote, when deforestation that accelerated beginning in the 1880s had led to an increase in flooding along the Mississippi.[8] It is this type of colonial economy, with Northern logging companies extracting Southern resources and leaving the South economically dependent and environmentally ravaged, that leads us to reintroduce a range of social histories into Faulkner's aesthetic experimentation. In particular, recent theorizations of the Anthropocene make it necessary to consider what happens to these human histories when placed alongside the quite different scale of natural history and epochal Time. A consideration of the relationship between these separate but related views of Time in Faulkner's novels allows us to sharpen an understanding of the demarcating quality of Faulkner's place in the literary imagination of the hemispheric Americas.

Only recently has this alignment of human and natural histories emerged as one of the more compelling challenges to traditional humanist thought, appearing in accounts of what has come to be called the Anthropocene. In this reframing of our current geological epoch, humans have become not simply passive inhabitants of an inert planet but a force in their own right capable of altering the fundamental structures and systems of the earth. According to the postcolonial historian Dipesh Chakrabarty, whose essay "The Climate of History: Four Theses" has helped to galvanize these conversations within humanist critique, the Anthropocene challenges traditional historical understanding by scaling up conceptions of the human into the category of the species, a shift that challenges attention to the individual and risks obscuring precisely the categories of difference to which scholars of both Faulkner and the Global South have productively attended. This is of course not to say that environmental crises such as climate change transcend social difference. With this in mind, Chakrabarty acknowledges that the Anthropocene necessitates thinking two temporal scales at once, moving between "recorded and deep histories of human beings" – the latter offering up the human as "a species dependent on other species for its own existence, a part of the general history of life," and the former aligning with "histories of capitalism and modernization" that pull social imbalances into the frame.[9] Thinking these scales at once is clearly not a simple task, for the species awareness that "arises from a shared sense of a catastrophe" like global warming "point[s] to a figure of the universal that escapes our capacity to experience the world."[10] Thinking at the scale of the species thus seems discordant with the specificities of human history.

If the Anthropocene poses a challenge for historical knowledge, we should also consider how it simultaneously challenges narrative form, necessitating ways of recognizing that its organizing environmental crisis – global warming – eludes the traditional temporal scales and cause-and-effect impulse of narrative. As Chakrabarty notes, "[w]e experience specific effects of the crisis but not the whole phenomenon,"[11] a formulation that echoes Rob Nixon's characterization of slow violence – "a violence of delayed destruction that is dispersed across time and space, an attritional violence that is typically not viewed as violence at all"[12] – and Timothy Morton's concept of hyperobjects, objects massively distributed across time and space.[13] Effects, in these formulations, become a more powerful form of knowledge than causes, because of the difficulty in locating a cause in the wide-ranging scales at which the Anthropocene necessitates thinking. The seriality of effects, their repeated appearance across space and time, lends them material validity, reshaping another form of knowledge of the real. Read against these formulations, Faulkner's stylistic and formal repetitions seem not only to reinstall an account of history more resonant with the Global South's resistance to the violent imposition of linear Western progress but to register another crisis of modernization, the asynchronous but simultaneous temporalities of progress and serialization embedded within industrialization.

Read in light of the Anthropocene's extensive temporalities and effect-based knowledge, Faulkner's interest in the effects – often of a singular event – that play out over and on generations begins to take on a new cast. And it is his representations of violence in and against the natural world that often dramatize the cyclicality of this violence, indeed, the cycle as a form of violence: hunting, flooding, logging. Charles Aiken has noted that "Faulkner witnessed a recurrent sequence in the delta: logging of the wilderness, drainage of the land, and establishment of the plantation system."[14] This sequence contributed to the Great Flood of 1927, but flooding itself was a recurrent structure in Faulkner's environment: floods in 1917 and 1937 made the event seem a type of generic structure, albeit one caused by the very "commercial nexus ... that imposed modernity upon the rural South."[15] Thus, it is unsurprising, given these repetitions on the land, that "nature in his writing gets filtered through the lenses of literary convention: stock romantic imagery of pastoral retreat from Andrew Marvell to A. E. Housman, American masculinist wilderness narrative from Cooper to Melville to Twain."[16] It is as if nature itself comes to follow certain plot structures. These repetitions are not the type of natural cycle that continues without end, however, for Faulkner's floods and hunts play out as repetitions only until they do not – that is, until they end in dramatically violent fashion. This teleological cyclicality marks the same type of temporal logic Chakrabarty sees in the Anthropocene, in which the repetition of certain modes of social being lead ultimately to global environmental crisis. It is, after all, the repetitive practices of colonialism, modernization, and industrialization – the extraction of resources to the point of exhaustion, the burning of fossil fuels – that carry us inevitably toward climate change's violent effects. In both the U.S. and the Global Souths, these practices began to ramp up in earnest in the late-nineteenth and early twentieth centuries, of which and in which Faulkner wrote.

Thus, at the very moment contemporary scholars have pointed to as an acceleration of the practices that have necessitated the demarcation of the Anthropocene, Faulkner's fiction registers the challenges we have only recently come to recognize, that this new epoch poses to both historical knowledge and human agency. In exploring the legacies of violence endemic to the American South, Faulkner found parallels between the exploitation of land and of peoples. This alignment is in part what has made Faulkner's work so compelling across the Global South, in regions whose relations of economic dependency, peripheralization, and immiseration resonate with that of the postbellum American South's history of resource extraction and large-scale displacements of people. Faulkner's narrative strategies for articulating this history, thoroughly modern in their interest in progress, challenge modernism's aesthetic turn toward cyclicality and repetition by seeing in these repetitions a type of alternative progress, rather than an alternative to progress. That he rooted this recognition in representations of wilderness does not make those representations an escape from history into myth but rather a more faithful depiction of a historical moment in which modernity's economic processes began to exploit natural resources at a staggering pace. Only as our own understanding of the interrelation of human and natural histories has grown more precise have Faulkner's aesthetic and narrative experimentations come to seem particularly prescient.

These concerns appear strikingly in two of Faulkner's stories that most explicitly inhabit the natural world, the "Old Man" section of *The Wild Palms* (*If I Forget Thee, Jerusalem*) (1939) and "The Bear," published in edited form as a short story but in its complete form in *Go Down, Moses* (1942). "The Bear," moving between Major de Spain's hunting grounds, Memphis, and the McCaslin plantation, recounts Isaac (Ike) McCaslin's series of hunting trips in quest of Old Ben, a legendary bear who has tormented both the farmers whose livestock he menaces and the hunters who repeatedly fail to kill him. After the hunters finally kill Old Ben, the narrative shifts to a conversation in which Ike, at twenty-one, explains to his cousin McCaslin Edmonds his reasons for relinquishing his inherited rights to the plantation, which he imagines cursed by the slaveholding of his ancestors. The story then returns once more to the hunting grounds, where Ike finds a wilderness irrevocably altered by the intrusion of a logging company to whom Major de Spain has sold off the timber rights. Unlike "The Bear," "Old Man" strays from Faulkner's Yoknapatawpha County as it narrates the travels and travails of an unnamed prisoner in the Mississippi State Penitentiary, referred to as the "tall convict." Temporarily released from the prison to aid in the rescue of flood victims in the wake of the 1927 Great Flood of the Mississippi, the convict loses control of his rescue boat and spends the next weeks, saddled with a pregnant woman he rescues from a rooftop, attempting to return to prison. By story's end, he succeeds in accomplishing his goal, but has ten years added to his prison sentence for what is deemed an attempted escape. In highlighting a natural history that intersects with the regional and familial histories long of interest to Faulkner scholars, both are thus uniquely positioned within Faulkner's oeuvre to speak to the interrelation between temporal and historical knowledge at a moment when natural and human histories irrevocably align, opening up glimpses of a history that stretches much longer than that to which Faulkner scholars have generally attended.

Throughout "The Bear," Faulkner establishes temporality as one of the central disjunctions between wilderness and city and as one of the key ways in which modernity imposes itself on regional and rural spaces. When Ike makes his final trip into the hunting grounds that are the setting for much of the story, he is immediately confronted by this asynchrony, a contrast the text emphasizes by setting his retreat into the wilderness on the heels of a trip to Major de Spain's office in town. Like the text, Ike moves from town to wilderness, where the timing of quotidian activities shifts: Ash, the hunting party's cook, tells Ike to return to camp in an hour for dinner, and after Ike replies by holding out his watch to insist it will be too early to eat, Ash replies, "That's town time. You aint in town now. You in the woods" (308). The "town time" to which Ash refers is structured here by Ike's watch, but throughout much of "The Bear" it most closely follows that other regulator of modern time, the train, as becomes clear when Ike and Boon go to Memphis for a bottle of whiskey in an earlier interlude. Dependent on the train's rigid schedule for their ability to return to the hunting grounds, Ike and Boon "[miss] the first train, the one they were supposed to take, but [Ike gets] Boon onto the three oclock train and they [are] all right again" (225). Here, the train both structures time and controls access to the wilderness. Susan Willis has linked Faulkner's use of the train to its similar appearance in much Latin American literature as an image of "the representation of exploitative progress," progress that, like the tracks of the train, evokes the linearity so often associated with Western industrialism.[17] In other words, progress comes to appear linear and routinized, an association Faulkner highlights with the train's "first and only curve in the entire line's length" appearing at the edge of the wilderness (304).

Against this linearity, the wilderness's spatio-temporality is cyclical and structured around repetitions, evidenced most explicitly by the hunt itself. Indeed, from its opening sentence, "The Bear" establishes environmental engagement as a form of repetition: "There was a man and a dog too this time," the temporal marker here nodding toward a series of preceding hunts (183). Hunting may seem an ambivalent form of environmental encounter from our contemporary vantage, but in the early twentieth century, hunters were often among the most ardent conservationists, an ethos exemplified by Teddy Roosevelt. Faulkner's own awareness of the changing Mississippi environment resulted, as Wiley C. Prewitt has argued, from his hunting excursions in an "environmental mix of diminished wilderness, disappearing large game, and the pursuit of predominantly small game."[18] For Ike McCaslin, who views the annual retreat into the wilderness in search of Old Ben as a "yearly rendezvous with the bear which they did not even intend to kill" (186), the hunt's outcome is secondary to its ritualized encounter with the wilderness. And it is this ritualistic, repetitive quality that Faulkner so often emphasizes. After an early brush with Old Ben, Sam Fathers, Ike's Native American hunting companion, muses that while they don't yet have the right dog for a successful hunt, they might "some day," a belief somewhat undercut by the narrator's addition: "Because there would be a next time, after and after," as if the hunt can continue ad infinitum, deferring the violent conclusion supposedly at its heart (195). The hunt's cyclicality comes to structure human activity in the wilderness, but because it does so at a moment when hunting itself had come to seem a threatened more than a threatening pastime, Faulkner's "after and after" takes on an ironic cast both within and outside the narrative, seeding repetition with a teleological structure that directs its violence inward.

Faulkner parallels the hunt's repetitions in the narrative structure and other formal elements of "The Bear" as well, grounding the text's experimental features in the material practices they represent. The first three sections each reenact the annual retreat into the wilderness, the encounters and near misses with Old Ben, at different points in time. Rather than progressing linearly, however, time loops forward and backward throughout these sections, so that in the first section, Ike is sixteen ("For six years now he had been a man's hunter" [183]) and then ten ("at the age of ten he was witnessing his own birth" [187]); when the second section opens, he is thirteen; and then he is once again sixteen in the third. Sentences, too, repeat. Sam's "We aint got the dog yet" in the first section becomes "We aint got that one yet" in the second, after Ike's too-small but incautious dog rushes straight at Old Ben (192, 203). In the second section, structured around Sam

Fathers's attempts to train the bear-hunting dog Lion, the text circles back three times – mimicking the first three sections of bear hunts – to Ike's recognition that Lion is a harbinger of the hunt's impending end: "So he should have hated and feared Lion" (201, 204, 216). Here, too, Faulkner's repetitions anticipate their own end, their conclusion inevitable in their structure.

This recursive narration, a cyclical progress analogous to environmental engagement, operates alongside the linearity of modernity rather than serving as a corrective to it. It appears in the "The Bear" as one element of a hybrid temporality in which cyclicality and progress coexist, with industrial modernization and wilderness serving as co-constitutive elements of a natural-historical knowledge able to reveal similarities between them that otherwise remain hidden. The most exemplary icon of wilderness within "The Bear," Old Ben himself, becomes visible to the recursive reader – a reader modeled by Ike – as a symbol of the very forces of progress leading to his own destruction. Early in the story, Ben lopes "with the ruthless and irresistible deliberation of a locomotive" (185), and in his final appearance, Ike remembers him not just moving like the train but taking its form: "the thick, locomotive-like shape which he had seen that day four years ago crossing the blow-down" (228). At the same time that Ben takes on the characteristics of a symbol of industrial modernity, Faulkner writes of the train in the repetitious sentences formerly associated with the natural world: first, "It had been harmless once" (304); next, "It had been harmless then" (305). The difference in the repetition here is telling: "once," signifying unrepeatability, is revised to "then," a temporal adverb that nods both forward, in its sequential meaning, and backward, in its demonstrative.

What "The Bear" learns by its final section is that "natural" cyclicality is not only unable to forestall forward progress but becomes actively complicit in a violence it seeks to obscure by assigning it to progress. The train's harmfulness comes not from any material change, for Ike notes in the final section that it is "the same train, engine cars and caboose" that carries him into the wilderness (306). But "this time it was as though the train ... had brought with it into the doomed wilderness even before the actual axe the shadow and portent of the new mill not even finished yet and the rails and ties which were not even laid" (306). Its harmfulness appears, retrospectively, to have been there all along, the "as though" marking the irony in Ike's belief that the train "had been" harmless. Significantly, this shift in meaning occurs after Major de Spain sells off the timber rights on the hunting grounds to a Memphis company, a sign of the dependent economic relations between semiperiphery and metropole and the increasing imbrication of the South in a modern economy. With that dependency made visible, Ike realizes that he cannot simply blame modernity for dooming the wilderness, for it is "not only the train but himself" that carries the "portent" of modernity into the wilderness (306). Thus, the final pages, focalized through Ike, take on a desperate cast as they attempt from within a knowledge of modernity's cyclical progress – "dark and dawn and dark and dawn again in their immutable progression" (313) – to unwrite the narrative: Ike first imagining the dead Sam Fathers aware of his visit to the woods, then "Old Ben too, Old Ben too; they would give him his paw back even, certainly they would give him his paw back: then the long challenge and the long chase" (313). Again the text repeats itself as if to ward off the violence it has already performed. This belated narration aligns the text's temporal understanding with history's interest in understanding the past but calls attention to repetition's insufficiency to forestall change, its own violent teleology made visible in retrospect. It also designates a profound epistemological shift in the narrative from what we have described earlier as knowledge based on causality – an action producing a decided effect – to understanding from accretions of effects rather than accomplished ends.

The necessity of a longer temporal awareness to recognize the violence that emerges through accretion leads Faulkner to offer glimpses of deep time, the *longue durée* of natural history. Thus wilderness in "The Bear" does not lie outside of History, as critics have often argued – there is no outside-History, we might say, in Faulkner – but rather pulls another mode of historical knowledge into the frame. Indeed, Faulkner's glimpses of this elongated temporal scale work precisely to align human and natural histories, for the woods are "bigger and older than any recorded document" (183). The woods may be "bigger and older" than the documents that record human history, but those spatio-temporal markers merely mask the fact that they have been made coextensive via the material history of Southern forestry, a fact echoed by the text's repetition of this assertion much later when we are told the wilderness is "older than any mill-shed, longer than any spurline" (307). Paper, a byproduct of a Southern lumber industry run primarily by Northern companies, was made from the seemingly valueless waste wood and sawdust.[19] Thus, recorded history itself comes to be both subordinated to natural history and associated with the cast-off refuse of Northern industry, a byproduct of a colonial economy that attempts to manage knowledge by managing time, literally writing over natural history with the violent histories, and in Faulkner's case *stories*, of man – a palimpsest in which the bottom layer, the material layer, is both the most visible and the least seen.

The material practices of the lumber industry, which highlight the increasing imbrication of the South in a colonial economy that shifted power to urban spaces and to Northern capital, contributed in no small way to the devastating 1927 flood in which Faulkner sets "Old Man." As Parrish writes of Ike's observation in "The Bear" that *man has deswamped and denuded and derivered*" the land, "what Ike McCaslin refers to here is a complex of anthropogenic changes such as wetlands drainage, cotton monoculture, massive deforestation by the timber industry, and the building of ever-higher levees to manage the Mississippi and its tributaries by straightening and containing their courses."[20] But "Old Man" inhabits this post-ecocatastrophe world more explicitly than "The Bear," even as it shares similar temporal schemes, allowing us to attend to the effects of Faulkner's cyclical progress.

When situated in the larger context of Faulkner's original plan for the publication of "Old Man" as one of the two alternating movements of *The Wild Palms* [*If I Forget Thee, Jerusalem*] the temporal characteristics "Old Man" shares with "The Bear" appear even more pronounced. In cycling between the two narratives of "The Wild Palms" and "Old Man," devoting five chapters to each of the intertwined segments of the novel, the entirety of *The Wild Palms* is like a modernist rendition of *Bleak House*, creating a composite whole out of two parallel but non-intersecting story vectors, which together emphasize the cycles of temporality rather than the disparities of narrative point of view. Set ten years apart, the narrative of "Old Man" begins "in the flood year 1927" (20) while "The Wild Palms" marks the historical moment of "this Anno Domini 1938" as its narrative present (118). Borges's translation emphasizes the interlocking temporality of the two stories by adding a table of contents page not included in Faulkner's original that names the dual phases of the combined temporality of the novel. And while both "Old Man" and "The Bear" employ the archetypal topos of the deep temporality of the wilderness as counterpoint to the cycles of modernization, "The Wild Palms" uses the temporal rhythms of the Louisiana and Mississippi Gulf Coast, the charted chaos of urban New Orleans and Chicago, and the spatial stasis of Utah and the Rocky Mountain west to similar effect.

As in "The Bear," human history appears in "Old Man" inseparable from natural history, and Faulkner uses the flooded Mississippi River to trace an awareness of this. With the first sight the inmates gain of the flooded river, the human and the natural scales appear coextensive. The water "sound[s] like a subway train passing far beneath the street" and appears "as if ... in three strata," a placid top layer of "frothy scum" that "screen[s] ... the rush and fury of the flood itself, and beneath this in turn the original stream, trickle, murmuring along in the opposite direction" (53). Here, the river, like Faulkner's narrative technique in "The Bear," moves backward and forward at once. Though the "original stream" is the least visible in Faulkner's tripartite articulation of the waters, its association with deep time is clear to the convict, whose boat is carried by the floodwaters into "the channel of a slough, a bayou, in which until today no current had run probably since the old subterranean outrage which had created the country" (122). The "until today" in the sentence, coming as it does after the flood, emphasizes that an understanding of deep time emerges as an effect of environmental disaster; without the flood, that is, deep time remains invisible and unknowable. Now situated within this longer span of time, the river asserts its agency, not just in its geologic capacity to carve out the landscape but because it "occur[s] to [the convict] that its present condition was no phenomenon of a decade, but that the intervening years during which it consented to bear upon its placid and sleepy bosom the frail mechanicals of man's clumsy contriving was the phenomenon and this the norm and the river was now doing what it liked to do" (135). The levees controlling the river's path during periods of calm are mere blips on the temporal radar. Rather, it is the cycles of flooding that become normalized, the river exceeding its pre-flood boundaries both spatially and temporally.

As the natural world gains agency, human agency comes to seem circumscribed by the type of circular progress evident in "The Bear." When the convict first loses control of his skiff, he attempts to paddle back upstream in search of his lost partner, who has been swept up into a tree. But the boat begins a "vicious spinning" before finally settling into the current and rushing away from where he hopes to go (123). And though the convict "[thinks] he must already be miles away from where his companion [has] quitted him ... actually he [has] merely described a big circle since getting back into the skiff and the object ... which the skiff was now about to strike was the same one it had careened into before when it had struck him" (124). Crucially here, the text links the boat's cyclical motion to violence, emphasized by the repetition of strike/struck, a theme that will recur throughout "Old Man" as this initial blow across the face leads the convict's nose to gush blood repeatedly. When he finally reaches the woman he has been sent to rescue, she comments, in recursive sentences, on precisely the type of circularity the text has foregrounded: "I thought for a minute you wasn't aiming to come back ... After the first time. After you run into this brush pile the first time and got into the boat and went on" (125). Eventually the convict learns "from experience that when [the flood's recurrent waves] overtook him, he would have to travel in the same direction it was moving in anyway, whether he wanted to or not" (143). He must fit himself into the river's flow, not fight this circular motion but "utilis[e] the skiff's own momentum to bring it through the full circle and so upstream again, the skiff travelling broadside then bow-first then broadside again" (127). While "being toyed with by a current of water," he finds that "it [does] not much matter just what he [does] or [does] not do" (124–5). In relinquishing a certain amount of his own agency, the convict is able to move more easily through the flooded landscape, but in a direction that rarely follows his own wishes.

This vision of human agency subordinated to the will of a natural world older and more powerful than humans is curiously at odds with the environmental history that lies behind the flood. Even as it opens up into a deep time that seems to normalize it, the flood gains its agency as a result of a complex of human action – the economic practices of industrial modernization that led to substantial environmental degradation. These communal actions exacerbated the conditions necessary to wreak havoc on the landscape and led to increased flooding in Faulkner's time. The tall convict's plight thus highlights two forms of human agency – societal and individual – for the flood operates contradictorily at these two scales. The flooded river is both determined by and determinative of human action.

The question of agency is a central concept throughout Faulkner's work, as characters so often find themselves living out the violent legacies effected by the actions of earlier generations – legacies of slavery, of incest, of poverty. In the fourth section of "The Bear," which interrupts the wilderness narrative with a long debate between Ike and his cousin McCaslin Edmonds over Ike's decision to give up his grandfather's land, Ike calls this inheritance a curse. In Ike's view, land ownership and slave ownership become inextricable, and thus any inheritance of one comes laden with the historical burden of the other, a legacy of violence that in his account encompasses the Civil War and Reconstruction along with complex histories of settler colonialism. At one point, Ike compares his inheritance of the land to the Biblical story of Noah, whose "grandchildren had inherited the Flood although they had not been there to see the deluge" (GDM 276). The flood, operating here as a symbol of cross-generational inheritance setting the limit on individual human behavior, thus calls attention once again to "Old Man," for in yoking agency in both texts to environmental disaster, Faulkner finds in ecocatastrophe a structure of dependency better able to articulate the challenges posed to human agency in industrial modernity, set against a backdrop of violence perpetrated both on and by the natural world.

The complex understanding of human agency that emerges in "Old Man" and "The Bear" thus resonates with what Dipesh Chakrabarty has argued are the two contradictory scales of agency in the Anthropocene: at one end, the individual human subject; at the other, the collective species operating as a geological force. As humans have collectively become powerful enough to alter planetary systems and cause widespread global warming, the human *qua* species becomes an actor alongside the more traditional modern subject. Visible only at a temporal scale in which earth-systems data can be tracked across millennia, this newly visible form of agency can be told through neither a purely natural nor a purely human history, necessitating the type of hybrid historical knowledge we have seen in Faulkner's understanding of modernity. This type of history, however, poses two issues for narrative of relevance to Faulkner's work. First, Chakrabarty's conceptualization makes clear that the Anthropocenic alignment of human and natural history requires a form of recursive narration: as soon as we entered the Anthropocene, we began to assert our agency at the scale of the species, but because the effects of that agency are visible only after hundreds of years, our achievement of species agency can only ever be narrated in retrospect. This formulation also brings up the second issue, which is that effect, more than event, becomes the Anthropocene's privileged site of knowledge. Because we can never experience ourselves as a species, we can only "experienc[e] the impact of it mediated by other direct experiences – of floods, storms, or earthquakes, for example."[21] These impacts, or effects, serve as both markers of our species agency and as the effects through which we can know of a temporally and spatially diffuse object like climate change – or colonialism. It is for these reasons that Faulkner's wilderness stories, written in a moment when the ramping up of industrial modernization was beginning to exacerbate the effects of species agency, strain against the type of linear narrative temporality of human history. Thus, in "Old Man," Faulkner's narrative style comes to register challenges to agency that emerge precisely at the intersection of modernity and nature we have come to call the Anthropocene.

Narrated in retrospect, "Old Man" calls repeated attention both to its retrospection and to the gap between how the convict remembers his time on the river and how he narrates it to the gathered inmates hearing tell of his time away from the prison. We are thrice told that the protagonist "didn't tell how he got the skiff singlehanded up the revetment and across the crown and down the opposite sixty-foot drop, he just said he went on," repetitions that return us, once more, to the narrative mode that dominates these works, for they include both the repetition and the conclusion (210).[22] The most extended disparity between narration and knowledge, however, comes in an extended passage in which the convict, his female companion, and her baby find in the Louisiana swamps near New Orleans a Cajun man who ekes out a living hunting alligators. To the gathered inmates, the convict says only, "'After a while we come to a house and we stayed there eight or nine days then they blew up the levee with dynamite so we had to leave.' That was all" (211). His memory of those days, however, becomes one of the longest passages in the story, detailing a utopian space that appears to transcend the type of relationships of dependency much of the rest of the text emphasizes.[23]

While the flood exposes the convict's subordination to the natural world, it simultaneously usurps another form of dependency, for the flood disrupts the labor practices that undergird economic relations. When the inmates first hear of the possible flood from newspaper reports, they are interested primarily in its ability to keep them from the fields. The Mississippi State Penitentiary, also called Parchman Farm, was a working plantation, where, mimicking slavery, "the land [the convicts] farmed and the substance they produced from it belonged neither to them who worked it nor to those who forced them at guns' point to do so" (26). With the flood threatening, the inmates are pulled from their fields to provide aid, and Faulkner makes clear repeatedly that theirs are not the only emptied farms: "A little later the motor launch with its train of skiffs came up across what was, fifteen feet beneath its keel, probably a cotton field" (63); "It's a right smart of cotton-houses around here. With folks on them too, I reckon" (127); "An hour later the skiff came slowly up an old logging road and … into (or onto) a cotton-field" (128); "if he had pondered at all about his present whereabouts … he would merely have taken himself to be travelling at dizzy and inexplicable speed above the largest cottonfield in the world" (134).

But when the tall convict and his companion come upon the Cajun, the two men form an alliance through labor that, rather than emphasiz-ing dependence, as do the cotton fields' allusions to slavery, transcend it. Though the man speaks only Cajun French and so the two cannot commu-nicate through language, they form an alligator-hunting partnership, agree-ing to split any profits from the skins equally. This utopian arrangement of labor freed from exploitation seems to offer one particularly optimistic extension of the flood's ability to nullify borders and boundaries – the two men, brought together by the flood, cooperate despite linguistic and cultural differences. Within this utopian space, time itself is effaced: the economic activity they enter into remains absented from the progressive temporal-ity and future orientation of modernity, aligning "hill-billy and bayou-rat, the two one and identical because of the same grudged dispensation and niggard fate of hard and unceasing travail not to gain future security, a balance in bank or even in a buried soda can for slothful and easy old age, but just permission to endure and endure to buy air to feel and sun to drink for each's little while" (214). The two work not for a secure future – a concept rendered suspect by the flood – but for a seemingly suspended present, the convict and the Cajun "stalking their pleistocene nightmares" (214). Even the recalcitrant space of fanciful romance, denoted throughout "The Wild Palms" by the "incontrovertible and plain, serene … clashing and murmuring dry and wild and faint" (272) of the wild palms symbolically shaken by disembodied memories of love, is consistently overridden by an elemental relationship to the natural world and prehistoric time. Thus what seem the most idealized of Faulkner's post-ecocatastrophe spaces exist curiously outside of time, enduring in a type of temporal suspension intruded on once again by both modernity and its environmental effects when the dynamiting of a nearby levee, a flood protection measure, forces their evacuation of the Cajun's home. This temporal suspension, then, accounts for the convict's later inability to narrate his time with the Cajun.

But in this failure of narration at the text's moment of absenting itself from progressive temporality, Faulkner seems to envision the modern world as so thoroughly imbued with the type of relations that circumscribe human agency – in economic relations as in environmental – that there is no language outside of those relations with which to make alternatives knowable. Agency *or* progress, the text seems to argue; agency *or* narration. Indeed, narrative comes to be associated not with freedom but with its opposite in "Old Man." The tall convict is serving a prison sentence for robbing a train, an act he decides on after reading dime-novel westerns: "he had saved the paper-backs for two years, reading and rereading them, memorising them, comparing and weighing story and method against story and method, taking the good from each and discarding the dross as his workable plan emerged" (21). Faulkner makes the dangers of repetition thus all the more explicit here, linking genre – narration's apotheosis of repetition – to incarceration. In telling of a man incarcerated for his adherence to outmoded narratives, Faulkner shows that not only are the old stories no longer sufficient, using them as a guide can do real harm. And yet, "Old Man" seems pessimistic about finding alternatives. At its end, the tall convict is once again an inmate of Parchman Farm, with ten years added to his sentence for the trumped up charge of attempting to escape.

At a time when modernist aesthetics had turned away from the linearity of nineteenth-century Realism, Faulkner recognized that its alternative, cyclicality and repetition, was not an escape from teleology but rather its own form of it. This inevitable forward motion seems in Faulkner's work to lead, again and again, to a violence that is at once material and psychic, a circumscription of individual agency within the confines of structures so large as to seem inescapable. A retreat into wilderness becomes not an escape from these structures or from the progression of history but instead a further embedding in the radical shifts of agency taking place in industrial modernity. Claiming Faulkner as an environmentalist may be a step too far – as Buell writes, "for Faulkner, environmental exploitation was one among a range of interlinked forms of regional pathology, among which …

racism would certainly have seemed more important"[24] – but his representations of the natural world help to reveal why certain formal strategies
in his work have resonated not just in the U.S. South but throughout the
Global South, where the exploitation of land and of people at the hands of
colonial economic relations have often gone hand-in-hand. The resonances
between his understanding of the interrelation of human and natural histories and recent accounts of the Anthropocene, a formulation that necessitates thinking across national boundaries, help us to see the importance
of reading Faulkner at these wider scales. They also help us recognize how
repetition – and with it, genre and serialization – seems to emerge within
the Anthropocene as a privileged site of knowledge formation, revealing
much about our contemporary understanding of human agency in a world
in which our repetitions of asserting that agency against the natural world
have increasingly shown us both how much and how little control we have.
But even if a certain pessimism exists in Faulkner's work over the ability to
escape our historical – and narrative – repetitions, the power he ascribes
to the old stories should make us consider all the more how necessary it is
to find the words to tell new ones, even if they require new forms in which
to speak.

NOTES

1 Hosam Aboul-Ela, "The Poetics of Peripheralization: Faulkner and the Question
of the Postcolonial," *American Literature* 77.3 (September 2005), 485.
2 Hosam Aboul-Ela, *Other South: Faulkner, Coloniality, and the Mariátegui
Tradition* (Pittsburgh: University of Pittsburgh Press, 2007), p. 134.
3 The 1940 edition was published by Editorial Sudamericana. We cite the 2002
Ediciones Siruela edition. Tanya T. Fayen notes that "*Las palmeras salvajes* is
one of the few early Latin American translations of Faulkner to be reprinted in
Spain" (*In Search of the Latin American Faulkner* [Lanham: University Press of
America, 1995], p. 230).
4 Saskia Sassen, "A Savage Sorting of Winners and Losers: Contemporary Versions
of Primitive Accumulation," *Globalizations* 7.1–2 (March–June 2010), 23–50.
5 Susan Willis, "Aesthetics of the Rural Slum: Contradictions and Dependency in
'The Bear,'" *Social Text* 2 (Summer 1979), 82.
6 Lawrence Buell, "Faulkner and the Claims of the Natural World," *Faulkner and the
Natural World: Faulkner and Yoknapatawpha, 1996*, ed. Donald M. Kartiganer
and Ann J. Abadie, Jackson: University Press of Mississippi, 1999, p. 10.
7 Susan Scott Parrish, "Faulkner and the Outer Weather of 1927," *American
Literary History* 24.1 (Spring 2012), 35.
8 Buell, "Claims of the Natural World," p. 181. On the region's environmental history, see also Parrish, "Outer Weather," 38–44.
9 Dipesh Chakrabarty, "The Climate of History: Four Theses," *Critical Inquiry*
35.2 (Winter 2009), 218–19.

10 Ibid., 222.

11 Ibid., 221.

12 Rob Nixon, *Slow Violence and the Environmentalism of the Poor* (Cambridge, MA: Harvard University Press, 2011), p. 2.

13 Timothy Morton, *Hyperobjects: Philosophy and Ecology after the End of the World* (Minneapolis: University of Minnesota Press, 2013).

14 Charles S. Aiken, "A Geographical Approach to William Faulkner's 'The Bear,'" *Geographical Review* 71.4 (October 1981), 455.

15 Thomas L. McHaney, "Oversexing the Natural World: *Mosquitoes* and *If I Forget Thee, Jerusalem [The Wild Palms]*," *Faulkner and the Natural World: Faulkner and Yoknapatawpha, 1996*, Donald M. Kartiganer and Ann J. Abadie (eds.) (Jackson: University Press of Mississippi, 1999), p. 38.

16 Lawrence Buell, *Writing for an Endangered World: Literature, Culture, and Environment in the U.S. and Beyond* (Cambridge, MA: Harvard University Press, 2001), p. 174.

17 Willis, "Aesthetics of the Rural Slum," 92.

18 Wiley C. Prewitt, Jr., "Return of the Big Woods: Hunting and Habitat in Yoknapatawpha," *Faulkner and the Natural World: Faulkner and Yoknapatawpha, 1996*, ed. Donald M. Kartiganer and Ann J. Abadie (eds.) (Jackson: University Press of Mississippi, 1999), p. 204. See also Judith Bryant Wittenberg, "*Go Down, Moses* and the Discourse of Environmentalism," in *New Essays on Go Down, Moses*, Linda Wagner-Martin (ed.) (Cambridge: Cambridge University Press, 1996), pp. 49–72.

19 See Michael Curtis, "Early Development and Operations of the Great Southern Lumber Company," *Louisiana History: The Journal of the Louisiana Historical Association* 14.4 (Autumn 1973), pp. 347–68.

20 Parrish, "Outer Weather," 34.

21 Dipesh Chakrabarty, "Postcolonial Studies and the Challenge of Climate Change," *New Literary History* 43.1 (Winter 2012), 12–13.

22 The second account of this elision in the convict's story occurs moments later: "He did not tell it that way, just as he apparently did not consider it worth the breath to tell how he had got the hundred-and-sixty-pound skiff single-handed up and across and down the sixty-foot levee" (211); the third, further on: "nor did he tell, anymore than about the sixty-foot levee, how he got the skiff back into the water" (231).

23 For a similar reading of labor in the novel, see Richard Godden and Pamela Knights, "Forget Jerusalem, Go To Hollywood – 'To Die. Yes. To Die?': A Coda to *Absalom, Absalom!*," in Godden's *Fictions of Labor: William Faulkner and the South's Long Revolution* (Cambridge: Cambridge University Press, 1997), pp. 179–232.

24 Buell, *Endangered World*, p. 188.

13

RANDY BOYAGODA

Reading Faulkner in and Beyond Postcolonial Studies: "There Is Nowhere for Us to Go Now but East"

The first thing to be said about Faulkner and postcolonial studies is that William Faulkner is not a postcolonial writer and he did not write postcolonial novels. Likewise, there are no immediately legible lines of influence or parallel historical-cultural experiences connecting him to the post–World War II writers and regions – primarily Asian and African – that we associate with postcolonial writing and experience. I offer this qualification at the outset for two reasons. First, reading Faulkner in postcolonial terms risks obscuring the profound gaps in economic and cultural advantage between him and many novelists emerging from postcolonial Third World sites: making your way from Mississippi to the Manhattan publishing world in the 1930s is meaningfully different in spatial and also racial terms than making your way from, say, Lagos to London in the 2010s. Second, reading Faulkner in postcolonial terms risks over-determining certain dimensions of his work and situation by privileging his Southern-ness and related, subaltern elements over his status as arguably the most prominent U.S. writer of the post–World War II era.[1] Given the decline of European imperialism, the rise of decolonization and independence movements, and the simultaneous rise of the United States to a preeminent, even unipolar global position during this period, Faulkner has always-already been received by global South writers as an author whose work emerges from the power matrices of a superpower nation – even if from an especially complex locale within it. Indeed, as a notable amount of critical work on Faulkner variously attests, exploring the relationship between Faulkner and postcoloniality is a complex project that resists singular assignments of relation and meaning.[2]

Of course, we can read Faulkner in productive relation to some of the structures and driving concerns of postcolonial studies and, to an extent, in similarly productive relation to certain postcolonial novelists themselves. Indeed, scholars and writers have been doing so for twenty years, particularly (and most persuasively) in Caribbean and Latin American contexts. Such readings seek to renew, renovate, and re-conceptualize our understanding of Faulkner's work beyond traditional national and regional frames of reference. Justifications for this project have been found in new approaches to U.S. national and U.S. Southern regional history and in new developments in literary and cultural theory, developments specifically evident in the shifting foci and imperatives of the New American Studies, New South Studies, and Faulkner Studies. Justifications have also come through claims of affiliation to Faulkner made by postcolonial writers and those made on behalf of these writers by various scholars. All of this has been made possible, at base, by the variegation and recalcitrance of Faulkner's own writing. Because as much as Faulkner can be understood in the binary terms that figure throughout his fiction and in writing about his fiction – North/South, black/white, urban/rural, local/national, local/global – his work inevitably resists, undermines, and interrogates these binaries. In other words, yes, Faulkner is an American writer, a Southern writer, a Mississippi writer. Yet, as *Absalom, Absalom!* suggests, he is also a hemispheric writer, and with late work like *A Fable,* he is further what we might call a globally Southern writer. He is even, to draw on Arjun Appadurai's most recent theorizing on globalization, a globalized writer, a writer whose work may lend itself to readings that "produce a preferred geography of the global by the strategic extension of local cultural horizons" into historico-cultural parallels elsewhere.[3] As we shall see, postcolonial concerns, articulated from multiple subject and power positions, thread through all of these potential designations for Faulkner, never finally winning out against any other but often adjusting and expanding our understanding of Faulkner's accomplishments and continued importance.

One notable postcolonial-framed articulation of this continued importance comes from Salman Rushdie, who has matter-of-factly proposed the widespread significance of Faulkner's fiction: "Outside the United States ... in India, in Africa, and again in Latin America ... Faulkner is the American writer praised most by local writers as an inspiration, an enabler, an opener of doors."[4] Rushdie's estimation is at once enticing and frustrating for those interested in making sense of Faulkner's position, indeed his role, in contemporary global literary production and specifically of lines of potential relation from Faulkner to postcolonial writing. The frustration is that Rushdie offers no evidence to substantiate his claim; he names no specific "local writers" and offers no elaborations as to what features of Faulkner's work provide such catalytic charge. A similar limitation characterizes André Bleikasten's passing observation in 1995 that "there are surely cultural and historical reasons for Faulkner's remarkably strong impact on Third World writers."[5] The vagueness in both of these instances is understandable – Bleikasten's note comes up in consideration of Faulkner in a European context, while

Rushdie's observation emerges in an anecdote about U.S. Southern writer Eudora Welty's telling him that Faulkner did not matter to her so much as might be expected. Nevertheless, these promising but limited overtures toward postcolonial-minded readings of Faulkner offer, in their very limitations, important cautions about the nature of evidence we choose to license our own, more expansive readings. Prudence is necessary to avoid making hasty or superficial claims for Faulkner's writing that in fact threaten to undermine the very effort toward a postcolonial understanding of his work and world that his writing sustains, as has happened with some early scholarship in this respect.[6]

Qualified by such cautions, however, Rushdie's and Bleikasten's remarks do anticipate the value of approaching Faulkner's work from global standpoints that are especially relevant today: for example, in the context of what Pankaj Mishra identifies as "the central event of the last century for the majority of the world's population ... the intellectual and political awakening of Asia and its emergence from the ruins of both Asian and European empires."[7] To acknowledge this as in fact the "central event," Mishra continues, is to restructure understandings of twentieth-century world history, politics, and culture independent of the (Euro-American) privileging of the two world wars and the Cold War. This reorientation in turn makes it plausible, Mishra proposes, "to understand the world not only as it exists today, but also as it is continuing to be remade not so much in the image of the West as in accordance with the aspirations and longings of former subject peoples."[8] As Mishra emphasizes, these aspirations and longings did not find voice and take shape in purist zones of Asian culture, sequestered from European and North American influences, and in fact it is in this mixture of what we conventionally regard as North and South, East and West, First and Third, that we can begin to identify how Faulkner may have influenced certain postcolonial writers seeking to give voice to "the aspirations and longings of former subject peoples" in Asia. Of course, Faulkner's importance to writers beyond the United States has long been attested to by the standing he enjoyed amongst the 1950s Latin American Boom generation, particularly Gabriel García Márquez. But in Rushdie's mentioning Faulkner's importance to Indian and African writers, he suggests that there are elements to Faulkner's writing that matter beyond his immediate geographic, racial, and national contiguities with these Latin American writers, elements that indeed matter, by way of Mishra's argument, in the context of the fall of European (and Asian) imperialism and the rise of postcolonial nations, politics, and culture. These elements, as we shall see, are in fact integral to Faulkner's sensitivities to the deep historical imperialist projects and colonial textures of his own immediate and adjacent environs.

Walter Johnson's recent *River of Dark Dreams: Slavery and Empire in the Cotton Kingdom* (2013) offers a substantial premise for considering the deep imperial history that Faulkner engages in his writing, especially with *Absalom, Absalom!* (1936), and in turn helps us account, in historical and materialist terms, for the many ways in which his work appeals to later postcolonial and Third World writers. As Johnson's work makes clear, the Mississippi Valley – first conceptualized by Thomas Jefferson out of his interest in growing a nation of white patriarchal yeoman citizens that, so composed, would anchor a greater "empire of liberty" – fostered a combination of spatial possibilities, racialized hierarchies, and economic opportunities, which in turn sustained a zone of imperial practice and production in the pre-Civil War South. The success of this imperialist project depended not just on local formulations of command and control that were consonant with European colonial models in Africa, Asia, and the Caribbean, or on those formulations operating in concert with the U.S. South's political and economic connections to East Coast and northern, industrial sites of production, but also on the U.S. South's early and direct connection to global centers of textile production: "the 'cotton market' about which [Southern planters] so frequently spoke," Johnson explains, "was in actual fact a network of material connections that stretched from Mississippi and Louisiana to Manhattan and Lowell to Manchester and Liverpool."[9] Not only did the American South play an important role in a nineteenth-century global economy dominated by European imperial powers, but in the decade before the Civil War, U.S. Southerners pursued an expansive empire of their own. By the 1850s, Johnson explains, slaveholding Southern planters were worried about two threats to their continued regime. First, they were concerned about potential slave rebellions, along the lines of U.S. and Caribbean precedents, what Johnson, riffing on James Baldwin, calls "fear of the fire next time – of Toussaint L'Ouverture, of Charles Deslondes, of Denmark Vesey, of Nat Turner, of Madison Washington."[10] Second, they were confronting mounting economic pressures: the rising prices of cotton and slaves made it hard, especially in Deep South states, to maintain or expand established plantations and likewise to extend the plantation franchise to white Southerners keen to become part of the local "empire for liberty." "In order to survive," Johnson argues, slaveholders had to expand, and so "they displaced their fear of their slaves [and need for more slaves] into aggression on a global scale," aggression that "increasingly took the form of imperialist military action."[11]

As his principal evidence for this, Johnson cites Mississippi Valley plant-ers' involvement in the invasions of Cuba and Nicaragua in the 1850s, and when these proved of limited success, their agitating, again unsuccess-fully, for the reopening of the Atlantic slave trade, banned by Congress in 1808. All of this, Johnson argues, was rooted in an ambition on the part of local planters to have the U.S. Southern "political economy of slavery [join] the global economy" in imperial terms and, in this joining, constitute a "South" that they would lead, a South whose circumference exceeded the national borders of the United States, a South that would cultivate their local plantation operations.[12] Crucial to their global aspirations was the strategic involvement of non-slaveholding whites, who were expected to be willing recruits for the Caribbean campaigns on the prospect of joining the slaveholding elites through the success of their shared imperialist efforts. As such, the expansive, imperialist South that Johnson describes in his his-tory of Cotton Kingdom slavery and empire is, in many ways, the South that Thomas Sutpen negotiates, in brutally ambitious and ultimately failed and fatal terms, in Faulkner's *Absalom, Absalom!*. A poor white Southerner intent on joining the planter class after a childhood experience of rejection and diminishment at a Virginia plantation house, Sutpen goes to Haiti of his own volition: "he ... had decided to go to the West Indies and become rich," we learn in one of the many layered narratives that make up the novel's tell-ing of Sutpen's life story (199). While in Haiti, working for a French planter, he plays a decisive role in the successful suppression of a local slave rebel-lion. He then returns to the United States to build a plantation of his own on the swampy outskirts of Jefferson County, Mississippi, to be worked by slaves he brings back with him from Haiti. In short, Sutpen is a one-man 1820s historical precedent-cum-literary antecedent of the global-local spa-tial integrations and efforts of 1850s pro-slavery Mississippi Valley imperi-alists, the figures that Johnson describes in his history.

Understood as the story of a representative deep historical-cultural fig-ure in this sense, *Absalom, Absalom!* could sustain framings as a post-colonial novel, in the following way: For many years, as is well known, discussions of the postcolonial novel in English have been routed through Fredric Jameson's 1986 "Third World Literature in the Era of Multinational Capitalism," in which he argued that stories of individual experience emerg-ing from postcolonial Third World contexts are best read as allegories of national trajectories and developments.[13] To be sure, Jameson's article has met with fierce resistance for its thoroughly Eurocentric presumptions about the intentions and meanings of postcolonial writing, and also for its uncriti-cal privileging of the nation – the most notable critique coming from Aijaz Ahmad.[14] More recently, however, Imre Szeman has offered a persuasive argument for a reconsideration and productive extension of Jameson's formulations, arguing that we should indeed explore the role of national allegory in postcolonial novels but as a form of "metacommentary" on the *project* of nation-making, rather than simply as narratives of nationhood to be taken at face value.[15] Were Faulkner readable exclusively as a Southern writer and not always-already as also a U.S. national writer, Szeman's model of metacommentary could lead to an unambiguous postcolonial interpretation of *Absalom, Absalom!*. Still, Szeman's approach does illuminate some of the features of the novel that lend themselves to a productive alignment with postcolonial concerns. This is nowhere more evident than in how Faulkner deploys Sutpen's career across the U.S. and Caribbean Souths to explore the making of the mythic great plantation South, specifically attending to its often grim and horrific elements and thereby exposing and unmaking the national allegory Sutpen embodies. This double action functions as the "metacommentary" Szeman identifies in postcolonial novels, and it is a role that *Absalom, Absalom!* substantially fulfills: the novel's account of Sutpen's life and work serves as a representative, critical account of U.S. national allegory-making that emphasizes the irreducibly regional and hemispheric elements to this project that persist in, alongside, and beyond the national frame.

It should come as no surprise that *Absalom, Absalom!* has probably sustained the most meaningful attention from critics interested in establishing the postcolonial dimensions of Faulkner's work. One notable effort in this respect is Vera Kutzinski's 2001 exploration of what she persuasively contends is the novel's "insistently trans-American reach," from Mississippi and Massachusetts up to Alberta and down through the Caribbean. "It is the Americas, not just the southern parts of the United States," she continues, "that constitute Faulkner's literary and cultural 'region,' and he, in turn, is reconstituted by the perspectives and claims of this larger territory."[16] Kutzinski develops this baseline claim for reading Faulkner in a postcolonial context out of her sympathetic commentaries on extensive readings of his work by two postcolonial Caribbean writer-critics, Édouard Glissant and Wilson Harris. Their engagements with Faulkner – Glissant's book-length *Faulkner, Mississippi* and Harris's literary essays on Faulkner's fiction (in 1983 and 1999 collections)[17] – are strong examples of self-conscious, self-critical, and sympathetic identifications with Faulkner on the part of postcolonial writers, made in terms of overlapping historical experiences, cultural practices, and narrative responses. Building in particular on Glissant's claims about *Absalom, Absalom!*, Kutzinski argues that the cultural, political, and historical implications of Sutpen's movements and actions in the novel most significantly emerge when we reveal the colonial context that is shared across the discrete regions and places – the plantations of the nationally bordered U.S. South and of nineteenth-century Haiti – that figure in his movements and actions.

More than a decade later, Kutzinski's work remains useful for its integrative contribution to understandings of Faulkner in a postcolonial context, insofar as it both gathered earlier postcolonial-minded Caribbean-framed readings of Faulkner (Glissant and Harris) alongside related work by notable Faulkner and Southern studies scholars, such as Barbara Ladd, Richard Godden, and George Handley, and in turn anticipated more substantial postcolonial readings of Faulkner and of *Absalom, Absalom!* in particular. These later readings include Taylor Hagood's *Faulkner's Imperialism: Space, Place, and the Materiality of Myth* (2008) and Hosam Mohamed Aboul-Ela's *Other South: Faulkner, Coloniality, and the Mariátegui Tradition* (2007), a work that makes an especially strong case for situating Faulkner in a postcolonial-framed Global (rather than only hemispheric) South.[18] Aboul-Ela argues persuasively for the significance of "Faulkner's role in [influencing] Arab writing, especially in the 1960s,"[19] and yet, as we shall see, his argument beyond this particular context at best attests to the challenges inherent in making a case for Faulkner's relationship to postcolonial writing outside the colonial spaces shared by the American South and the Caribbean South or the common hemispheric/continental space occupied by the United States of America and Latin America that Deborah Cohn and Ramón Saldívar have respectively explored.[20]

To be sure, Aboul-Ela advances a formidable reading of *Absalom, Absalom!*. He argues for the importance of "geohistorical location" in determining the terms and textures of Sutpen's trajectory, given the planter's circulation through the routes of what Aboul-Ela maps as a "colonial economy" linking "northern New England, western Virginia, plantation states, and the West Indies."[21] But Aboul-Ela is interested in contributing more than this broadened geography to our understanding of Faulkner's postcolonial relevance. Sympathetic to what he describes as the rising "innovative scrutiny" over "William Faulkner's relationship to writers of the Global South," Aboul-Ela effectively goes a step further than Glissant (who reads Faulkner as a Creole writer rather than a U.S. national writer because his writing mixes European and New World storytelling modes and materials).[22] Aboul-Ela argues that peripheralization, understood as a cultural position, as a historical condition, and as a program of poetics, is central to Faulkner's work. In this sense, he further contends, "Faulkner is more strongly connected to the ideology of structure found in the work of ... Global Southern novelists" than to the ideologies of structure found in canonical Euro-American modernist works.[23] In other words, Faulkner may better be understood less as a Mississippi answer to James Joyce and other High Modernists than as a remote but influential ancestor of Arundhati Roy and other postcolonial South Asian writers.

Pursuing this potential argument, Aboul-Ela identifies Roy as a writer who "falls into the category of postcolonial novelists often linked to Faulkner who claim not to have read him," a claim Aboul-Ela reframes to his own purposes by plotting out a genealogy of influence based on "comparisons between Faulkner's project and those of many earlier Indian writers in English [that] offer[s] a partial explanation for Roy's familiarity with certain narrative strategies and conceptual issues" prominent in Faulkner's fiction. Such writers include N. K. Narayan, Anita Desai, and Salman Rushdie.[24] Appealing as a premise, Aboul-Ela's argument about Faulkner's significance for Asian postcolonial fiction ultimately fails to persuade because it is rooted only in speculative claims of literary influence on Roy through intermediate writers: Narayan's space may be comparable to Faulkner's but also, of course, to Thomas Hardy's Wessex; Desai at best "seems to be rewriting" a Faulkner novel with one of her own but obviously not to the exclusion of other influences; Rushdie at most "indirectly" brings Faulkner into South Asia by way of Latin America; these are "undoubtedly familiar" to Roy, "whether she has read Faulkner or not."[25]

Only one major South Asian writer has in fact written substantially about Faulkner: Pakistani novelist Zulfikar Ghose. In his 1991 book *The Art of Creating Fiction*, however, Ghose offers little more than an extended textual analysis of Faulkner's writing, specifically his short story "Barn Burning," under the pretext of providing the reader with "an example of perfection in the art of creating fiction."[26] By deciding to read Faulkner in exclusively, almost obsessively textual terms – with a devotion to formalism worthy of New Critic Cleanth Brooks – Ghose tacitly rejects any claim of cultural-historical identification with Faulkner's world. The only identification happens on the generalized plane of a writer responding to another writer. We never learn, for instance, of the autobiographical, historical or material contexts in which Ghose first came upon Faulkner's work. Moreover, for Ghose, Faulkner's situation within local, regional, national, hemispheric, and even global problematics seems incidental to the nature, concerns, and accomplishments of Faulkner's work, rather than integral to them. Ghose's decision to write about Faulkner in strictly formalist terms rather than in either a more personal or broader cultural vein is all the more puzzling in light of his longstanding position in the United States as a professor of literature at the University of Texas-Austin dating to the late 1960s, as well as his authorship of a series of novels set in South America that employ magic realist techniques reminiscent of Márquez and others.

Ghose in effect triangulates his own origins in postcolonial Asia through a double relocation: as a writer in the American South, with subject matter drawn from South America. Faulkner may serve Ghose in mediating a web of global postcolonial Deep Souths.

Indeed, one of Ghose's novels suggests an especially strong affinity to Faulkner, *A New History of Torments* (1982). Populated by a cast of Native Americans, Europeans, and native-born creoles of European descent, the novel is a saga whose events extend across the South American continent. Through the fevered memories and obsessive imaginings of its characters, the novel traverses the centuries-long history of South American colonialism and maps a tangled relationship to an era of postcolonial revolution and the voracity of oligarchs. These elements coalesce around a convoluted storyline that involves a gold-obsessed revolutionary's attempt to trade bullion meant to aid a political insurrection for a seventeenth-century map that apparently points the way to the mythic El Dorado. Ghose explores all of this through the intense and fractured relationships of the wealthy Jimenez clan, whose driven patriarch, Jorge Rojas, destroys the family (his son and daughter aid the revolutionary in his bullion-for-El Dorado gambit) and the family's ranching empire out of a combination of lust and pride, selfishness and nihilism. The novel's prose never attains a density comparable to Faulkner's, and the novel's magic realist elements (Biblical plagues, vampire bats) point to Marquez as a direct influence. Nevertheless, it is not hard to find plausible evidence of Faulkner's influence in the novel's combustible fusions of history and memory, in the past-haunted obsessions and fixations that drive its heterogeneous cast of characters, and in the fatalism that dooms the prospects of a single powerful family and its surrounding village, region, and continent. Indeed, *A New History of Torments* reads very much like a novel whose sensibility, scale, and concerns – so much of which takes shape as conjoined private and public wreckage wrought by what Ghose describes as the "florid imaginations of ... succeeding generations" – seem profoundly informed by Faulkner's work, most notably *Absalom, Absalom!*.[27]

Appreciating Faulkner primarily as an imaginative precursor who explores the hubris of dynastic imperialism and colonial greed may moot questions of direct influence. Ghose himself underplays the issue by speaking of Faulkner as having perhaps been an "unconscious" influence because he "read him ardently as an undergraduate" at a British university in the late 1950s.[28] Yet what would it mean for a Pakistani student to be reading (in the seat of the British Empire itself) a writer from a colonial South? Perhaps we cannot get farther than Rushdie's vague statement about Third World writers looking to Faulkner's work for inspiration and enablement because division, resistance, and dislocation persist as the cultural effects of western colonialism around the world.

And so I wish to turn to other ground for claims about Faulkner's direct relationship to postcolonial concerns by examining their appearance in Faulkner's own later work. A revealing pair of sequences from his novel *A Fable* (1954) signal Faulkner's interests in the world emerging after World War II – a world that, as Mishra suggests, is more decisively characterized by the fall of empires and rise of Southern nations, cultures, and literatures than by responses to the (Cold War) third act in a century of European-based conflicts.

Near the end of *A Fable*, a dense and, even for Faulkner, often difficult novel set during World War I that operates in part as an allegory of the Christ story, a French soldier notices that at one particular Allied position, the demographics are different from those dominated by the European and American troops otherwise involved in the war. This is so much the case,

> It's like another front, manned by all the troops in the three forces who cant speak the language belonging to the coat they came up from under the equator and half around the world to die in, in the cold and the wet – Senegalese and Moroccans and Kurds and Chinese and Malays and Indians – Polynesian Melanesian Mongol and Negro who couldn't understand the password nor read the pass either.... No man's land is no longer in front of us. It's behind us now. Before, the faces behind the machine guns and the rifles at least thought Caucasian thoughts even if they didn't speak English or French or American; now they don't even think Caucasian thoughts. They're alien. They dont even have to care. They have tried for four years to get out of the white man's cold and mud and rain just by killing Germans, and failed. Who knows? by killing off the Frenchmen and Englishmen and Americans which they have bottled up here, they might all be on the way home tomorrow. So there is nowhere for us to go now but east – (959–60).

John T. Matthews rightly reads this passage as evidence of Faulkner's presenting "the war as a curtain call of Western imperial history," a claim he supports with textual evidence taken from elsewhere in the book that suggests the novel is "preoccupied with matters of empire, repeatedly coming back to the term itself: the 'scrap or fragment of an empire' (899), 'empire's carapace' (905), 'the vast glorious burden of empire' (915)."[29]

But Faulkner was far more than preoccupied; he was intent on exposing, I argue, the internal contradictions and fractures inherent to the imperial project in its full-dressed European iteration, a critique advanced for its own sake and also as a framing, cautionary tale for a 1950s United States rapidly ascending into a position of global dominance. This much is especially evident in a key passage that appears earlier in the novel and critically frames the passage just quoted that details the crumbling imperial demographics of the European front. In this important preceding moment in the novel, Faulkner details the longings, delusions, frustration, and despair that inform the thoughts of a French military man's consideration of his work and prospects as an ambitious, romantic, if finally despairing cog in France's African imperial machinery. It is here that we learn about the colonial experiences that the "old general," one of the novel's main characters, had as a younger man. Before leaving to take up his assignment – which he imagines will involve a plum posting in French Algiers, where he will parade around Oran seated beside the local governor-general – he predicts the standing he will enjoy among his colleagues and his stature in France itself following his efforts abroad. He expects that he will be regarded as nothing less than "invincible Man," having come back to Paris from his colonial assignment looking young and vital "even after two years of African sun and solitude," perhaps leading someday to a grand military parade through the heart of Paris and thereafter to promotions, even a colonial governor-generalship of his own (899). But, in Faulkner's handling, we soon learn that the military man's service to the French nation and empire affords no such invigoration, no such ascendancy. When he actually departs, he "crossed the Mediterranean and disappeared," meaning, he entered France's African imperial system and certainly not via Algiers; in fact, he is sent to a place more than "remote merely because it was far away and impossible to reach, like Brazzaville say" (899–900). In other words, rather than going only into the established, verifiably distant heart and center of the French Congo – a situation that would serve simply as an obvious parallel to the Belgian Congo trajectories of Conrad's characters in *Heart of Darkness* – Faulkner sends his character to "a place really remote":

> He had left the port base the same day he arrived, for a station as famous in its circles as the Black Hole of Calcutta – a small outpost not only five hundred kilometres from anything resembling a civilised stronghold or even handhold, but sixty and more from its nearest support – a tiny lost compound ... a single building of loop-holed clay set in a seared irreconcilable waste of sun and sand which few living men had ever seen, to which troops were sent as punishment or, incorrigibles, for segregation until heat and monotony on top of their natural and acquired vices divorced them permanently from mankind. He had gone straight there from the post base and (the only officer present, and for all practical purposes, the only white man too) [served more than two years] ... in the shock of that first second of knowledge ... that earth itself had faltered, rapacity itself had failed. (900)

With a framing reference to an eighteenth-century anti-imperial insurrection in India directed at the British East India Company followed by an overwhelming sense of (racialized) isolation and futility that devastate the character's romantic delusions of personalized imperial grandeur, Faulkner here exposes the useless prospects, even absolute futility of the imperial project itself. He does so not just in personal but also in systemic terms, and nowhere more starkly than when he simultaneously glosses and condemns the vain imperative driving imperialism itself; as one would-be champion of European colonialism discovers when he becomes directly involved with maintaining and advancing the effort, "rapacity itself had failed."

This sequence can be productively read as informing the novel's subsequent representations of the American presence in a world of receding European imperial power, a presence personified in part by three American soldiers (then serving as executioners) in the novel whom Matthews describes as representatives from "the world's newest empire," a characterization he bases on the passage from *A Fable* that I quoted to begin this closing section.[30] In fact, I argue, Faulkner's representation of the American presence in this "nowhere for us to go but east" passage – particularly when read in light of the old general's youthful and despairing experiences in French imperial Africa – calls into question the newness and viability of that newest of empires.

In looking back at Faulkner from the unipolar moment of the early twenty-first century, Matthews may undervalue just how forward-looking Faulkner was in conceptualizing a geopolitical situation beyond the Euro-American parameters of successive European and American empires. Note how Faulkner groups together, as *all* already outmoded, those who speak and think in English and French and also in American, as opposed to those from the remote Eastern and Southern places named in this passage. The Kurds, Chinese, Malays, Indians, and others "don't even have to care" about the concerns of the (fading, receding) imperial powers that brought them to this place to become fodder and pawns, because these men "might all be on [their] way home tomorrow," back, that is, to the emerging loci of twentieth-century geo-historical significance. Beyond whatever immediate military-logistical connotations there are to the French soldier's thoughts on the necessity for a new orientation, I propose that there are greater historical, cultural, and political implications informing Faulkner's suggestion, "So there is nowhere for us to go now but east." The likelihood of these implications is evident in part from the context of the book's composition: the early 1950s were at once the beginning of the Cold War and the end of European Empire. And while we may understandably also identify the historical overlap between these events as the rise of American empire – which is the persuasive premise informing Matthews's reading of this passage, writing as he does from a much later and more developed moment in that empire's rise – I would nevertheless argue that Faulkner envisioned the end of even that empire's story already vouchsafed in the more immediately evident ending of its predecessor empires' stories, stories that reveal the hollowness and despair of the ostensibly "Invincible men" of empire as they themselves discover the very failure of rapacity itself in trying to keep it going to feed the imperial center and maintain a global system of command and control.

Moreover, and here anticipating Mishra's claims about the non-Eurocentric events of greatest significance to twentieth-century history, Faulkner effectively suggests with this sequence in A Fable that should we seek to envision and know the places and peoples who would form the new locus of global politics and culture, then "there is nowhere for us to go now but east." In a coinciding act of humility, Faulkner recognized that this story, their stories, were beyond his imagining and position to tell. He could but point to them and identify their trajectories as running through and persisting beyond both European and American imperial frames. At most, he could go one step further and articulate a sympathetic account for why such peoples might in fact try to forcibly break themselves free from those frames. "Senegalese and Moroccans and Kurds and Chinese and Malays and Indians – Polynesian Melanesian Mongol and Negro": these are soldiers from the global South and East, brought into a European conflict through colonial structures that will not hold them for much longer ("empire's carapace," etc.). They speak and think in different terms than their diminishing superiors. They make no great effort to ape, mimic, or otherwise slavishly follow the lead of these superiors; in fact, they "don't even have to care." Indeed, having failed to find escape from the "white man's cold and mud and rain just by killing Germans," they might next try "killing off the Frenchmen and Englishmen and Americans": by staging, in and as a small scale military mutiny, a kind of anti-imperial insurrection against the combined power of both old and new Western empires.

The work of postcolonial writing and postcolonial studies is to describe precisely these actions, events, stories, and trajectories, mindful of the multiple, often fractured and asymmetrical lines of influence, overlap, and relations that continue to develop between First and Third World, North and South, East and West. Contemporary scholars of Faulkner's work can productively explore the many ways that his writing contains all of this without having to assign any conclusive, singular, static claims of influence. Perhaps it is in this sense, ultimately, that Faulkner remains of lasting significance for postcolonial writers: his fiction critiques and resists totalizing accounts of people and places, and in this way offers visions of a future beyond old and new empires both, as evidenced both in *A Fable* and also in *Absalom, Absalom!* In its closing moments, Quentin Compson's Canadian roommate Shreve predicts a future world originating from the descendant of the only family member to have escaped the destruction of Sutpen's failed personal empire: "I think that in time the Jim Bonds are going to conquer the western hemisphere. Of course it wont be in our time and of course as they spread towards the poles they will bleach out again like the rabbits and the birds do, so they wont show up so sharp against the snow. But it will still be Jim Bond; and so in a few thousand years, I who regard you will also have sprung from the loins of African kings" (302). Coming from a Canadian to a Mississippian in a Massachusetts dorm room and imagining a future self as nothing less than the scion of the eventual African conquerors of the Western hemisphere, this is a racially, temporally, politically, and geographically convoluted prophesy meant to suggest that Jim Bond, and the formerly colonized peoples of the world, will not just endure but indeed shall prevail. In 1936, in a sense, Faulkner imagined partly what Appadurai argues is now, in the 2010s, taking place, as we live out a globalization marked by "unexpected new cultural configurations in which locality always takes surprising new forms."[31] Describing those surprising new local forms, telling the stories that give shape and force to them – displaced Canadians heralding the Massachusetts sons of conquering African kings – was not finally up to Faulkner, as he himself knew, but to the writers and scholars who have come after him.

NOTES

1 A representative reading of Faulkner as almost exclusively a Southern writer (rather than as both a major American writer and a Southern writer), as a means of justifying a postcolonial reading of his work, is Sean Latham's "An Impossible Resignation: William Faulkner's Post-Colonial Imagination," in *A Companion to William Faulkner*, Richard C. Moreland (ed.) (London: Blackwell, 2007), pp. 252–68.

2 Postcoloniality itself – whether in theoretical, historical, cultural, or literary terms – is the focus of a scholarly movement marked by internal disruptions and disputes over the term's own continued meaning and relevance. See, for instance, "The End of Postcolonial Theory?" a *PMLA* roundtable discussion in which a series of leading theorists question the current status and future viability of postcolonial theory. Among the responses, Simon Gikandi's is the most salient for the concerns here over a too sanguine reading of Faulkner in a postcolonial context, specifically his calling out of "an epistemological error – namely, the confusion of postcolonial theory and the condition of postcoloniality, the assumption that a theory developed to account for the place of the 'other' subject in the narrative of European identity has anything to do with 'other' geographies and their cultural traditions" (635). In this spirit, we should also avoid placing Faulkner's narratives

too simplistically in such "'other' geographies and their cultural traditions." See Agnani et al., "Editor's column: The end of postcolonial theory? A roundtable with Sunil Agnani, Fernando Coronil, Gaurav Desani, Mamadou Diouf, Simon Gikandi, Susie Tharu, and Jennifer Wenzel," *PMLA* 122.3 (2007), 633–51.

3 Arjun Appadurai, *The Future as Cultural Fact: Essays on the Global Condition* (London: Verso, 2013), p. 198.

4 Salman Rushdie, "Influence," *Step Across This Line: Collected Nonfiction, 1992–2002* (New York: Random House, 2002), p. 63.

5 André Bleikasten, "Faulkner from a European Perspective," in *The Cambridge Companion to William Faulkner*, Phillip M. Weinstein (ed.) (New York: Cambridge University Press, 1995), p. 76.

6 Unfortunately, surface applications of postcolonial theory and simplistic historical characterizations are among the more notable features of the first book-length effort to read Faulkner in postcolonial terms, Charles Baker's *William Faulkner's Postcolonial South* (New York: Peter Lang, 2000). Drawing on the now-canonical ideas of Edward Said's *Orientalism* about postcolonial cultural and political production emerging from a colonial subject's effort to claim his local space – imaginatively, linguistically, and so on – back from the colonizer, Baker frames Faulkner in uncomplicated terms as a polemical and patriotic postcolonial writer, working in a domestically colonialist U.S. historical context defined by post-Civil War North-South relations running along a colonizer-colonized axis. Baker ignores, in other words, the substantially colonial formations internal to the U.S. South itself, which have received their most comprehensive and authoritative treatment of late from Walter Johnson's recent work, discussed later in this chapter.

7 Pankaj Mishra, *From the Ruins of Empire: The Revolt Against the West and the Remaking of Asia* (Toronto: Doubleday Canada, 2012), p. 8.

8 Ibid, p. 8.

9 Walter Johnson, *River of Dark Dreams: Empire and Slavery in the Cotton Kingdom* (Cambridge, MA: Harvard University Press, 2013), p. 10.

10 Ibid., p. 14.

11 Ibid., p. 14.

12 Ibid., p. 15.

13 Fredric Jameson, "Third World Literature in the Era of Multinational Capitalism," *Social Text* 15 (Autumn 1986), 65–88.

14 Aijaz Ahmad, *In Theory: Classes, Nations, Literatures* (London: Verso, 1992).

15 Imre Sizeman, *Zones of Instability: Literature, Postcolonialism, and the Nation* (Baltimore: Johns Hopkins University Press, 2003), p. 20.

16 Vera M. Kutzinski, "Borders and Bodies: The United States, America, and the Caribbean," *CR: The New Centennial Review* 1.2 (Fall 2001), 59.

17 Édouard Glissant, *Faulkner, Mississippi*, Barbara B. Lewis and Thomas Spear (trans.) (Chicago: University of Chicago Press, 1999), Wilson Harris, *The Womb of Space: The Cross-Cultural Imagination* (Westport, CT: Greenwood Press, 1983); *The Unfinished Genesis of the Imagination: Selected Essays of Wilson Harris*, Andrew Bundy (ed.) (London: Routledge, 1999).

18 Taylor Hagood, *Faulkner's Imperialism: Space, Place, and the Materiality of Myth* (Baton Rouge: Louisiana State University Press, 2008); Hosam Mohamed

Aboul-Ela, *Other South: Faulkner, Coloniality, and the Mariátegui Tradition* (Pittsburgh: University of Pittsburgh Press, 2007).

19 Aboul-Ela, *Other South*, p. 131.

20 Cohn considers the political implications of Faulkner's influence on Latin American writers and attends to Faulkner's difficult position there as both a fellow "Southern" writer based on shared historical-cultural experiences of plantation slavery and so on but also as a representative figure and voice of the neo-colonial United States exerting its controlling influence on its Latin American neighbors. Deborah Cohn, "Faulkner, Latin America, and the Caribbean: Influence, politics, and academic disciplines," in *A Companion to William Faulkner*, Richard C. Moreland (ed.) (London: Blackwell, 2007), pp. 499–518. Twelve years earlier, Saldívar published an article comparing Faulkner's *Absalom, Absalom!* to Américo Paredes's "Mexicotexan" novel *George Washington Goméz* (composed in the 1930s, published in 1990), given the two works' parallel explorations of subject formation in the context of characters living in historical moments and places (the American South, Mexico) marked by transitions from colonial to postcolonial relationships to the United States' imperial presence pressuring both. Ramón Saldívar, "Looking for a Master Plan: Faulkner, Paredes, and the Colonial and Postcolonial Subject," in *The Cambridge Companion to William Faulkner*, Philip M. Weinstein (ed.) (New York: Cambridge University Press, 1995), pp. 96–120. The only other notable postcolonial context for reading Faulkner is in terms of his representations of Native Americans and their (subjugated and colonized) experience in the American South: see, for instance, Annette Trefzer's "Mimesis and Mimicry: William Faulkner's Postcolonial Yoknapatawpha," a chapter in her *Disturbing Indians: The Archeology of Southern Fiction* (Tuscaloosa: University of Alabama Press, 2006), pp. 145–79; see also Melanie Benson Taylor's important works on reading the place and position of Native Americans and related domestic colonial and postcolonial experience in Faulkner's fiction: *Disturbing Calculations: The Economics of Identity in Postcolonial Southern Literature, 1912–2002* (Athens: University of Georgia Press, 2008) and *Reconstructing the Native South: American Indian Literature and the Lost Cause* (Athens: University of Georgia Press, 2012).

21 Aboul-Ela, *Other South*, p. 141.

22 Ibid., p. 130.

23 Ibid., p. 140.

24 Ibid., p. 132. As one recent example of a Faulkner-Roy reading, see Alfred J. López, "The Plantation as Archive: Images of 'the South' in the Postcolonial World," *Comparative Literature* 63.4 (2011), 402–22. Reading Roy and García Márquez alongside Faulkner as part of a "genealogy of the plantation," López argues that "Subaltern writers ... are beginning to find in each other ... scraps and fragments of a shared condition of subjection to the imperatives of globalization as the refinement and further elaboration of imperialism" (420).

25 Aboul-Ela, *Other South*, p. 133.

26 Zulfikar Ghose, *The Art of Creating Fiction* (London: Macmillan, 1991), p. 128.

27 Zulfikar Ghose, *A New History of Torments* (New York: Holt, Rinehart, and Wilson, 1982), p. 161.

28 As quoted in Chelva Kanganaykam, *Structures of Negation: The Writings of Zulfikar Ghose* (Toronto: University of Toronto Press, 1993), p. 67; see this book more generally for a definitive reading of his work and its relationship to magic realism. Biographical details about Ghose are taken from http://www.utexas.edu/cola/depts/english/faculty/ghoseza.

29 John T. Matthews, *William Faulkner: Seeing Through the South* (London: Blackwell Publishing, 2012), p. 273.

30 Matthews, *Seeing Through the South*, p. 274.

31 Appadurai, *Future as Cultural Fact*, p. 299.

FURTHER READING

Biography

Blotner, Joseph, *Faulkner: A Biography*, New York: Random House, 1984.

Gray, Richard, *The Life of William Faulkner: A Critical Biography*, Malden, MA: Wiley-Blackwell, 1996.

Minter, David, *William Faulkner: His Life and Art*, Baltimore: Johns Hopkins University Press, 1980.

Sensibar, Judith, *Faulkner and Love: The Women Who Shaped His Art, a Biography*, New Haven, CT: Yale University Press, 2010.

Weinstein, Philip, *Becoming Faulkner*, Oxford: Oxford University Press, 2009.

Williamson, Joel, *William Faulkner and Southern History*, New York: Oxford University Press, 1995.

Selected Critical Studies

Aboul-Ela, Hosam, *Other South: Faulkner, Coloniality, and the Mariátegui Tradition*, Pittsburgh: University of Pittsburgh Press, 2007.

Aiken, Charles S., *William Faulkner and the Southern Landscape*, Athens: University of Georgia Press, 2009.

Atkinson, Ted, *Faulkner and the Great Depression: Aesthetics, Ideology, and Cultural Politics*, Athens: University of Georgia Press, 2006.

Bibler, Michael P. *Cotton's Queer Relations: Same-Sex Intimacy and the Literature of the Southern Plantation, 1939–1968*, Charlottesville: University of Virginia Press, 2009.

Bleikasten, André, *The Ink of Melancholy: Faulkner's Novels from 'The Sound and the Fury' to 'Light in August,'* Bloomington: Indiana University Press, 1990.

Brooks, Cleanth, *William Faulkner: The Yoknapatawpha Country*, New Haven, CT: Yale University Press, 1966.

Davis, Thadious M., *Faulkner's "Negro": Art and the Southern Context*, Baton Rouge: Louisiana State University Press, 1983.

Doyle, Don, Faulkner's County: *The Historical Roots of Yoknapatawpha*, Chapel Hill: University of North Carolina Press, 2001.

Duck, Leigh Anne, *The Nation's Region: Southern Modernism, Segregation, and U.S. Nationalism*, Athens: University of Georgia Press, 2006.

Dussere, Erik, *Balancing the Books: Faulkner, Morrison, and the Economies of Slavery*, New York: Routledge, 2003.

Duvall, John N., *Faulkner's Marginal Couple: Invisible, Outlaw, and Unspeakable Communities*. Austin, TX: University of Texas Press, 1990.

Glissant, Édouard, *Faulkner, Mississippi*, Barbara B. Lewis and Thomas C. Spear (trans.), Chicago: University of Chicago Press, 1999.

Godden, Richard, *Fictions of Labor: William Faulkner and the South's Long Revolution*, Cambridge: Cambridge University Press, 1997.

William Faulkner: An Economy of Complex Words, Princeton, NJ: Princeton University Press, 2007.

Gwin, Minrose, *The Feminine and Faulkner*, Knoxville: University of Tennessee Press, 1990.

Howe, Irving, *William Faulkner, A Critical Study*, New York: Ivan R. Dee, 1991.

Irwin, John T., *Doubling & Incest / Repetition & Revenge*, Baltimore: Johns Hopkins University Press, 1975.

Kartiganer, Donald, *The Fragile Thread: The Meaning of Form in Faulkner's Novels*, Amherst: University of Massachusetts Press, 1979.

Kawin, Bruce, *Faulkner and Film*, Ungar: New York, 1977.

Ladd, Barbara, *Nationalism and the Color Line in George W. Cable, Mark Twain, and William Faulkner*, Baton Rouge: Louisiana State University Press, 1996.

Loichot, Valérie, *Orphan Narratives: The Postplantation Literature of Faulkner, Glissant, Morrison, and Saint-John Perse*, Charlottesville: University of Virginia Press, 2007.

Lurie, Peter, *Vision's Immanence: Faulkner, Film, and the Popular Imagination*, Baltimore and London: Johns Hopkins University Press, 2004.

Matthews, John T., *William Faulkner: Seeing Through the South*, Malden, MA: Wiley-Blackwell, 2009.

Moreland, Richard, *Faulkner and Modernism: Revision and Rewriting*, Madison: University of Wisconsin Press, 1990.

Polk, Noel, *Children of the Dark House: Text and Context in Faulkner*, Jackson: University Press of Mississippi, 1996.

Ross, Stephen M., *Fiction's Inexhaustible Voice: Speech and Writing in Faulkner*, Athens: University of Georgia Press, 1989.

Schwartz, Lawrence H., *Creating Faulkner's Reputation: The Politics of Modern Literary Criticism*, Knoxville: University of Tennessee Press, 1988.

Sundquist, Eric J., *Faulkner: The House Divided*, Baltimore: Johns Hopkins University Press, 1983.

Towner, Theresa, *Faulkner on the Color: The Later Novels*, Jackson: University Press of Mississippi, 2000.

Urgo, Joseph. *Faulkner's Apocrypha: A Fable, Snopes, and the Spirit of Human Rebellion*, Jackson: University Press of Mississippi, 1989.

Watson, Jay, *Reading for the Body: The Recalcitrant Materiality of Southern Fiction*, Athens: University of Georgia Press, 2013.

Weinstein, Philip, *Faulkner's Subject: A Cosmos No One Owns*, Cambridge: Cambridge University Press, 1992.

Other Resources

Blotner, Joseph (ed.), *Selected Letters of William Faulkner*, New York: Random House, 1977.

Cowley, Malcolm, *The Faulkner-Cowley File: Letters and Memories 1944–1962*, New York: Viking Press, 1966.

Hamblin, Robert W. and Charles A. Peek (eds.), *A William Faulkner Encyclopedia*, Westport, CT: Greenwood Press, 1999.

Fagnoli, A. Nicholas and Michael Golay, *William Faulkner A-Z*, Facts on File, 2001.

Faulkner, William, *Essays, Speeches, and Public Letters*, New York: Random House, 2011.

Meriwether, James B. and Michael Millgate (eds.), *Lion in the Garden: Interviews with William Faulkner, 1926–1962*, Lincoln, NE: Bison Books, 1981.

William Faulkner on the Web (University of Mississippi): http://www.mcsr.olemiss.edu/~egjbp/faulkner/faulkner.html

Faulkner at Virginia (University of Virginia): http://faulkner.lib.virginia.edu/

INDEX

Cambridge Companions to...

AUTHORS

Edward Albee edited by Stephen J. Bottoms

Margaret Atwood edited by Coral Ann Howells

W. H. Auden edited by Stan Smith

Jane Austen edited by Edward Copeland and Juliet McMaster (second edition)

Beckett edited by John Pilling

Bede edited by Scott DeGregorio

Aphra Behn edited by Derek Hughes and Janet Todd

Walter Benjamin edited by David S. Ferris

William Blake edited by Morris Eaves

Jorge Luis Borges edited by Edwin Williamson

Brecht edited by Peter Thomson and Glendyr Sacks (second edition)

The Brontës edited by Heather Glen

Bunyan edited by Anne Dunan-Page

Frances Burney edited by Peter Sabor

Byron edited by Drummond Bone

Albert Camus edited by Edward J. Hughes

Willa Cather edited by Marilee Lindemann

Cervantes edited by Anthony J. Cascardi

Chaucer edited by Piero Boitani and Jill Mann (second edition)

Chekhov edited by Vera Gottlieb and Paul Allain

Kate Chopin edited by Janet Beer

Caryl Churchill edited by Elaine Aston and Elin Diamond

Cicero edited by Catherine Steel

Coleridge edited by Lucy Newlyn

Wilkie Collins edited by Jenny Bourne Taylor

Joseph Conrad edited by J. H. Stape

H. D. edited by Nephie J. Christodoulides and Polina Mackay

Dante edited by Rachel Jacoff (second edition)

Daniel Defoe edited by John Richetti

Don DeLillo edited by John N. Duvall

Charles Dickens edited by John O. Jordan

Emily Dickinson edited by Wendy Martin

John Donne edited by Achsah Guibbory

Dostoevskii edited by W. J. Leatherbarrow

Theodore Dreiser edited by Leonard Cassuto and Claire Virginia Eby

John Dryden edited by Steven N. Zwicker

W. E. B. Du Bois edited by Shamoon Zamir

George Eliot edited by George Levine

T. S. Eliot edited by A. David Moody

Ralph Ellison edited by Ross Posnock

Ralph Waldo Emerson edited by Joel Porte and Saundra Morris

William Faulkner edited by Philip M. Weinstein

Henry Fielding edited by Claude Rawson

F. Scott Fitzgerald edited by Ruth Prigozy

Flaubert edited by Timothy Unwin

E. M. Forster edited by David Bradshaw

Benjamin Franklin edited by Carla Mulford

Brian Friel edited by Anthony Roche

Robert Frost edited by Robert Faggen

Gabriel García Márquez edited by Philip Swanson

Elizabeth Gaskell edited by Jill L. Matus

Goethe edited by Lesley Sharpe

Günter Grass edited by Stuart Taberner

Thomas Hardy edited by Dale Kramer

David Hare edited by Richard Boon

Nathaniel Hawthorne edited by Richard Millington

Seamus Heaney edited by Bernard O'Donoghue

Ernest Hemingway edited by Scott Donaldson

Homer edited by Robert Fowler

Horace edited by Stephen Harrison

Ted Hughes edited by Terry Gifford

Ibsen edited by James McFarlane

Henry James edited by Jonathan Freedman

Samuel Johnson edited by Greg Clingham

Ben Jonson edited by Richard Harp and Stanley Stewart

James Joyce edited by Derek Attridge (second edition)

Kafka edited by Julian Preece

Keats edited by Susan J. Wolfson

Rudyard Kipling edited by Howard J. Booth

Lacan edited by Jean-Michel Rabaté

D. H. Lawrence edited by Anne Fernihough

Primo Levi edited by Robert Gordon

TOPICS

CPSIA information can be obtained
at www.ICGtesting.com
Printed in the USA
LVHW031650240621
691066LV00002B/245